THE JEWS OF THE *TITANIC*

A REFLECTION OF THE JEWISH WORLD ON THE EPIC DISASTER

ELI MOSKOWITZ

Published by
Hybrid Global Publishing
301 E 57th Street, 4th fl
New York, NY 10022

Manufactured in the United States of America, or in the United Kingdom when distributed elsewhere.

Moskowitz, Eli
    The Jews of the *Titanic*: a reflection of the Jewish world on the epic disaster
    LCCN: 2018931142
    ISBN: 978-1-938015-96-0
eBook: 978-1-938015-97-7

Cover design: Joe Potter
Front cover photo source: Wikipedia Commons
Back cover photo credit: Hebrew Publishing Company
Copyediting and typesetting: Claudia Volkman

In memory of my father, Jeffrey Moskowitz

CONTENTS

FOREWORD

A number of books have been written with a focus on specific nationalities of passengers on the *Titanic*, and some even centering on a particular region or locale. But Eli Moskowitz has written an entire book on people of a particular faith. As a result, it encompasses both passengers and crew, and a variety of nationalities.

Beyond simple biographies, although some of these life stories are far from simple, Mr. Moskowitz has gone into great detail not just about the lives of these people, but about how their faith impacted the story of the *Titanic*. He goes into fascinating detail about why these people were on board – the pogroms and forced military service that drove them from their countries, despite the efforts of their religious leaders to keep them from emigrating and possibly leaving their Jewish traditions behind as they settled into new countries and cultures.

The story of the Jews on the *Titanic* goes beyond the night of the disaster. The coverage of the sinking by Jewish newspapers is described. Some of the greatest stories of heroism the night of the sinking, those of Benjamin Guggenheim and, more importantly, Isidor and Ida Straus, were performed by Jewish passengers, and were eagerly picked up by newspapers everywhere.

This book doesn't end with the sinking, but continues on with the Jewish involvement in the recovery of so many of the bodies and how they were identified as either Jewish or Gentile. There is also the dilemma widows faced when their husbands' bodies were not recovered, which resulted in issues and restrictions placed upon them by their faith. Like other cultures and religions, the Jewish community saw an abundance of sermons, songs, ballads, essays, and the like resulting from this terrible tragedy.

Everyone reading this book will learn something. It details aspects of the disaster that no previous book has described. The *Titanic* community is indebted to Eli Moskowitz for tackling this subject, and covering it so well.

—Don Lynch

Author's Introduction

The discovery of the wreck of the *Titanic* in September 1985 gave the world a new wave of interest in the everlasting story of the lost ocean liner. I was a boy, and all I knew about the *Titanic* is that the ship had four funnels or smokestacks, as I called them. The story of the disaster intrigued me, and I wanted to know more about the ship, so I wrote letters to museums in America and England asking for information about the *Titanic*. A few answered me and sent timelines, maps, and other relevant documents.

In Judaism when a boy turns thirteen, he becomes responsible for keeping the commandments of the Jewish faith. He is called a *Bar Mitzvah,* and this term also describes the ceremonies which commemorate this milestone. For my *Bar Mitzvah* I received my first *Titanic* book: *The Discovery of the Titanic* by Dr. Robert Ballard, and my interest and passion in the *Titanic* grew and developed.

Later when I took a course about Contemporary American Jewry while studying for my master's degree in Jewish history in Jerusalem, I wrote a paper about the Jewish passengers on the *Titanic*. I started to thoroughly research the topic. The course was in Hebrew, and therefore the paper was in Hebrew. After I graduated, I decided to research the topic further and develop the paper into a book.

Coincidently the book in Hebrew was published in Israel soon after the *Titanic* came to Israel. In the summer of 2014, the *Titanic* exhibition visited Tel Aviv during its world tour. This was my first chance to see artifacts that were retrieved from the site of the wreck. The organizers of the Israeli exhibition requested my assistance in giving the Israeli visitors an Israeli point of view of the *Titanic* story. They wanted something unique for the Israeli audience. For the first time Israelis were exposed not only to the *Titanic* in general but also to the Jewish story of the *Titanic*. My cooperation with the *Titanic* exhibition expanded when I guided groups in both Hebrew and

English at the exhibition. I consider myself a Titaniac: a fan of the *Titanic* story; a person who is very enthusiastic about the *Titanic*. In the summer of 2014, my interest and knowledge about the *Titanic* was put to good use.

I have a collection of over fifteen *Titanic*-related books. This collection includes a rare copy of *The Sinking of the Titanic and Great Sea Disasters* published in 1912, several months after the sinking. My dream is to dive down to the bottom of the Atlantic Ocean and see the wreck of the *Titanic* in person.

As a Jew, it is natural that I would focus on the Jewish aspects of this epic story. A year after my book was released, I decided to translate it to English for the benefit of the English-speaking audience. As I was translating the book, I decided to rewrite the whole thing. I did more research, added information, and found and added more names to the Jewish passenger list. Now is the time to have an English version of the Jewish story of the *Titanic,* and here it is. May this book be a commemoration for the 1,500 souls who died in the world's most famous maritime disaster.

PROLOGUE

The drama that took place on the decks of the *Titanic* on that fateful night of April 14, 1912, was unimaginable. Up until that night, the *Titanic* was endlessly praised. She was the largest and most luxurious ship ever built. She was said to be unsinkable, yet she sank on her maiden voyage. The *Titanic* was heading straight through an iceberg field despite the never-ending warnings of ice that were received during that day. The Atlantic Ocean was calm. It was a moonless night, and the sky was lit with stars.

After the collision with the iceberg, it seemed as if something mystical was happening on the decks of the *Titanic*. The band played relaxing tunes as women were torn from their husbands' arms. The passengers did not rush to leave such a large ship for so small a lifeboat, so the first lifeboats left the *Titanic* half full as water was filling the hull of the great ship.

The tale of the *Titanic* contains all the elements that make a story epic. The sinking of the *Titanic* has fascinated the world for over a century. Numerous books have been written and numerous films have been made about her. The *Titanic* disaster has been researched from almost every possible angle and aspect. The *Titanic* was not only a large ship. She was a phenomenon, a myth.

With the sinking of the *Titanic,* over 1,500 souls were lost, including many Jewish people. On the *Titanic's* maiden voyage were wealthy Jews from the elite of American Jewry, while down in steerage there were many Jews from Eastern Europe, hard workers who were on their way to America to try and start a better life in the Promised Land. On the *Titanic* were rich Jews on their way back home from their winter vacations in Europe and Jewish immigrants fleeing the pogroms, persecution, and anti-Semitism of Russia and Eastern Europe.

This book tells the story of the *Titanic* from a Jewish prospective. It deals with aspects unique to Jews. It focuses on the life and death of the Jewish passengers and examines the influence of the disaster on the Jewish world. This book covers Jewish immigration, the *Kashrut* issue, Jewish burial, the reaction of the Jewish press to the disaster, and other topics.

1

THE MYTH

In the beginning of the twentieth century, a tale circulated in the Jewish world. It was the story of a young Jewish man from a *shtetl* in Eastern Europe. In this story the youth wanted to leave his hometown and go to America, which he heard was the land of opportunity. His father objected to the idea and asked his local rabbi for advice. The rabbi told the father to tell his son not to go to America. The young man disobeyed both his father and the rabbi, left his family, and sailed to America. The ship sank, and he died. The father went to the rabbi and complained to him for not stopping his son. He asked the rabbi why he did not warn his son that such a disaster would happen. Why did he not say that the ship would sink? Why did he not save his son? The rabbi answered the grieved father and said that he did not know the ship would sink, but when a rabbi says not to go to America, one needs to obey the rabbi.

This tale was told in the beginning of the twentieth century, but after the sinking of the *Titanic*, more details were added to the story. In the new and updated story, the rabbi was actually Rabbi Shalom Dovber Schneersohn (1820–1920), the fifth Rebbe of the Chabad Lubavitch Hasidic movement. The ship in the story was obviously the *Titanic*. In the new story Rabbi Schneersohn told the young man: "Well, if you insist on going to America, at least take the *Tanya* book with you." He obviously did not take the book with him, therefore the rabbi said: "One thing leads to another. If you disobey the rabbi and go to America, you will also forget the *Tanya* at home."

This tale was told by rabbis, preachers, and Hasidic leaders in order to discourage young Jews from leaving their communities in Europe and immigrating to the United States. It was thought that leaving the little

1

European *shtetl* meant leaving Jewish tradition and assimilating in America. The sinking ship is an allegory of losing the religion, a spiritual threat that was largely connected with immigration to the United States. This was an actual problem since many Jewish immigrants who fled Europe eventually did leave their Jewish traditions and assimilate in America. Tragically many of the rabbis who opposed leaving Europe were murdered along with their faithful followers and communities in the Holocaust only a few decades after the sinking of the *Titanic*. The main haven for many of the Jewish survivors of the Holocaust ironically was the United States.

A similar message was given by Rabbi Yosef Ber Soloveitchic (1903–1993), who was the spiritual leader for American Jews for many years. The Soloveitchic Rabbi acted greatly in order to save young Jewish souls in the United States and helped the Zionist cause, especially after the establishment of the State of Israel. He wrote many articles about his concern over the loss of Jews who left their traditions in the Diaspora. The Soloveitchic Rabbi distinguished between two kinds of diasporas: the exile of Egypt and the exile of Assyria. While in Egypt the Jews toiled in anguish and suffering, in Assyria the Jews were free. They were not enslaved and enjoyed civil rights. They settled, flourished, and became wealthy. They refused to return to Israel. The Assyrian exile was far worse than the exile of Egypt. Over the years, the Jews in the Diaspora established themselves in big houses and they surrounded themselves with luxuries. The sparkle of the materialistic world blinded them. The Soloveitchic Rabbi tried to warn the American Jews (especially those who were nonobservant ones and the ones who did not follow Jewish law) about the arrogance and overconfidence similar to the cheerfulness and smugness of the *Titanic* passengers before the disaster. The Soloveitchic Rabbi and others explained that the people on the *Titanic* acted as if it would never sink, yet it did, taking many of the rich with it down to the bottom of the Atlantic Ocean.

One of the stories the Soloveitchic Rabbi discussed was a *Talmudic* story about a boat with a group of people. Among the travelers there was a scholar named Rabbah Bar Bar Hana. During their voyage the boat drifted away from shore, and the people tried to row back. After several days of traveling, they saw a green surface in the distance. Thinking it was land, they started rowing toward it. When they reached it, they assumed it was a small island. Most of the travelers climbed onto the "island" and started to establish a new home. Only Rabbah Bar Bar Hana stayed on the little boat. One day the "island" awoke and turned itself upside down. It was a whale, not an island, and everyone fell off and drowned. This *Talmudic* story, with all its symbolism – the boat, the drowning, the survivor – tells the story of the spiritual loss related to leaving the homeland and Jewish tradition in the same way as the *Titanic* allegory.

In general many European and American rabbis saw the construction of the *Titanic* in a negative light. They heard the shipbuilders boasting about a mighty ship that was practically unsinkable. (Although the newspapers described the *Titanic* as unsinkable, which is how the public perceived it, the shipbuilders never said such a thing.) Rabbis compared the *Titanic* to the biblical Tower of Babel. The comparison was obvious. Rabbis saw the *Titanic* as a symbol of arrogance, of people who believed they could build ships so large, so huge, that could cross the mighty oceans with great speed and comfort. Those rabbis saw the building of the *Titanic* as challenging the forces of nature and testing God himself. Even the name *Titanic*, taken from the world of imagery of Greek mythology, was seen as inappropriate. After the sinking of the *Titanic,* some rabbis continued to compare the end of the Tower of Babel to the end of the *Titanic*, where God prevented the human race from achieving their goal. In the biblical story God intervened and stopped the humans from completing the tower. With the *Titanic* God caused the ship to sink, preventing it from completing its maiden voyage to show people how humble they should be. The shock that circled the world with the news about the *Titanic* sinking was evidence to those rabbis who saw the *Titanic* as a war between men and God.[1]

The *Titanic* disaster was one of the biggest maritime disasters before World War I. It symbolized the end of the era prior to the world wars. In England, the sinking of the *Titanic* was viewed as an event that ended the Victorian era, an era of innocence, although Queen Victoria passed away in 1901. The *Titanic* disaster was a turning point. From that day, men lost their innocence.

Many myths were connected to the *Titanic*. What makes the *Titanic* story so special? Why does the *Titanic* attract so much attention even a century later? As terrifying as the sinking was, the *Titanic* was not the only incident where so many people lost their lives. Jews were killed in so many tragedies, many of which were natural disasters such as earthquakes, but also fires, pogroms, blood libels, and other anti-Semitic incidents. In the second half of the nineteenth century and the beginning of the twentieth century, thousands of Jews were killed in natural disasters and human-made disasters, including the famous Kishinev pogrom in 1903, the Bialystok pogrom in 1906, and the Hebron massacre in 1929, where many dozens of Jews were murdered and many more wounded.

The Jewish people experienced many tragedies and disasters far worse than the sinking of the *Titanic*. In 1837 a mighty earthquake hit Galilee and destroyed much of Safed and Tiberias. In Safed, over 1,700 Jews died, and in Tiberias, about six hundred Jews died. In 1911 a fire destroyed the Triangle Shirtwaist Factory in Manhattan. The fire was the worst industrial disaster ever in New York City. One hundred and forty five people were killed, most of whom were young Jewish workers, such as the young, hardworking immigrant women who were barely making a living. Every day when the workers arrived at the factory, the doors were locked to prevent the workers from leaving the building without authorization. When the fire broke out, the workers were trapped. Many were killed from the flames and fumes, and some died when jumping from the high floors of the burning building.

Many Jews died at sea. In 1904 the *Norge* sailed from Copenhagen, Denmark, to New York. During the voyage it ran aground and sank. Six hundred and thirty five people died, including many Jewish immigrants from Russia. Similar to the *Titanic,* one reason many died was the shortage of lifeboats. In October 1913, only a year and a half after the sinking of the *Titanic*, the *Volturno* caught fire and sank during a voyage from Rotterdam, the Netherlands, to New York. Many of the 140 casualties were Russian Jews. The ship sank on Yom Kippur night, and many saw that as punishment for traveling on the holiest day of the Jewish year.

Compared with other maritime disasters, the *Titanic* was not the worst. The *Empress of Ireland* collided with a Norwegian coal ship and sank in the Saint Lawrence River, killing one thousand people. In World War II, four thousand died when Germans bombed and sank the British liner *Lancastria*. Four thousand more were killed when a Russian submarine torpedoed the German ship *General von Steuben* in 1945. That same year the largest loss of human life in a single ship ever accrued when the German ship *Wilhelm Gustloff* was torpedoed and over 9,300 people were killed – six times as many as the *Titanic* victims.

And after World War II, many people died at sea too. In 1949 the Chinese steamer *Taiping* sank and over 1,500 people died. In 1991 an overcrowded

Saudi passenger steamer hit a reef and over 1,400 people returning from pilgrimage to Mecca drowned. In 1987 more than 4,300 died when the *Doña Paz*, a Philippine passenger ferry, collided with an oil tanker. And the list goes on and on. So why is the *Titanic* so famous? Why is the *Titanic* so remembered? What makes the *Titanic* disaster so special?

The *Titanic* story has been told many times in books and films. The first film about the disaster was released only twenty-nine days after the sinking. It was a silent motion picture called *Saved from the Titanic*. It starred a *Titanic* survivor, actress Dorothy Gibson, who wore the same gown during the filming as she did the night of the disaster. Several films were made between the 1920s and the 1950s. One of the more interesting films was made in 1943 during World War II. It was a Nazi propaganda film, and it was anti-British, anti-American, and personally overseen by the Reich Minister of Propaganda Joseph Goebbels.

One of the best known and most accurate and successful films about the *Titanic* was *A Night to Remember*. It was an adaptation of a book with the same title written by historian and author Walter Lord. The opening scene of the film is the launching of the *Titanic* and shows an elegantly dressed woman, who announces the name of the new ship: "I name this ship *Titanic*. May God bless her and all who sail in her." The woman broke a bottle of wine on the hull and the *Titanic* started to move.[2]

This scene did not really happen. There were ceremonies on *Titanic's* launch on March 31, 1911, and on the *Titanic's* maiden voyage on April 10, 1912. There were boats and ships honoring the *Titanic* by honking as the *Titanic* started on its way from Southampton, but there were no ceremonies as depicted in the film. Although the opening scene is not realistic, *A Night to Remember* was the most accurate film ever made at that time. It was the first major *Titanic* film without any fictional characters.

Water Lord was born in 1917, five years after the *Titanic* disaster. At age nine he crossed the Atlantic Ocean from New York to Southampton on board the *Olympic*, *Titanic's* sister ship. He studied law, joined the United States Army during World War II and served as a code clerk in the intelligence corps. He wrote many books about important events in United States history, such as the battle of the Alamo, World War I, and exploring the North Pole. *A Night to Remember* is his most noted book. For his research he interviewed sixty-three *Titanic* survivors and based his book on their experiences. During the film's production Lord and his team were guided by several survivors who helped out on the set. After the film's debut Lord kept in touch with some of them.

The myth of the *Titanic* story has thrilled many people and still does. One century after the disaster, people are still hooked on the *Titanic* story. Two big events that brought the *Titanic* back to the center of attention were the discovery of the lost *Titanic* on the bottom of the Atlantic Ocean in 1985 and the release of the blockbuster film *Titanic* in 1997. It was one of the most expensive films ever made, topped the highest grossing films for twelve years, and won eleven Academy Awards. It was the most accurate *Titanic* film ever, and only the use of fictional characters put a damper on its accuracy.

The sinking of the *Titanic* was a tragedy to the shipping world and to hundreds of families around the globe. The *Titanic* was a microcosm of the world at that time. The passengers included millionaires, industry moguls, writers, actors, politicians, athletes, and many hundreds of immigrants on their way from Europe to the land of endless opportunities. The passengers of the *Titanic* included thirty-three nationalities from six continents and people from many religions.

Among the Jewish passengers, the youngest was ten-month-old Frank Philip Aks. He was traveling with his mother, Leah, age eighteen. Their story is quite typical for many Jews of that time. Leah Aks (nee Rosen) was born in 1894 in Warsaw, Poland, and immigrated to England. She met and married Samuel Aks, a Polish immigrant as well who was a tailor. He worked hard and barely made a living. A friend of the family who left England and immigrated to the United States told them about the good life in the new land. Samuel and Leah decided to immigrate to the United States, but like many other young families, they decided that Samuel would go alone, start making money, and then send for Leah, who was pregnant at the time. Leah's father, Moshe Rosen, did not want his daughter to travel by sea while she was pregnant. Only after the baby was born while Samuel was already in the United States was Leah able to travel. They nicknamed the baby "Filly," and his Hebrew name was Ephraim Fishel Aks.

Leah wanted to leave in early April but postponed their trip so they would not have to travel during Passover. The *Titanic* left Southampton two days after Passover ended. Leah and Frank boarded the *Titanic*, and their ticket cost them 7£ 9s. Leah was surprised when she saw the relatively good

Samuel, Leah, and baby Frank Aks. Photo credit: Michael Findlay Collection

conditions in steerage. Leah and Frank had their own cabin, so they did not have to share a room with strangers. Such a thing was evidence of the luxury of the *Titanic* in comparison to third-class conditions of other ships during that era. Leah was on her way to a new and better life in America, and one of the most colossal human dramas of the beginning of the twentieth century was only a few days away. Did these poor immigrants have any chance to be saved? Did those steerage passengers such as Leah Aks deep in third class have any idea how to make it to the Boat Deck and into a lifeboat? Would she be stopped by stewards on her way to safety?

Many questions about the disaster remain unanswered. Was the disaster inevitable? Why did so few people survive? Why did the *Californian*, a ship that was visible to the *Titanic* that night, not come to the rescue? Was there any discrimination between the three classes during the evacuation?

Regarding the Jewish passengers, there are also many questions. How many Jews were on the *Titanic*? How many survived? How many died? Did the Jewish passengers have *kosher* meals during the voyage? What did they eat? Where did they pray? Was there a synagogue on board? Did they have Sabbath services? Was there any anti-Semitism on the *Titanic*? Some of these questions will forever remain unanswered. The exact number of Jewish passengers is unknown, and it is only possible to assume with what is known, which is that fewer than forty Jews survived. There may have been a hundred Jews on board, and maybe more.

Isidor Straus and Benjamin Guggenheim were the most prominent and most famous Jews on the *Titanic*. Most wealthy American Jews during that era suffered one way or another from anti-Semitism. In some social circles it was standard to discriminate against Jews. Even Isidor himself suffered from anti-Semitism in America.[3]

By life and by death, Jewish passengers were exposed to prejudices. Stories of the ultimate altruistic sacrifice of some of the Jewish victims could be a proper response to anti-Semitic claims based on selfishness. After centuries of exile, humiliation, persecution, and a suspicious and hostile environment, the bravery of the Jewish victims is a testimony that the Jewish passengers deserve honor and pity as much as the other *Titanic* passengers without discrimination of religion. Shortly after the disaster the story of the deaths of Ida and Isidor Straus, for example, was known to the entire world and encouraged admiration and astonishment among Jews and gentiles alike.[4]

It seems that the heroic acts of Ida and Isidor Straus and other Jewish passengers on the night of the sinking addressed anti-Semitic claims while making that ultimate sacrifice which led to their deaths.

The acts of Benjamin Guggenheim and the Straus's in their final hour could have been caused by their subconscious desire to respond to the anti-Semitic claims of Jewish egocentricity. The fact is that prominent Jews such as Guggenheim and Straus did not enter the lifeboats although they could have been saved.*

Jews from all three classes performed heroic acts of personal sacrifice. In second class, Benjamin Hart put his wife and child into a lifeboat. He told them to be brave. His exact words to his seven-year-old daughter were: "Hold Mummy's hand and be a good girl." He then turned away with the other men and accepted his fate. His body was never found. Is that not heroic? In steerage there were no incidents of Jews trying to escape at the expense of other people.

---

*Titanic *researcher Richard Davenport-Hines described this theory in his book* Titanic Lives *(2012). He claims that it is possible that the actions of Straus and Guggenheim during the* Titanic *disaster were a response to anti-Semitic claims.*

In research made about Jews fighting alongside the German Army during World War I and World War II, it was apparent that many Jews volunteered for elite units and fulfilled dangerous missions in order to express their loyalty to their superior officers. Relative to the number of Jews who served in the *Wehrmacht*, the number of Jewish casualties was high. One of the reasons for that is the fact that many Jews felt the need to prove their loyalty to their country beyond the loyalty their gentile neighbors showed. Doing so cost their lives, and they died in honor. Over the years Jews had to prove their loyalty over and over again in order for them to feel trusted by the public and the governments. Many times it ended in their deaths.[5]

The reaction of the Jewish world to the *Titanic* disaster was one of partnership and collaboration. This feeling embodied the will to be accepted among the nations. The fact is that the *Titanic* was a world disaster, one that befell all mankind. In some way the disaster made the Jews belong.

What makes the *Titanic* story so fascinating? The fact that the *Titanic* was the largest and most luxurious ship of her time? The fact that she was considered unsinkable? The stories of valor of the victims? The great loss of life?

On the other hand maybe the *Titanic* fascinates us so much because we know that the disaster could have been avoided. If only there were more lifeboats. If only there was more time. If only the *Titanic* would have reduced its speed. If only the iceberg was seen sooner. If only the crew had been able to steer around the iceberg. If only the *Carpathia* would have arrived sooner. If only the radio operator of the *Californian* would have heard the S.O.S. messages in time. If only the *Californian* had reacted to the distress rockets fired by the *Titanic*. There were so many possible scenarios. Something about the *Titanic* draws our attention. Interest in the *Titanic* started while the ship was being built, when the public learned that the largest and most luxurious ship ever was being built, a ship larger and more luxurious than any ship before her. That is when our story of the *Titanic* begins.

2

SHIP OF DREAMS

In 1907 there was a competition for passengers on the North Atlantic route. Two major British shipping companies (Cunard and White Star Line) as well as several German and American shipping companies competed over the privilege to ferry passengers and immigrants from Europe to America. In June 1906 the Cunard Line launched a new luxury ship named *Lusitania*. At the time, the *Lusitania* was the world's largest passenger ship and held the Blue Ribbon for crossing the North Atlantic with the highest record speed. Thanks to the *Lusitania* and her sister ship, the *Mauritania*, Cunard Line controlled the route between England and the United States.[6]

Bruce Ismay, a British businessman, was the owner and director of the White Star Line, which he had inherited from his father. In the summer of 1907, Ismay met with Lord Pirrie (William James Pirrie), chairman of Harland & Wolff shipbuilders, to discuss how to prevail over Cunard Line. Ismay and Lord Pirrie decided to build three new and much larger passenger ships. With these new ships, the White Star Line would become the victor on the North Atlantic route. The *Lusitania* and the *Mauritania* were each 240 meters long. The ships to be built were designed to be 270 meters long and the most luxurious ships ever built with amenities such as an

Jewish shipbuilder Gustav Wolff, co-founder of Harland and Wolff, builder of the Titanic.
Source: Wikimedia Commons

indoor swimming pool, squash court, Turkish bath, gymnasium, and several high-class restaurants. One was a French café with French-speaking waiters.[7] The White Star Line planned that the ships would be able to travel at a top speed of twenty-four knots using sophisticated machinery. The new vessels would require over nine hundred crew members each.[8]

Harland & Wolff was the British ship-building company that built most of the ships at the shipyard in Belfast, Ireland. Gustav Wolff, one of the company's founders, was born a Jew but converted from Judaism. He was also a member of the British Parliament.

The three new ships were given names derived from Greek mythology to reflect their size and might: *Olympic, Titanic,* and *Gigantic.* After the sinking of the *Titanic,* the *Gigantic* was renamed the *Britannic.*

Harland & Wolff built additional shipyards in Belfast Harbor that were large enough to build two new ships at once. The *Titanic* and *Olympic* were built side by side. The keel of the *Titanic* was laid on March 31, 1909. The first of the ships, the *Olympic,* was launched in October 1910 and then work started on building the *Britannic,* while the *Titanic* was soon to be finished.

Half a year later on March 31, 1911, the *Titanic* was launched. She was

Construction of the Titanic, *Belfast, 1910. Source: Library of Congress*

Titanic docking in Southampton, April 1912. Source: Wikimedia Commons

somewhat larger and heavier than the *Olympic* and had a few more staterooms. She was 270 meters long and twenty-eight meters wide. At the launch she was the largest man-made moving object ever built, with first-class staterooms and suites more luxurious than any other ship in the world. Second-class rooms were more luxurious than the second-class accommodations of any other ship. Even third-class passengers, most of them poor immigrants, enjoyed excellent amenities unlike steerage on any other ship. On the *Titanic* some third-class cabins had six beds, some had four, and some had only two beds. To compare, most steerage cabins on other ships had ten beds each. The *Titanic* really was the ship of dreams.

The captain of the *Titanic* on its maiden voyage was Captain Edward John Smith who had a long career with the White Star Line. He also commanded the *Olympic* on its maiden voyage. He was due to retire after *Titanic's* maiden voyage. He was liked by many of the wealthy passengers who traveled on White Star Line ships. Smith dined with the passengers and participated in cultural events with them during the voyages. Many prominent passengers insisted on traveling only on ships commanded by Captain Smith.[9]

Countless businessmen and public figures, most of them British or American, wished to sail on the *Titanic's* maiden voyage. The wealthiest felt pride in joining such a journey. The richest man on the *Titanic* was John Jacob Astor, whose estimated worth was $150,000,000 at the time. Astor was on his way back home to New York with his young and pregnant bride, Madeleine. The second-richest man on the *Titanic* was Benjamin Guggenheim, a Jewish businessman and heir to a mining and smelting company. Thomas Andrews, the ship's lead designer, boarded the *Titanic* with some of his employees from Harland & Wolff. Bruce Ismay also boarded. Two passengers worth noting are Sir Cosmo Duff Gordon and his wife, Lucy, (also known as the fashion designer Lucile).

Another famous passenger was Major Archibald Butt, adviser to the United States President William Taft. Also on board was Margaret (Molly) Brown who would later be known as "the unsinkable Molly Brown." Other prominent passengers were Army Major Arthur Peuchen, actress Dorothy Gibson, Countess Noelle of Rothes, and Swiss tennis player Norris Williams. Besides Guggenheim, the most famous and well-known Jews on the *Titanic* were Isidor and Ida Straus, a philanthropic couple and co-owners of Macy's department store in New York.

Jewish couple Isidor and Ida Straus. Ida's immortal words are: "Where you go, I go."
Source: Wikimedia Commons

One of the most colorful characters on board was fashion importer, stylist, and journalist Miss Edith Louise Rosenbaum, who sailed alone. She was born in 1879 to a wealthy Jewish family in Cincinnati, Ohio. She wrote a column in a weekly fashion newspaper, imported fashion merchandise, and served as an advisor for clothing stores in the United States and France. In 1910 she worked for a New York company in Paris.

In 1911 she was slightly injured in a car accident in France. In April 1912 she decided to return to the United States. She boarded the *Titanic* at Cherbourg, France. She

First-class Jewish passenger Edith Rosenbaum. Courtesy: Randy Bryan Bigham

took a double suite for personal use and a third room for her trunks of clothing as she did not want to leave her belongings in the cargo hold. Her ticket cost her 27£ 14s and she was placed in stateroom A11 (on A Deck). When she requested insurance for her valuables, she was told that it was unnecessary because the *Titanic* was unsinkable. One important item she had with her was a little toy pig she named "Maxixe" because it played the tune La Maxixe whenever its tale was wound up. It was a gift from her mother after the car accident.

Many prominent passengers embarked with their personal valets, servants, maids, secretaries, chefs, and chauffeurs. Some had their personal staff quartered with them in first class, but others sent their personal staff to second-class cabins or even steerage cabins. Guggenheim's personal valet was quartered with him, but his chauffeur was sent to second class.

In addition to the rich and famous, hundreds of businessmen and passengers of various occupations were in all three classes. The *Titanic* was a luxurious passenger liner and an immigrant ship with a capacity of over one thousand in steerage. The *Titanic* did not sail at full capacity. There were a total of 2,200 people aboard: 329 in first class, 285 in second class, 710 in steerage, and 890 crewmembers.[10]

Titanic's maiden voyage started with the departure from Southampton en route to New York with stops in Cherbourg, France, and Queenstown, Ireland. Both stops were for collecting additional passengers and dropping off bags of mail. The *Titanic* was due to arrive in New York within a week. Sailing day was April 10, an excellent time for the White Star Line. Many passengers cancelled their plans with other ships in order to book tickets for the *Titanic*.

The *Titanic* sailed in the midst of a coal strike that caused shipping companies to reduce usage of passenger ships, and many ships were grounded. The White Star Line transferred coal from other ships to ensure that the *Titanic* could sail to New York and return to England.

Still, the *Titanic* was not full, because even with all the enthusiasm about this great ship, some were concerned about its safety and ability to sail. Not all of the senior officers were experienced enough to handle such a large ship. Only several months earlier, the *Olympic* had collided with a British warship named the HMS *Hawke*. The collision caused damage to both vessels. Although there were no casualties, the *Olympic* was out of use for several weeks for repairs. The repairs on the *Olympic* caused a delay with *Titanic's* maiden voyage. People thought that large ships such as the *Titanic* and the *Olympic* were not safe.[11]

To make the two ships safe, the White Star Line took various safety precautions, including installing watertight compartments divided by bulkheads that reached one deck over the waterline. The doors between the watertight compartments could be electronically controlled from the ship's bridge. The ship was divided into sixteen such compartments. If water flooded two of the first compartments, the ship would stay afloat if the doors were shut in time.

According to the original plan of the shipbuilders, in case of a collision with another vessel, an iceberg, or a reef, the *Titanic* would survive if the watertight doors were shut, even if some compartments were damaged. The builders of the *Titanic* did not envision a scenario that would cause damage

Titanic *leaving Southampton, April 10, 1912. Source: Wikimedia Commons*

Eli Moskowitz, third-class cabin, Titanic *Exhibit, Tel Aviv, 2014. Photo credit: Reuven Kastro, Courtesy: Makor Rishon*

to more than four compartments, which is why they thought the watertight system was good enough to call the ship practically unsinkable. The White Star Line owners never claimed that the ship was unsinkable, yet that was the impression made to the public.

Another safety issue was the number of lifeboats. According to the British Board of Trade, the *Titanic* had to carry sixteen lifeboats, which would hold a third of the passengers, to meet regulations. The *Titanic* designers wanted to add more lifeboats – at first sixty-four boats, then thirty-two, and then only twenty boats: the original sixteen and four collapsible boats, two of which were stored on the roof of the officers' quarters.[12]

In the early morning of April 10, 1912, the crew of the *Titanic* started boarding the ship at the harbor in Southampton: officers, stewards, cooks, chefs, engineers, firemen, seamen, and bellboys. Some of the crewmen boarded the day before to start the coal bunkers and the engine. Mid-morning, passengers started arriving on special trains from London. The first-class passengers were kindly escorted to their staterooms and suites. Stewards welcomed them and took good care of their luggage, which was sent to cargo. Second-class passengers were also warmly greeted. Steerage passengers, however, were not greeted by stewards. Instead they had to pass medical inspection and immigration processing before boarding. After they boarded, many steerage passengers could not find their cabins, getting lost in the labyrinth of corridors and stairways.

The third-class cabins were divided into three separate sections of the ship: one for single women, one for single men, and one for families. The third-class public rooms (dining room, general room, and smoking room)were open from morning until 22:00, as was the open space on Poop Deck. The third-class passengers could mingle during the day, but at night they had to return to their cabins. Third class-passengers were separated from the rest of the passengers, and steerage areas were closed by gates.[13]

At noon the largest man-made moving object ever built started its maiden voyage. Minutes after the *Titanic* left the pier, the unexpected almost happened. As the *Titanic* was moving away from the dock into the canal, she passed by two ships that were tied with mooring lines to the dock. These ships, the *Oceanic* and the *New York* were grounded because of the coal strike. The *Titanic* created a maelstrom of suction that caused the mooring lines of the *New York* to snap, and the vessel swung toward the *Titanic*. The quick thinking and actions of the crew on the tugboats pulled the *New York* away when she was only one meter from colliding with the *Titanic*. Many onboard who knew about the *Olympic* and *Hawke* incident thought that the two incidents were quite similar. The incident with the *New York* emphasized the importance of safety precautions at sea, especially when maneuvering large behemoths such as the *Titanic*.[14]

The first stop was Cherbourg. The *Titanic* arrived at the French coast an hour later than expected because of the near collision with the *New York*. At Cherbourg, 270 passengers boarded the *Titanic*. The ship spent an hour and a half at Cherbourg before leaving for her next stop.

The *Titanic* reached Queenstown (known today as Cobh), Ireland, on the morning of April 11. Before noon a few hundred passengers boarded. Most of them were Irish immigrants on their way to America. Later that day the *Titanic* left Queenstown. She sailed along the Irish coast and then turned west and disappeared beyond the horizon, never to be seen from land again.

The journey began. The first few days were uneventful, and the passengers enjoyed good weather. The first-class passengers could stroll on the promenade, have a drink at the café, smoke and play cards in the smoking rooms, enjoy a swim in the swimming pool, or exercise in the gym. Second-class passengers had an open deck to stroll; they could enjoy a good book in the library, go to the smoking room, and more. Even third-class passengers had their open deck (the Poop Deck). Steerage passengers were a mix of nationalities.

On the morning of April 14, the passengers felt a difference in the weather.

The air became colder. Many of the passengers preferred to stay indoors rather than strolling outside.

In the radio room, the two operators were very busy that day. The *Titanic* was close enough to the east coast of North America that it was possible to send telegrams to the continent. Many first-class passengers sent private messages to acquaintances and relatives. To add to the traffic, any ship that was in range with the *Titanic* sent the new liner welcoming messages and wished the vessel a successful voyage. To make things even busier, the *Titanic* received several ice warnings during the day. There was no set policy for forwarding ice warnings to the ship's bridge. Some warnings were sent directly to the bridge and posted in the log; some were not. Some were directed to Captain Smith and delivered to him personally. One message from the *Baltic* was delivered to the captain, who, instead of sending it to the bridge, handed it to Bruce Ismay, who put the message in his pocket. Only later that day was the message returned to the captain. Because of the lack in policy, none of the officers on the bridge knew that the *Titanic* was headed directly into an ice zone. Had all the messages been collected, it would have been possible to know the danger that lay straight ahead.[15]

At 22:00, with the changing of the officers and posts at the bridge, the new officers in charge received explicit instructions to watch for icebergs and growlers and to be sure the fresh water supply did not freeze in the tanks. It became freezing cold; the temperature dropped to nearly zero. The ocean was flat and smooth. There was no glare from the bottom of icebergs, so it was difficult to spot them from a distance. When water becomes wavy, the waves hit the icebergs and make them easier to spot. But not that night. The water was calm and flat like glass. It was the end of the Hebrew month of Nissan.* There was no moon in the sky. The lookouts were supposed to have a pair of binoculars, but they had been forgotten in Southampton.[16]

Twenty minutes before midnight, Frederick Fleet, one of the two lookouts in the crow's nest, noticed something in the distance. As soon as he understood that what he saw was an iceberg, he rang the emergency bell and phoned the bridge. Sixth Officer James Moody was on duty on the bridge, and he picked

---

*Calculating the moon's shape and size is easy for Jews who follow the Hebrew calendar. The beginnings of the Hebrew months are marked by the birth of a new moon. Toward the end of every Hebrew month, the moon is nearly invisible. In 1912, April 14 was two days before the end of the Hebrew month of Nissan, so there was no moon that night.

up the phone and heard Fleet yell: "Iceberg right ahead!" Moody called First Officer William Murdoch, who sent an order to the engine room to stop the ship and turn it astern. He ordered Quartermaster Robert Hichens at the helm to turn the ship "hard a'starboard." Murdoch was trying to avoid a head-on collision and turn the ship around the iceberg. He also gave an order to shut the watertight doors. The *Titanic* was still going straight towards the iceberg, but twenty seconds later the ship started to turn. It seemed as if the ship would not hit the berg, but thirty-seven seconds after Fleet rang the bell, there was a grinding jar as the *Titanic* swiped her starboard side against the iceberg.

From the impact, some of the rivets popped open and the plates of the hull on the starboard side buckled inward, which caused a gash in the hull. The damage was below the waterline, and some of the boiler rooms and cargo holds started to flood. As soon as Captain Smith knew about the collision, he rushed to the bridge and started to evaluate the damage to the ship. Then, and even an hour later, people on the *Titanic* still believed that this was a minor event and the *Titanic* would soon start on its way again to New York. One rumor was that the *Titanic* lost a propeller blade, but the voyage would continue, and the passengers were safe.

The watertight doors were closed, but the bulkheads were only one deck above the waterline. When the flooded compartments were full, the water went over the bulkheads and into the next compartment, flooding them as well. Thus the ship started to sink, bow first. Slowly the ship sank deeper and deeper, and the water flowed from one compartment to the next. When it was clear to Captain Smith and to the ship's head builder, Thomas Andrews, that the ship would sink, Captain Smith gave the order to uncover the lifeboats and prepare the passengers for evacuation. The stewards woke the passengers and told them to put on life vests and go to the Boat Deck. An hour after the collision, most passengers still believed the *Titanic* would not sink, although there was a tilt to port. Smith gave the order to start loading the lifeboats with women and children. In the far distance, lights of a ship were seen. As it turns out, those were the lights of the Leyland Line *Californian*, a cargo ship that had stopped for the night because of the ice field. The *Titanic* radio operators tried to contact the ship, but the *Californian*'s radio operator was off duty and his radio was shut down. Today there is much controversy about the *Californian*. The captain of the *Californian*, Captain Stanley Lord, insisted until his last days that his ship was not the ship that was seen from the *Titanic*. He claims that there was another ship, an unidentified vessel, between them. Most researchers today agree that it was in fact the *Californian* and that not waking the radio operator was a fatal mistake. The *Titanic* fired distress rockets. The *Californian* crew saw rockets from the ship in the distance. Nevertheless, no one woke the radio operator.[17]

Over an hour after the collision, the first lifeboat with capacity for sixty-five people left the *Titanic* with eighteen passengers and crew. The people still felt more comfortable on the great ship with all the lights and warmth and did not feel the urgency of leaving the deck and climbing into a tiny boat to bobble in the freezing water. One lifeboat with a capacity of forty left the *Titanic* with only twelve people. There were ten lifeboats on the port side and ten on the starboard side. The captain's order was women and children first. On the starboard side, with First Officer William Murdoch in charge, the rule was women and children first, and if there was room, men could join. On the port side, with Second Officer Charles Lightoller in charge, the rule was women and children only, with no exceptions. The chances of a man surviving depended upon the side of the ship he was on during the evacuation.

As time went by, the panic began. The pressure to rush to the lifeboats was getting greater. The *Titanic* was tilting forward. The bow was under water. The radio operators were desperately calling for assistance from nearby ships. The first to respond were the *Carpathia* and the *Olympic*. Both ships started heading toward the *Titanic*. Another ship, the *Mount Temple*, was nearby but could not come to the rescue because she was stuck in a field of ice.

Two hours after the collision, the only lifeboats still remaining on the *Titanic* were the collapsible ones. The *Titanic* was listing so greatly that it was difficult to attach the boats to the davits. Mayhem began as passengers desperately triedto make it to the lifeboats. The crewmen linked arms and formed a human barrier. At this point, many of the steerage passengers finally made it to the Boat Deck and swarmed the lifeboats. It is said that with the beginning of the loading of the lifeboats, some of the gates between third class and the rest of the ship were closed. Most third-class passengers never made it to the open decks. While the lifeboats were loaded with first-class and second-class passengers, some women from steerage were allowed to reach the upper decks and get into lifeboats. Some steerage men were able to pass the closed gates but got lost in the corridors of first and second class. Few third-class men made it to the lifeboats. Many women tried reaching the lifeboats from third class but never made it. In one case a steward led a group of women from third class into a lifeboat, but most of the steerage passengers were on their own. Toward the end, many men rammed the gates and broke through. When the large group of steerage men finally reached the Boat Deck, the lifeboats were gone. One officer tried to keep order by shooting a few bullets in the air. According to some survivors, one of the officers shot a man who tried to jump into a lifeboat.*

To the very last moments, deep in the engine room, the engineers were pumping water, feeding coal into the furnaces, and keeping the electricity going. To the very last moments, the radio operators tried repeatedly and desperately to call for help using the internationally known C.Q.D. and the famous S.O.S. distress calls. To the very last moments, the band played cheerful tunes on the Boat Deck. In those last desperate moments, people started jumping into the water, throwing deck chairs and trying to make rafts. Many people turned to prayer.

While the bow was filling with water and sinking, the stern was rising up into the air. The pressure of the weight of the stern and the sunken bow caused the *Titanic* to break in two. When this happened, the bow was already submerged. The bow sank to the bottom of the Atlantic Ocean and hit the seabed. Although the impact was great, the bow section stayed intact with minimal damage. The stern of the ship, with its propellers and all, was out of the water for a while. The stern stayed afloat for a minute or two and then sank as well. The *Titanic* disappeared at 02:20. The stern hit the bottom of the ocean at great speed and was severely damaged from the impact. The decks collapsed one on top of the other. Much of the hull was twisted and bent. Around the two sections, there was a great debris field.

The lucky ones who survived found themselves in little lifeboats, shocked and confused in the icy waters of the Atlantic Ocean. Many survivors (mostly women) feared for the lives of their loved ones that were not with them in the boats. Some women and crew members wanted to return to the scene and try to rescue a few of the hundreds of drowning people in the water calling for help. In Lifeboat 6, Quartermaster Hichens decided not to return, although many of the women in the lifeboat asked to. Some of these women

---

Writer and Titanic *researcher Walter Lord wrote about this in his book* The Night Lives On *(1987). Lord suggests that shots were fired by an officer or maybe even by two different officers. This happened very close to the* Titanic's *last moments, and there are conflicting accounts about who did the shooting. Lord concludes that the shooter was probably First Officer William Murdoch. Murdoch died, and all of the surviving officers claimed that he couldn't have done the shooting. It remains a mystery.*

testified against Hichens at the inquiry. The women said that Hichens was given a direct order from the captain to try to rescue people from the water. He was reportedly quoted as saying: "It is our lives now, not theirs." One of the occupants of Lifeboat 6 was Army Major Arthur Peuchen, who was allowed into the lifeboat because of his experience in rowing, as there was not enough crew in the lifeboat. He, too, testified against Hichens. Peuchen claimed that throughout the night he tried to mediate between the women and the quartermaster, but in vain. After the disaster and inquiry, Hichens was condemned for his behavior.[19]

Lifeboat 6 did not return, but Lifeboat 4 did and picked up five survivors, two of whom died during the night. Lifeboat 14 also returned and saved three more people.[20]

Toward dawn, the *Carpathia* was finally seen in the distance. Her captain, Arthur Rostron ordered to light the night sky with rockets to signal the lifeboats. Some survivors burned newspapers to make torches to signal the other lifeboats. Some officers used green flares. At 03:30, the *Carpathia* saw the first of the lifeboats. At 04:10, the first lifeboat reached the rescue ship. It was Lifeboat 2 with twenty five survivors. It was now dawn, and the dark night was beginning to give way. The lifeboats started to row toward the *Carpathia*. Four hours later, the last survivors boarded the *Carpathia*. It was Lifeboat 12 loaded with its own survivors and with the survivors of overturned collapsible Lifeboat B whom they picked up during the night. The last survivor to board the *Carpathia* was Second Officer Charles Lightoller, fourth in command of the *Titanic* crew and the highest-ranking surviving officer. In total 712 people boarded the *Carpathia* while over 1,500 died. The *Carpathia* sailed to the reported site of the *Titanic* but only found a few floating deck chairs and one body.[21]

Three days later the *Carpathia* reached New York. She docked at the harbor on Thursday, April 18. By then the disaster was well known worldwide. At first it was thought that the *Titanic* hit an iceberg but all the passengers were safe. Within days, the real news made it to the newspapers and special editions reported the truth about the disaster. Some newspapers had lists of survivors.

The White Star Line chartered a few small ships to search for bodies and possible survivors. The cable ship *Mackay-Bennett* left Halifax, Canada, on April 17. For nine days she searched the area and collected 300 bodies, all wearing life vests. Later, more ships were sent to the scene, and a total of 330 bodies were recovered. Of those, over one hundred were buried at sea because the bodies were too damaged to be identified. The rest of the bodies were taken to Halifax. Sixty bodies were claimed by relatives. The remaining bodies were buried in Halifax in three cemeteries: Catholic, Protestant, and Jewish. Many graves were marked "unknown."[22]

After the disaster two inquiries were made: one in the United States and one in England. Bruce Ismay, the White Star Line owner, was a lead witness for both inquiries, as was Second Officer Charles Lightoller. Both inquiries decided to increase the number of lifeboats required by large ships and issue new regulations regarding radio messages at sea and the height of watertight bulkheads. One theory mentioned was the possibility that if the *Titanic* had hit the iceberg straight on and not swiped against it, the *Titanic* would not have sunk. Today, using simulators, the same conclusion is reached. If the *Titanic* had hit the iceberg with her bow, only the first couple of compartments would have been flooded, but the ship would not have sunk.[23]

The American inquiry started a day after the survivors arrived. The Americans wanted to be sure the British survivors (crew and passengers) did not return to England before they were called to testify. The first witness was Bruce Ismay who escaped on one of the lifeboats while so many women were still on board. Because he was a British citizen, it was thought that he might flee to England, so he was called first. Only after the American inquiry finished with Ismay and the other British survivors were they permitted to leave the country. The British inquiry began on May 2 and continued until July. There were differences between the inquiries, and there was not much cooperation between the Americans and the British. One example is the conclusion regarding the number of lifeboats required on ships. The Americans were very clear on the need to match the needed number to the capacity of the ship, but the British were not eager to change regulations. (The regulations were old and nonrelevant because of the increase in the size of new ships). That is also why the British did not find the White Star Line negligent. The British were also concerned about relatives suing the White Star Line for damages.[24] Both inquiries decided that there needed to be a radio operator stationed around the clock. Both inquiries agreed that neither the White Star Line nor the crew were responsible for the disaster.

One hundred and eighty witnesses testified at the two inquires. Over two thousand pages of testimony were compiled. Some testimonies contradicted each other, such as those regarding whether the ship broke in two or not and

Captain Smith's behavior during the evacuation. In the British inquiry, the most interesting witnesses besides Bruce Ismay were Sir Cosmo Duff Gordon and his wife, Lucy. There was gossip and rumors about their escape. They were questioned about this but were not accused of anything.[25]

Another male survivor that suffered from bad public opinion was Bruce Ismay. He was shunned for the rest of his life and forbade anyone to mention the *Titanic* in his presence.[26]

The *Titanic* disaster affected both of her sister ships. The *Britannic* was never used as a passenger ship as designed. Before her launch, many modifications and safety precautions were made. However, with the outbreak of World War I, the ship was converted to a hospital ship. She was the largest ambulance ship ever, a record that still stands today. In December 1916 she was sunk by a German mine off the coast of the Greek island of Kea and sank within an hour. Thanks to the quick evacuation, all 1,100 people on board the *Britannic* made it into lifeboats, but thirty people died when their lifeboat was caught in one of the ship's mighty propellers.[27]

The *Olympic* was converted to a troop ship in World War I. She was camouflaged and carried a total of over 119,000 American and Canadian troops during the war. After the war she reverted to being a passenger liner and sailed for the White Star Line until the mid-1930s. By then there was a substantial decrease in traffic across the Atlantic, and the *Olympic* was no longer profitable. In 1935 she was scrapped and her furnishings and fittings sold at auction.

In the 1970s and 1980s, there were attempts to search for the remains of the *Titanic*. One was funded by a Texas millionaire named Jack Grimm who planned to find the *Titanic* and salvage valuable artifacts from the wreck. He also sponsored searches of *Noah's Ark*, the Loch Ness Monster, and the legendary Bigfoot in the 1970s. In 1980 he organized an expedition and sailed from Florida to the area where he assumed the *Titanic* would be found. He used wide-sweep sonar and oceanographic experts. Grimm was not an expert himself and did not use a specific search method. He skipped from one point to another, making many strategic mistakes. The expedition suffered from bad weather and technological problems, and failed.

Grimm went on three expeditions, and although he spared no expense, he searched in the wrong places and never found the wreck. His second expedition was in 1981. In 1983 during his last expedition, he claimed to have found one of the *Titanic's* propellers and shared photos of his "discovery" at a press conference when he returned. It turned out to be false, and he became unreliable. When asked to give coordinates of the *Titanic* wreck, he lied.[28]

A joint American and French research group went to search for the wreck of the *Titanic* in 1985. The head of the group was an American researcher, former United States Navy expert Dr. Robert Ballard, a professor of oceanography and underwater archaeology. He spent many years in the depths of the oceans searching for shipwrecks and had found many wrecks, including the American aircraft carrier *USS Yorktown* in 1988 and the German battleship *Bismarck* in 1989. Dr. Ballard also found the wreck of the Israeli submarine *INS Dakar* in the Mediterranean Sea in 1999.[29]

An expedition led by Dr. Ballard and French researcher Jean Louis Michel left Woods Hole Oceanographic Institution, Massachusetts, in July 1985. The expedition was funded by private investors and the United States Navy. The search had two phases. The first phase was led by the French on board the research vessel *le Suroit*. The *Titanic* was not found during the first phase, and the search entered the second phase, led by the Americans on the research vessel *Knorr*. This time, Dr. Ballard led the search.[30]

The research team spent several weeks at the site. The team used highly advanced equipment, including an unmanned submarine that could reach the ocean floor equipped with high resolution cameras. The submarine was named *Argo*, after the famous ship from Greek mythology, the ship that Jason and the Argonauts sailed on their journey to retrieve the Golden Fleece.

In the beginning of Dr. Ballard's research, the team based their strategy on the information they had received from Jack Grimm, but the information they had was false. Later the team used a method known as "mowing the lawn." *Argo*, connected to the *Knorr* with a long cable, was towed back and forth in straight lines, much like a reverse kite.

After a month at the site, on September 1, soon after midnight, the team in the command van of the ship was watching the monitors with images sent by *Argo*. Suddenly they noticed round, man-made shapes on the screen. The crew realized they were staring at one of the *Titanic's* boilers. The *Titanic* had been found! From that moment, it was relatively easy to find the rest of the wreck. After several more days of searching and filming, Dr. Ballard and his team were able to solve some of the *Titanic's* most intriguing mysteries. One was: did the ship break in two or did she sink in one piece? The answer was right there. The *Titanic* had indeed broken in two, and the two sections – the bow and the stern – were 600 meters apart. All around was a huge debris field. Up until the discovery, most people believed that the *Titanic* sank in one piece. That was the official resolution made by the inquiries, and that is how it was depicted in books and film. A few days later after filming the wreck, the team returned to the United States and shared photos of the *Titanic* with the world.[31]

A year later Dr. Ballard returned to the wreck site. This time he had only fourteen days for diving and filming. He and his team dove to the ocean floor in a tiny submarine named *Alvin* where they took thousands of photos and hundreds of films. The photos showed a wonderful mosaic of the ship. The larger half of the wreck, the bow, was fairly intact and easy to get near to and film. The stern was in a terrible mess, and it was dangerous for the *Alvin* team to get too close. Still, both parts of the ship enabled Dr. Ballard, and later other researchers, with the ability to study the wreck and understand what had happened to the *Titanic* the night she sank. They saw the damage caused by the impact of crashing into the iceberg and hitting the ocean floor.[32]

One of the questions that researchers asked was the extent of the damage caused by the iceberg. Until the 1980s most researchers believed that the iceberg had torn a long gash

Dessert spoons recovered from the wreck, on display at the Titanic *exhibition, Tel Aviv, summer of 2014. Photo credit: Eli Moskowitz*

along the starboard side of the hull which caused the water to penetrate the "unsinkable" ship. Using simulators, it was hard to see how the *Titanic* sank so fast (two-and-a-half hours) with one continuous gash. The data received from photos after the *Titanic* was found gave the researchers a new and more accurate theory. The iceberg did not tear a continuous gash; instead, the pressure of the iceberg on the hull caused rivets to pop and plates to buckle, and so a noncontinuous gash had doomed the ship.[33]

The discovery of the *Titanic* enabled researchers to solve many mysteries regarding the sinking. One of the questions concerned the the tragic saga of the third-class passengers. When the *Titanic* was found, there was evidence that some of the gates between steerage and the rest of the ship were indeed locked. Such evidence contradicted the claim by the White Star Line that there was no discrimination between the classes on the night of the disaster. Another question, more eerie than others, was: would they find any bodies at the wreck site? After many hours of filming and searching, no human remains were found.

Ever since the *Titanic's* last resting place was found, many search groups have wanted to photograph the ship and salvage parts of the wreckage and debris field. Within the next few years, thousands of artifacts were salvaged, including chunks of coal, cutlery, metal pieces of the hull, floor tiles, and other pieces of the ship. Personal belongings were salvaged as well, including watches, pairs of glasses, suitcases, and much more. Even the memorial plaque that Dr. Ballard left on the *Titanic's* bow in 1986 was stolen several years later. Occasionally *Titanic* artifacts are sold at auction to private collectors or museums. The *Titanic* lies in international waters, and there is no jurisdiction over the wreckage area. To prevent grave robbers and fortune hunters, an international protective body was established under the UNESCO Convention on the Protection of the Underwater Cultural Heritage Law. Today the rights to the *Titanic* wreck and debris field belong to Titanic Inc., and all artifacts that are salvaged are kept safe in storage. Some are displayed in museums and exhibitions.[34]

Not many scientists and researchers have visited the wreck. Two, Bob Blumberg and Kirk Wolfinger, were Jewish and shared a visit to the wreck. While at the site, Blumberg prayed a Jewish prayer in respect for the dead.[35]

The last of the *Titanic* survivors, Millvina Dean, who was only two months old when she sailed on the *Titanic*, passed away in 2009 at the age of ninety-seven. In 2012 there were countless ceremonies around the world to commemorate the 100th-year anniversary of the *Titanic* disaster. A special ceremony was held at sea at the site where the ship sank.[36]

The *Titanic* story is not only about a famous sunken ship or about a series of coincidences that led to the collision with an iceberg. It is a story about people who died and people whose lives were changed forever on the cold North Atlantic night of April 14, 1912. It is a story about rich travelers who sailed the biggest, most luxurious ship of her day, and it is also a story about hundreds of immigrants who wanted to start a new life away from religious persecution in Europe.

3

IMMIGRATION

Eliezer (Leslie) Gilinski was twenty-two years old when he boarded the *Titanic*. Gilinski was born in 1890 in a *shtetl* called Ignalina in eastern Lithuania. He had four brothers and one sister. Gilinski, whose Hebrew nickname was Leizer, was a mechanical engineer and a professional locksmith. For a short time he served as a locksmith in the czarist Russian regime but escaped Lithuania to avoid serving in the Russian Army. His father, Shlomo, served in the Russian Army for twenty-five years. To avoid serving in the army like his father, he immigrated to England. He stayed with his brother David and family in Abercynon, South Wales, and worked as a locksmith.

Third-class Jewish passenger Eliezer Gilinski (right) with his brothers David and Louis. Courtesy: Stanly Gilinski

Later, more family members joined them. His parents, Shlomo and Sarah Gitel, remained in Lithuania but wanted the whole family to eventually immigrate to America. Eliezer, the youngest and the only bachelor, was chosen to be the first to immigrate to the United States and settle in Chicago. The rest of the family would follow. After making enough money as a locksmith, Eliezer Gilinski purchased a third-class ticket that cost him 8£ 5s on the *Titanic*. He was a Jewish immigrant on his way to America.[37]

The *Titanic* was a luxurious

ship but also an immigrant ship. Most first-class American passengers were returning to the United States after a winter vacation or business trip to Europe. In steerage, hundreds of passengers were immigrants from Eastern Europe. As technology advanced and ships grew larger and faster, the number of passengers in steerage grew. At the same time the conditions in steerage became better, and crossing the Atlantic became shorter with better accommodations for the passengers. During the period of time in which the *Titanic* sailed, the gates to the United States were wide open to immigration. Tens of millions flocked to America, including over 2.5 million Jews.

Jewish immigration to what is now the United States started 250 years before the *Titanic* sunk. The first Jews, a group of twenty-three people, came to North America in the mid-1650s. During the Spanish Inquisition many Jews fled Spain and Portugal and settled in the Spanish-Portuguese colonies along the South American coast. When the Inquisition reached Brazil, some Jews fled north by ship. The first group of Spanish and Portuguese Jews to do so had a hard journey. Their ship was attacked by pirates, and their belongings were stolen. Eventually the group made it in 1654 to the Dutch colony in what was then New Amsterdam. A Jewish enclave was established, and so began the continuous era of Jewish settlement in North America.[38]

At first the Jews in North America faced discrimination, but as the Jewish community grew, so did their independence and civil rights. For example, they were granted permission to trade in fishing. In 1656 the Jewish community was authorized to establish a Jewish cemetery. Only in 1728, when the Dutch colonies were traded to British hands, were Jewish communities given full rights, including the right to pray and practice Judaism in public. The Jewish community started to build a synagogue. Two years later, in 1730, the first synagogue was founded in the settlement that was renamed New York. The synagogue was called *Shearit Israel*, also known as the Spanish and Portuguese Synagogue, and today it is one of the oldest Jewish synagogues in North America.

When the American Revolution broke out in 1777, there were three thousand Jews scattered around the thirteen colonies. One hundred and sixty Jews fought with General George Washington and the Continental Army. Many were killed in fierce battles. In 1840, at the beginning of a wave of immigration from England, Germany, Russia, and Poland to America, there were around 15,000 Jews living in the United States. Another big

Jewish milestone was in 1849 when a group of Jewish settlers established a community in San Francisco, California, during the Gold Rush.

In the middle of the nineteenth century, the twelfth American president, Zachary Taylor, opened the gates of the United States to mass immigration. He called upon citizens of foreign countries to come and settle in the United States. The Jewish American poet Emma Lazarus (1849–1887) called to the people of the old world:

> Give me your tired, your poor, your huddled masses yearning to breathe free… I lift my lamp beside the golden door!

This quote was later inscribed on a bronze plaque on the pedestal of the Statue of Liberty. Emma Lazarus symbolizes great pride and honor to American Jewry. She was from an aristocratic Jewish family that immigrated to America from Portugal. She supported Jewish pride by helping to establish the Hebrew Technical Institute, and she assisted poor Jewish immigrants in becoming self-supporting. Most immigrants were refugees and survivors of pogroms in Russia. Lazarus was a big supporter of the Zionist movement and called for a Jewish homeland many years before Theodor Herzl used the term *Zionism*.[39]

Most non-Jewish immigrants came to the United States to improve their financial situation. The Jewish immigrants, on the other hand, came to America because of persecution, religious discrimination, and anti-Semitism. They came to America to flee massacres, pogroms, and riots. While most of the non-Jewish immigrants were single men without their families, most Jewish immigrants were families with children.

Eventually within the United States there was a cultural conflict between the new Jewish immigrants, who came from Eastern Europe (especially from Russia and Lithuania) to escape persecution and the American Jews who had settled, assimilated, integrated, and were part

Jewish immigrants being examined, Ellis Island, early twentieth century.
Source: Library of Congress

of American society. There was conflict between Sephardic Jews and Russian Jews. Some of the Jewish American leaders saw the new immigrants as a burden on the Jewish community in particular and on American society in general. There was a strong objection to absorbing these new immigrants, who clung to traditions such as speaking Yiddish and wearing Hasidic clothing, kept kosher, and observed the Sabbath, in established Jewish communities. Between the years 1787–1820, around six thousand immigrants came to America every year. From 1820 on, the rate of immigration rapidly increased. By 1830 more than 23,000 immigrants were arriving every year. By 1840 there were sixty thousand new immigrants every year. Most immigrants were from England, Ireland, Germany, and France. In 1849, with the discovery of gold in California (known as the Gold Rush), a wave of immigrants began, not only from Europe but also

Immigrants approaching New York, early twentieth century. Source: Wikimedia Commons

from China, Mexico, and South American countries. At first, the percentage of Jews among the immigrants was low, but between the years 1870–1880, a new wave of 125,000 immigrants arrived from the Russian and Austro-Hungarian empires. The percentage of Jewish immigrants became significant. In the beginning of the twentieth century, 30 percent of new immigrants per year were Jewish. The mass immigration came to an end in 1921 when the United States Congress passed the Emergency Immigration Act to decrease the number of immigrants from Europe. Immigrants still arrived but in smaller numbers. The period between 1880 and 1920 is known as the "great immigration era."

Within forty years an estimated 2.7 million Jews immigrated to the United States, most from Eastern Europe.

Many Jewish immigrants who came from Eastern Europe were penniless. They worked hard in sweatshops. Some made it the hard way to the peak of American society in various fields. Henry Morgenthau (1856–1946) was born in Germany and immigrated with his family at age ten. He studied law, befriended President Woodrow Wilson, and eventually became the American ambassador to the Ottoman Empire. Another Jewish immigrant who succeeded in the American financial world was Jacob Henry Schiff (1847–1920). He was born in Frankfurt, Germany, and immigrated with his family at age eighteen. He became a banker and a businessman. He was also a noted philanthropist who contributed to the welfare of Jewish immigrants. In literature there is Isaac Asimov (1920–1992), who was born in Russia, immigrated to the United States at age three, studied biochemistry, and became an author of science fiction and a professor at Boston University. In the field of entertainment, there is Al (Asa) Jolson (1886–1950), who was born in Lithuania, immigrated at age eight, and became an actor, singer, and comedian. Jews have succeeded in almost every field in America, including politics, entertainment, and banking.

Descendants of Jewish immigrants have always played important roles in American politics, and the influence is noticeable even today. At one point in 2012, all three mayors of the three largest American cities were Jews: Michael Bloomberg (New York) whose Jewish grandparents immigrated from Belarus, Eric Michael Garcetti (Los Angeles) whose Jewish grandfather immigrated from Russia, and Rahm Emanuel (Chicago) whose Jewish grandfather immigrated from Moldova. On the national level there is Joe Lieberman, the 2000 election vice president nominee whose Jewish grandparents immigrated from Poland and Hungary, and Bernie Sanders, one of the 2016 presidential candidates, whose Jewish parents immigrated from Poland.

The contribution of American Jews to the economy was great, and so was their influence on American culture, science, literature, and media. One of the main reasons for the mass immigration at the end of the nineteenth century and the beginning of the twentieth century was the rise of anti-Semitic incidents in Eastern Europe. Many incidents were encouraged by the governments themselves. In 1903 during the Kishinev pogrom, fifty Jews were massacred by a mob led by priests and supported by the governor, who gave an order not to stop the rioters for three days. Nicholas II, the Russian Tsar, allowed local Chris-

A poor Jewish immigrant living in a dirty cellar, New York, 1890. Source: Library of Congress. Photo credit: Jacob Riis

tian leaders to harm the Jews. The Kishinev pogrom was an expression of hate that had been fermented for many years by the anti-Semitic Christian leadership and backed by the authorities. Similar to other organized anti-Semitic riots and massacres, the Kishinev pogrom was a turning point in the Jewish world, especially for American Jewry. In the aftermath of these pogroms, many Jews realized that life in Europe was no longer sustainable and immigrated to the United States and other countries. Until 1903 Eastern European Jews were seen by American Jews as old-fashioned and inappropriate to the Reform movement that was rising in the Jewish communities in the United States. The increasing anti-Semitic persecution changed all that, and new refugees were more welcomed into America. The pogroms in Eastern Europe caused American Jewry to feel compassion toward the poor Jewish immigrants.

Another influential factor that increased the flow of immigration to the United States was the Cantonist decree. The decree was a method used by the Russian regime to cause Jews to convert by forced service in the Russian Army for twenty-five years. The main goal behind the forced military service was to re-educate the Jewish population by integrating them into Russian society. The decree that was made by Tsar Nicholas II was to recruit Jewish boys aged twelve to eighteen. During their service the Cantonist boys would be forced into Christianity and eventually assimilate. Other than bribes and ransoming, the only way to avoid recruitment was to flee Russia. It was very difficult to leave Russia in legitimate ways, and many Jews forged documents and fled Russia to neighboring countries under assumed identities.[40]

The deterioration in enforcement of the decree started in 1827. Until that year, many Jewish communities had paid the Russian government bribes to avoid the forced recruitment of Jewish boys. From that year forward, all the benefits and privileges were cancelled, and many Jews were under the threat of immediate recruitment. The recruitment was done by force and Jews were kidnapped by the Russian Army and recruited unwillingly. The biggest threat to the Jewish communities and for the boys was the fear of forced christening. Indeed, most of the Cantonist Jews were eventually baptized against their will or re-educated and left the Jewish religion out of fear of punishment by their officers and commanders. A few Jews still kept their Jewish traditions despite the hostile environment. Many lost their lives from disease or anguish, especially the ones who insisted on keeping kosher. Herzl Yankel Tsam was one of the only known Jewish Cantonists that never converted from Judaism, yet he became a captain in the Russian Army, where he remained a Jew and served for forty-one years. Nevertheless, most Jews did not survive the pressure and converted. To avoid Jews from escaping the draft, the Russian government appointed the rabbis and heads of the communities to be in charge of recruiting and forced them to fill the quota of draftees.

One who described the Cantonist situation was the Jewish and Yiddish author Shalom Yaakov Abramovich (1836–1917), widely known as Mendele Mocher Sforim, in his satirical story *The Travels of Benjamin the Third* (written in 1878). The story tells the tale of Benjamin of Batelon, a fictional town. Benjamin is the town fool. He and his friend Sendrel set out to find the ten lost tribes of Israel. The two friends were captured by the Russian Army and forced to be soldiers. Mendele Mocher Sforim describes the two poor Jewish friends while they are in the barracks:

> It was difficult to recognize the two. Their faces were changed. Heads shaven, no beards or *pe'ot* (side curls). Their eyes sad and doleful. Their forehead full of sweat. Shadow of death on their faces. They are bent and twisted, shaken and shivering and all around them there are armed men with evil faces.

Benjamin and Sendrel's fate turned to the good side after a failed escape attempt. The two were recaptured and reported to a military court but eventually were discharged. Although this satire has a happy ending, it was not so for thousands and thousands of Jews who were kidnapped by the Tsarist Russian Army for enslavement and forced conversion.

The Russian government put much pressure on the heads of the communities. There was also much pressure from wealthy Jews who did all they could to save their sons from the draft. In practice, most of the recruited Jews were from poor families that could not pay a ransom. Many Jewish families fled their hometowns to prevent the Russian authorities from taking their sons. In many cases the families would falsely report the deaths of their sons to avoid capture.

The Cantonist Decree was only one of the hundreds of anti-Semitic decrees and laws that the Tsarist regime issued against the Jews. The purpose of all those laws was to uproot the Jewish foundations and undermine the rabbinical institutions. During that period, there were many anti-government riots against the Tsar. The peak of the uprising was the assassination of the Russian Tsar Alexander II and several of his government officials in 1881. The assassination was used as an excuse for more anti-Semitic propaganda, and the incident resulted in more pogroms and riots against the Jews. One of the slogans of the riots was "Kill the Jews and Save Mother Russia." Many of the riots ended with Jews being murdered. Within the next few years, the Russian authorities became even more hostile to the Jewish communities. In 1882 more anti-Semitic laws and decrees were announced. The decrees included the prohibition of Jews owning land and banning Jews from practicing medicine and law. In 1891 all twenty thousand Jews were expelled from Moscow.[41] The pogroms, the Cantonist decree, the anti-Semitism, and the government hostility all caused millions of Russian Jews to leave Russia and immigrate to Western Europe, England, and the United States.

Most Jewish immigrants who came to America were poor. They saved all the money they could in order to purchase a one-way ticket for them and for their families on one of the ships that sailed to America. Usually they took a train to England or France from where most ships sailed. Some ships sailed from Germany. Usually the father went first to make some money in America and then sent the money to his family so they could join him. Many Jews saw their exodus from Europe to the United States as an opportunity to start a new life. Many Americanized their names, the men shaved their beards and *pe'ot*, the women dumped their wigs, and many tossed their *tefillin* overboard as they sailed to America. This mass immigration and assimilation was also connected to the new movement that was spreading in the United States and in Europe: Reform Judaism.[42]

During this period many Jews in the United States continued to be observant Jews and kept the Jewish traditions they brought with them from Europe. They hung on to their Jewish Hasidic attire, their Yiddish, their Jewish identity and dignity. They were not troubled by anti-Semitism and persecution. They felt safe continuing to be Jews just as they had wanted to be in Europe. Meanwhile many other Jews assimilated into American society. Some hung on to Jewish tradition but felt that they were more American than Jewish. Generally most Jews in America considered themselves Jews and, although assimilated, belonged to a Jewish congregation. Many Jews, whether Hasidic or Reform, observant or secular, were proud to be Jewish in America. Most were immigrants, but many travelers were businessmen who had already established themselves in America or were American-born descendants to Jewish immigrants. Some Jewish businessmen had dealings in Europe and traveled frequently on the European-American route. Some had businesses in France, Belgium, the Netherland, England, and Germany.

One of the many immigrant Jews who arrived in America was Swiss-born (from an *Ashkenazi* ancestry) Meyer Guggenheim (1828–1905). In Switzerland his family suffered from persecution and poverty. Guggenheim left Switzerland in 1847. The family arrived in Philadelphia, and Meyer started working as a merchant. He sold shoelaces, hair bands, and spices. Then he opened a vegetable store. He married his stepsister Barbara. During the American Civil War, his business became quite successful. After the war he purchased some shares of a prosperous train company, and by 1879 his fortune was $300,000. He began investing in mining in Colorado. Within a few years in the mining industry, his fortune grew an additional $250,000 per year. Meyer Guggenheim became one of the richest Americans in the mining industry as the owner of the American Smelting and Refining Company. Meyer and Barbara Guggenheim had ten children: seven sons and three daughters. The Guggenheims became philanthropists and donated money to the expanding New York Jewish community. They contributed to the Mount Sinai Jewish Hospital in New York for the benefit of many poor Jewish immigrants. The Guggenheim family also invested in an art museum and an aviation research institute.

Meyer and Barbara Guggenheim's fifth son was Benjamin, who was born in Philadelphia in 1865. He married Florette Seligman (1870–1937), daughter of businessman and banker James Seligman, a descendant of German-Dutch Jews. Benjamin and Florette had three daughters: Benita (1895–1927), Marguerite (1898–1979), and Barbara (1893–1995). Benjamin Guggenheim joined the family business in mining and smelting and was sent to Colorado to manage the mining industry. He developed the refining industry, which became one of the most prosperous businesses in the family. He was in charge of the men who operated heavy machinery for mining metals such as silver and copper. He was an interesting character who walked around the mines carrying a revolver and lived in a hut amongst the miners. One of his acquaintances was Margaret (Molly) Brown, a wealthy businesswoman who struck it rich from the mining industry. The two became business associates and met again in Cherbourg while boarding the *Titanic*. Molly Brown became the character later known as "the unsinkable Molly Brown."

In 1901, after marring Florette, Benjamin Guggenheim was the first member of the family to leave the family business. He moved to New York and developed an independent business in the mining and smelting industry. After his father's death in 1905, Benjamin received a large inheritance that was added to his personal fortune and bought a mansion on the corner of Fifth Avenue.[43]

First-class Jewish passenger Benjamin Guggenheim. Richest Jew on board. Source: New York Public Library

In 1909 Benjamin Guggenheim was appointed executive manager of an international company that dealt with pumping steam. Because of his many businesses, he traveled frequently on the New York to Paris route. He opened an office in Paris and occasionally lived there, but then he lost money in unsuccessful projects and failed businesses. In the winter of 1911–1912, he was in Paris, planning to return to the United States on the Cunard luxurious liner *Lusitania*. The ship was in repairs, however, so he purchased a boarding ticked on another ship, the *Carmania*. That trip was delayed because of the coal strike, so he decided to purchase a ticket on the *Titanic*. He took a train from Paris to Cherbourg to board the ship. With him were his valet, his chauffeur, his mistress, and her maid. Benjamin Guggenheim was the richest Jewish passenger on the *Titanic*; the only passenger richer than him was Colonel John Jacob Astor. Guggenheim's ticket cost him 75£ 4s for him and his valet. They occupied stateroom B84 on the B Deck.

Isidor Straus is another example of a Jew who prospered in the United States. Isidor, whose Hebrew name was Abraham, was born in Otterberg, Bavaria, Germany, in 1845. He was the eldest son of Lazarus (1809–1898) and Sarah (1823–1876). Lazarus, whose Hebrew name was Eliezer, immigrated to the United States in 1852, and Sarah joined him two years later, bringing Isidor and the rest of the family with her. Isidor had four brothers: Hermine (1846–1922), Nathan (1848–1931), Jacob (1849–1851), and Oscar (1850–1926). The family settled in Georgia. As a child, Isidor helped his father in the family business in a small grocery store.[44]

When the American Civil War broke out in 1861, Isidor tried joining the Confederate Army, but he was too young at age sixteen and thus was denied. In 1864 he joined a group of merchants who tried to break the northern blockade on the south. The army of the north had many more ships and was able to surround the southern ports and form a blockade. Eventually the Confederate Army noticed Isidor's skills and posted him in Europe to help break the blockade from there. Eventually he was appointed lieutenant. Among his duties and missions was smuggling merchandise and food products from Europe to the besieged southern ports.

Isidor Straus, who was a successful businessman, proved his worth and was able to smuggle many shipments of goods from Europe to the south. He was also in charge of finding successful smuggling routes and raising funds. He is well remembered within the confederate loyalists for his resourcefulness and for his contribution to the cause. Even today, Isidor Straus is considered a confederate hero, a patriot loyal to the confederacy.

First-class Jewish passenger Isidor Straus, who refused to enter a lifeboat before other men. Source: Library of Congress

Isidor Straus was not the only Jewish soldier to serve in the American Civil War. Jews fought both in the union and in the confederacy. It is estimated that over three thousand Jews fought for the union and seven thousand Jews fought for the confederacy. Many Jews died in combat, and their contribution to their armies was well appreciated. In total over six hundred Jewish soldiers were killed in combat during the war. Some are buried in the Cemetery for Hebrew Confederate Soldiers in Richmond, Virginia, the only Jewish military cemetery not located in the State of Israel.

By the end of the American Civil War, Isidor Straus had made a small personal fortune of $12,000 from the smuggling business. After the war the Straus family left Georgia and moved to New York. In 1871 Isidor married Rosalie Ida (nee Blun). She was born in 1849 in Worms, Germany, to a Jewish family. Her parents, Nathan and Mindel Blun, and their family immigrated to New York later that year when Ida was an infant.

Lazarus Straus and two of his sons, Isidor and Nathan, owned a store for kitchenware, houseware, and crockery. They called their shop L. Straus & Sons. In 1874, the family expanded their little storehouse and moved into the basement of Macy's department store. The Straus's business thrived, and by 1896 they gained full ownership of the department store.

Isidor Straus joined the Democratic Party and was elected as a congressman (1894–1895), after which he did not run another term. He was a close friend and adviser to President Grover Cleveland but declined the offer to serve as Postmaster General.

Isidor Straus kept Jewish traditions and co-founded the Jewish Seminary in New York. Isidor saw himself as more of an American than a Jew. In a letter he wrote in 1909, he stated that although he was born a Jew, he did not belong to any synagogue. He also opposed the Zionist movement. In 1907 he said that Zionism was an unrealistic and dangerous faith. He said: "If the meaning of Zionism is a homeland for the Jewish people, I object strongly."[45]

Although he did not want to be seen as a Jewish figure, he was very generous with donations to Jewish organizations and education. He was head of the Montefiore Medical Center in the Bronx, New York, which was described as the largest Jewish hospital in the United States.

Isidor Straus also was involved in assisting Jewish immigrants arriving in New York. In 1889 he founded The Educational Alliance, the Jewish social institution for Eastern European Jewish immigrants. The main purpose of the institution was to help the Jewish immigrants find jobs, study English, and learn about American history and culture.

Isidor and Ida had seven children. The couple was very devoted to each another. When Isidor served in Congress and went on business trips, he wrote to Ida every day.

Two of Isidor's brothers were also known in the political and business world. His brother Oscar (Solomon) Straus had a long political career. He practiced law and served as the United States ambassador to the Ottoman Empire. He also served as United States secretary of commerce and labor under President Theodore Roosevelt, the first Jew to serve in that position. Oscar Straus also ran for governor of New York.

Of Isidor's brothers the best known was probably Nathan. After the American Civil War, Nathan helped their father in the family business. Until the end of the 1880s he served as an executive in the family business and then retired to run his own businesses and engage in activities which included philanthropy.

In the late 1880s he donated much of his wealth to the healthcare of

Jewish Philanthropist Nathan Straus.
Source: Library of Congress

New York citizens. Nathan Straus was among the founders and funders of the laboratory to provide pasteurized milk, an organization that saved tens of thousands (especially children) from diseases and infant mortality. He also visited the Holy Land which was under Ottoman rule several times. His first trip to the region was in 1904.[46]

While in Israel he supported the local Jewish pioneers by donating money to their welfare and assisted with milk-pasteurizing efforts in Jerusalem. Nathan Straus gave two-thirds of his personal fortune to the people of Israel. Nathan's philanthropic activities in Israel made such an impact on the Jewish people that an Israeli city established in 1929, Netanya, was named after him. Today, Netanya is a large city with a population of over 200,000. In addition, several Israeli medical centers are named after Nathan Straus, including the Nathan and Lina Medical Center on Straus Street in Jerusalem which is still in operation today. All the Straus family members were involved in many aspects of the Jewish community in New York and the American public as well as with the Jews in Jerusalem.

Isidor and Ida spent most of the winter of 1911–1912 in Cape Martin on the French Riviera. Later the couple visited Germany, Paris, and London. On April 4, a week before departure, Ida wrote a letter from the Claridges Hotel to their sons:

> Dear children … you may not know that this is already the third day of *Pesach* and that you should all be eating *Matzos*. Claridges does not serve them so we cannot do our duty.[47]

Nathan and Lina Straus visited Jerusalem in February with their good friend Rabbi Judah Magnes, a prominent Reform rabbi and Zionist activist. The purpose of the visit was to aid the Jews in Jerusalem and other Jewish communities by building soup kitchens to feed hundreds daily.

It is possible that there was another reason Nathan insisted in staying in Israel.

41

He had a good friend named Aaron Aaronson who was a Jewish agronomist, botanist, and Zionist activist who at the time was in mourning over his mother who passed away that winter, and Nathan wanted to pay his condolences to his friend. Also while in Israel Nathan met with Rabbi Abraham Isaac Kook and agreed to give another contribution to the welfare of the Jewish settlers. In April Lina and Nathan went to Rome.

Isidor and Ida were scheduled to sail back to America on a German ship, but they were transferred like many others to the *Titanic* because of the coal strike. Isidor planned to meet up with Jewish investors on the ship. On Wednesday morning, April 10, the couple arrived at the White Star Line dock at Southampton with their new maid, Ellen Bird, and Isidor's valet, John Farthing. Their tickets cost them 221£ 15s, and they occupied staterooms C55–C57.

Not all the Jews who immigrated to the United States prospered and succeeded as did the Strauses and the Guggenheims. Nathan Goldsmith did not become wealthy in America. He was born to a Jewish family in 1875 in a small Latvian town named Kreutzburg and lived there most of his life. He married Sarah, a neighbor's daughter, and they had two children. In 1908 his family immigrated to the United States.[48]

Nathan Goldsmith was a shoemaker, but it was difficult to find a steady job in New York. He left the United States in 1911, leaving his young wife and children in New York, and moved to South Africa where he was able to make some money as a shoemaker in Cape Town. He used to send money to his wife every week.[49]

Eventually it became too difficult for him in South Africa as well, and he decided to return to New York. The Boer War ruined his business. He sailed to England, and there he bought a third-class ticket which cost him 7£ 17s for the only available ship sailing to America, the *Titanic*. Before he boarded at Southampton, he wrote a letter to his wife telling her he was on his way via the *Titanic*.[50]

Some immigrants made it only to England and stayed there. Some stayed in England for a while to make money to be able to continue the journey to America. Many immigrants bought tickets for the *Titanic* directly from White Star Line officials, but others bought tickets through agents and paid a higher commission. Some sailed under assumed names. Some bought tickets for other ships but were transferred to the *Titanic* because of the coal strike.

Eliezer Gilinski, Nathan Goldsmith, Isidor and Ida Straus, Benjamin Guggenheim, and many others had two things in common. They were all sailing to America on board the *Titanic,* and they were all Jews.

4

SAILING DAY

Who were the *Titanic* Jews? How many Jews were on the *Titanic*? We know that the most famous Jews on board were Benjamin Guggenheim and the Straus couple, Isidor and Ida. We know the story of Ida Straus, who refused to get into a lifeboat without her husband. Isidor was offered a seat but declined and said that he would not go before other men. The couple was last seen on deck. We know that Benjamin Guggenheim realized that he was going to die, so he took off his life vest, got dressed in his best suit, and prepared to die like a gentleman. Besides Straus and Guggenheim, there were many other Jewish passengers on the *Titanic,* and they were all very excited to sail on the largest ship ever built.

Sailing day was scheduled for April 10, 1912. The ship arrived at Southampton on April 3. On the evening of April 9, most of the senior officers arrived and started preparing the ship. In addition, the engineers and firemen had arrived a day before to get the engines running and the electricity going.

On April 10 Captain Edward Smith arrived with most the crew, about 890 people including seamen, saloon stewards, bedroom stewards, chefs, firemen, engineers, stokers, bellboys, and pursers. There were eight band players that were not employees of the White Star Line and two wireless operators who worked for the Marconi Radio Company and were not official crew members. Most of the crew members were British, and many of them lived in Southampton. Two mailmen were American. The waiters in the Café Parisien were French. The White Star Line hired a team of Harland & Wolff employees, headed by Thomas Andrews, to inspect the ship during the maiden voyage. The senior officers came from all over Britain. Almost all crew members were Christians.[51] Herbert Klein, the barber for second-class passengers, was the only crewmember who was definitely Jewish. Klein lived in Leeds, England, and had a wife and two daughters.[52]

Later that morning the passengers started to arrive. The wealthy came by special trains or private cars from London with trunks that were loaded into cargo. The passengers strolled nonchalantly alongside the great ship, enjoying the beauty of the huge vessel. The passengers walked up the gangway that was specially built for the *Titanic* and the *Olympic*. As they entered the ship, every first-class male passenger was given a flower to put in his lapel.[53] When the passengers arrived to their staterooms, the White Star Line surprised them by giving them a pamphlet with the names of all the first-class passengers. Many first-class passengers knew each other and made plans to socialize or meet for business matters.

A Titanic *first-class stateroom (B Deck), decorated in Louis XVI style. Source: Wikimedia Commons*

Besides Guggenheim and Straus, there were many Jews in first class.[54] Among them were John Baumann, an importer of rubber and timber returning from a business trip to London; Adolphe Saalfeld, a chemist carrying a leather bag with perfume samples on his way to immigrate to America from Manchester; Emil Brandeis, a dry goods merchant returning from a business trip in Europe; Edger Josef Mayer and his wife, Leila (Leah); Herman Klaber, a businessman returning to Portland, Oregon; Emil Taussig, his wife, Tillie, and their nineteen-year-old daughter Ruth; Erwin Lewy, a jeweler returning from Amsterdam; and Henry Harris, a theater manager and his wife, René.

Traveling first-class were many American-born Jewish passengers, whose parents had immigrated from Europe. Many of the passengers had crossed the Atlantic before, and the *Titanic* was just another trip home. Some first-class Jewish passengers had been on vacation trips to Europe and the Middle East. Many Jewish passengers knew each other and were friends. Emil Brandeis, for example, was a good friend of John Baumann and Henry and René Harris. Edger Mayer and Benjamin Guggenheim were both members of the same congregation: Temple Emanuel in New York City.

The first-class Jews were businessmen, merchants who dealt with imports, chemistry, fashion, theater, and many other enterprises. Walking up the gangway, they entered the *Titanic* from B Deck and were welcomed by an army of stewards who escorted them to their staterooms. The passengers settled in and waited for the ship to depart. Many strolled around, visited the various public rooms, or went on deck.

At the same time, the passengers of the other two classes arrived. In second class, many of the passengers were relatively wealthy but did not want to spend too much money on first-class tickets. They settled for second-class staterooms that were just as luxurious. In addition there were many second-class passengers who were hard workers. Many of them had purchased first-class tickets for different ships but were transferred to the *Titanic* because of the coal strike. As far as luxury goes, the upgrade served them well.

Jewish theatric couple and first-class passengers Henry and René Harris. Source: Wisconsin State Historical Society. Courtesy: Don Lynch

Second-class public rooms were just as luxurious and could compete with first-class luxury on any other ship. They had their own smoking room, reading room, and reception rooms. The second class had open decks filled with deck chairs. The *Titanic* and *Olympic* were the first ships with elevators for second-class passengers.[55]

Second class held a variety of Jewish passengers. There were couples, single men and women, a widow, and families with children. The Jewish passengers in second class were from many nationalities: Polish Jews, Russian Jews, French Jews, English Jews, and American Jews. There were chemists, engineers, and businessmen. In total there were fewer than twenty Jewish passengers in second class. Among them were Polish-born Rosa Pinsky who had visited relatives in Poland; Israel Nesson, an electrician going to Boston, Massachusetts; businessman Samuel Greenberg who was going to New York; French born chemist René Jacques (Jacob) Lévy, who immigrated to Canada and was on his way back home from a visit to Europe; and Moses Aaron

Troupiansky, a shop assistant immigrating to America. Also in second class were Leopold (Aryeh) Weisz and his Catholic wife, Mathilde. Leopold was born in Hungary, immigrated to France, became an architect, and was on his way to immigrate to Canada. Before sailing, his wife had sewed gold coins into his pockets.[56]

Also sailing were Jewish lawyer Sydney (Samuel) and his wife, Amy

Jacobsohn. The two were traveling with Amy's sister, Rachel Juli Cohen, and their mother, Alice Frances Cohen Christy. Sydney Jacobsohn was born in Cape Town, South Africa, and then moved to London. The four were on their way to Quebec to visit relatives. Alice's Jewish husband (the father of Rachel Juli and Amy), Moreno Cohen, had died in 1890. Following his death, she and Rachel Juli were baptized in 1891. Alice remarried, this time to a Catholic man. Other Jewish passengers in second class were Benjamin Hart, his wife, Esther, and their daughter, Eva, age seven. Russian-born Jewish couple Miriam and Sinai Kantor also traveled second class.

Second-class Jewish passenger Leopold Weisz. Source: Encyclopedia Titanica

We know approximately how many Jews there were in first class and second class, but we do not know exactly how many Jews were in third class. The registration by the United States Ministry of Immigration was not always accurate. Mistakes were made when compiling the lists of passengers, and even more mistakes were made when listing casualties and survivors after the disaster. Names were written more than once; names were erased; names were misspelled. Leah Aks is a good example. On some lists her family name is misspelled as Oks and her son, Philip (Frank), is misspelled as Tilli (a typo of the name Filli). These mistakes were later seen on survivors' lists and in many English language newspapers. There were communication gaps between the non-English-speaking immigrants and the immigration office, much confusion, and many misunderstandings. Furthermore, during registration, officers requested passengers to state their nationality but not their religion.

The first serious attempt to locate Jews among the passengers in recent years was in 1998. That year a list of Jewish-sounding names was published. The list was based upon the passengers' list and composed of Jewish-sounding first and last names. The first names on the list included Jacob, Benjamin, Ruth, Hannah, Esther, Leah, Nathan, Shimon, and so on. Surnames included: Lehman, Jacobsohn, Goldberg, Wiseman, Rothschild, Salomon, Greenberg, Spector, and of course Cohen and Levy. The list of Jewish-sounding names had a hundred names on it, but at least half of the people on the list were not Jewish. For example, Leopold Weisz is on the list, but so is his wife, Mathilde, and while Leopold was Jewish, Mathilde was not. In addition there were plenty of Jews on the *Titanic* who were not listed. Some of them even had Jewish-sounding names. Rachel Juli Cohen was born Jewish but converted to Christianity. Her surname remained Cohen, a typical Jewish name.

The list was composed by Gertrude Ogushwitz and is an excellent starting point for any researcher trying to find Jewish passengers on the *Titanic*. Unfortunately the list has no names from the crew list.

One obstacle to an accurate list is those passengers who traveled for various reasons with assumed names. Jews changed their names to avoid authorities while escaping Russia and other Eastern European countries. Some changed their names to ease registration at the immigration office. Some "Americanized" their Jewish names, like Edith Rosenbaum who changed her name to Edith Russell in 1918.

Not only Jews, but many other passengers traveled with assumed names. Traveling with an assumed name were also those engaged in illegal acts such as gambling. George Brayton, an alias, was a well-known gambler. He sailed the Atlantic route on luxury liners and would sit with his con buddies in the first-class smoking room to stalk wealthy players and gamble with them. On the *Titanic* several stewards recognized him, but Brayton bribed them and was not reported to the captain.[57]

Alfred Nourney was another con man. Nourney had a second-class ticket, but when he boarded the *Titanic*, he convinced the stewards that a mistake had been made and he was a first-class passenger. To be in character, he had an assumed name fit for a first-class passenger: Baron Alfred von Drachstedt. Eventually he was transferred to a first-class stateroom. The name Alfred Nourney appears on the *Titanic's* passenger list as a first-class passenger.[58]

One of the weirder incidents of a passenger with an assumed name on board the ship was the case of Michel Navratil. Navratil was born in 1880 in Nice, France. He was married and had two little boys. He and his wife were getting divorced, and she had custody of the children. In April 1912 Michel Navratil visited his children and took them for Easter weekend. Instead of returning them to their mother, he abducted them and fled to London. He forged new identification documents for himself and his children and went on the *Titanic* with second-class tickets and an assumed name: Louis Hoffman. The new name sounds Jewish. On board he claimed to be a widower.[59]

Hundreds of third-class passengers lost their lives when the *Titanic* sunk. Many of them died without leaving a trace. Most bodies were never found. Of the bodies that were found, about half were not recognized. Over one hundred of the bodies were buried as "unknown."

One of the most peculiar mysteries involving the identity of Jewish passengers was the story of Typkia Friedberg, born in Germany to a Jewish family. She immigrated to England and married. She and her husband (name unknown) planned to immigrate to America and join her two sisters in Chicago. The young couple performed in Piccadilly Circus as an accordionist and a dancer, collecting coins tossed at them. They accumulated enough money to purchase two steerage tickets and boarded the *Titanic* with assumed names which are unknown. The surname Friedberg does not appear on the passengers list. Some researchers believe that Typkia and her husband traveled under American-sounding names to ease the immigration process. No other information is known about the two. It is also possible that Friedberg was not their real name but the name of her birth town in Germany.*

The official passengers list is available to anyone who wishes to search for a passenger's name. In most cases the names that appear on the list are as given by the passengers when boarding. If a passenger decided to travel with a fake name, there would be no way to find out who he really was unless he survived the disaster or his body was recognized by relatives or friends. Many unidentified bodies were buried at sea or in Halifax, Nova Scotia. Relatives of third-class victims were unable financially to travel to Canada (especially from Europe). It is

---

Alexander Levi, a relative of the family (great-grandson of one of Typkia's sisters) tried to find the whereabouts of Typkia Friedberg, but he could not discover any new information either. Furthermore, there is a theory that the Friedbergs were not even on the Titanic.

possible that there are dozens of Jewish passengers who died in the tragedy and we will never know who they really were. It is also probable that many anonymous Jews were buried with the inscription "unknown" on their tombstones. Therefore we will never know exactly how many Jews were in third class. The numbers vary between seventy and four hundred. Evidence of a significant amount of Jewish passengers in third class can be found in a letter from a crew member to his mother. His letter was written in Cherbourg and sent ashore while the *Titanic* was in Queenstown. In his letter, electrical engineer William Kelly wrote:

> We have a large crowd of passengers on board, the first and second class are just what you would expect but the third class are terrible. They include everything from a Christian to a Jew, not excluding Chinese and Japanese, with children of all ages.[60]

Researchers occasionally find passengers' names that are thought to be Jewish. One of them was Russian-born Josef Murdlin, a third-class passenger who perished in the disaster. First-class passenger George Rheims is another example. Apparently his in-laws did not accept him into the family because he was Jewish. It is also possible that George Rheims was not Jewish and was not accepted by his in-laws for other reasons. Furthermore, he probably had a brother named Leon who was killed by the Nazis in the Holocaust. Nevertheless George Rheims was probably not Jewish.[61]

Another example would be a crew member (a bathroom steward) named Thomas Frederick Pennal, who was not Jewish although his mother's name was Mary Jane Cohen, a typical Jewish name.

Another possible Jewish name on board the *Titanic* is first-class passenger Antoinette Flegenheimer, although some researchers claim she was in fact Christian, as she was probably baptized as a child in 1863. Antoinette's husband, Alfred, was Jewish, but he died in 1907. Other possible Jewish names include Julia Cavendish (nee Siegel),

First-class Jewish passenger Ruth Dodge. Source: San Francisco Call, 9 April 1906

who married a British aristocrat. Julia was born in Chicago, and her father was Henry Siegel, probably a Russian Jew.*

Another Jewish first-class passenger was Ruth Dodge (nee Vidaver). She was married to Washington Dodge (who was not Jewish). Ruth's father, Rabbi Falk Vidaver, officiated the wedding. Rabbi Vidaver was a Reform rabbi who served in several congregations in the United States, including congregation *Beit Yisrael* in New York.

Ruth boarded the *Titanic* at Southampton with her husband and their four-year-old son, Washington Dodge Jr., who by Jewish law was considered a Jew. They occupied stateroom A34, and their ticket cost them 81£ 17s.

So, how many Jews were on board the *Titanic*?

Some sources from after the disaster give clues regarding the amount of Jewish passengers. Several Jewish newspapers wrote about the *Titanic's* Jewish passengers. In Krakow, *Hamitzpe* mentioned that there were four hundred Jewish immigrants from Eastern Europe on their way to America on board the *Titanic*, a hundred of them from Mogilev County (in what is today Belarus). A month after the disaster, *Hatzvi* published (in Jaffa) a notice saying that on the *Titanic* there were many Jewish immigrants from Mogilev County. Two months after the disaster, *Hamitzpe* wrote that seventy-one Jews died in the *Titanic* tragedy. *Titanic* survivor Gershon Cohen said in an interview that there were about forty Jews with him in third class.[62] In 1962 an article published in *Herut* (in Jerusalem) stated that thirty-six Jews survived the disaster.[63] In 2012, an article opened with the words: "Over a hundred Jews died in the disaster."[64] Unfortunately, we know of fewer than thirty Jewish names in third class. If there were more, we will probably never know.

It is hard to believe that there were so few Jews in third class. *Titanic* researchers Charlie Haas and John Eaton have a theory for the low number of Jews in third class. As it turns out, the *Titanic* sailed a day and a half after Passover. That year, *Seder* night was on March 31 and the last day of Passover was on April 8.* It is possible that many observant Jews did not want to travel

*Titanic *historian Phil Gowan claims that both Antoinette Flegenheimer and Julia Cavendish were Jewish. Other historians claim that neither of the two were.*

In Israel, Passover is a seven-day holiday. The first and last days are days of Yom Tov, and on these days one is forbidden to do any manual labor, including traveling. In the Diaspora Passover is an eight-day holiday. The first two days and the last two days are Yom Tov. The eighth day of Passover was on April 8, which means observant Jews found it difficult to sail so close to the end of Passover.

to Southampton on the last day of Passover, so they did not buy tickets for the *Titanic*. It is also possible that many immigrants, including observant Jews, avoided the trouble of going to Southampton during the coal strike and waited a few more weeks in England before they continued to America.

What makes the two assumptions more interesting is the fact that the *Titanic* did not sail at full capacity. The *Titanic* could accommodate over three thousand passengers. With all the publicity and advertising of the greatest and most luxurious ship, the *Titanic* sailed on her maiden voyage with only 2,200 people, including 890 crew members – well below full capacity.

Third-class Jewish survivor Bella Moor and her son Meyer five years after the disaster. Photos taken during Meyer's Bar Mitzvah celebration. Photo credit: HIAS Photo Archive

Among the Jewish passengers in third class that we do know about were two young mothers with little children. One was Leah Aks with her ten-month-old son, Frank, as mentioned. The second was Bella (Beila) Moor and her seven-year-old son, Meyer. Bella was born in Russia in 1882. Unfortunately her husband, who was in the Russian Army, was killed in 1905 in the Russo-Japanese War, and Bella had to raise her son alone. Later she was persecuted and experienced anti-Semitism, so she decided to flee to England where she worked as a seamstress. Eventually she took her son and sailed to America, following relatives, but in New York she could not find them, so she returned to England. In 1912 she made a second attempt to immigrate to America. She bought a ticket for the *Adriatic*, but because of the coal strike, she was transferred to the *Titanic*. She, just like Leah Aks, was accommodated in a private room for herself and her son. Her ticket cost her 12£ 9s. She did not expect the ship to be so luxurious or the food to include delicacies such as fresh fruit.[65]

Other Jewish third-class passengers included Harry Sadowitz, who was traveling to Providence, Rhode Island; Leo Zimmerman, traveling to Canada; Simon Kutsher, Zalman Francis Slocovski, Jacob Cook, Woolf Spector, and Maurice (Moshe) Sirota, who were all on their way to New York. Most of them were from Russia.

After all the third-class passengers went through medical examinations, they were questioned and registered by the United States Ministry of Immigration. Once they were processed, they walked up the gangway and entered the *Titanic* on E Deck. The stewards did not escort them to their cabins. They had to find their own way in the endless labyrinth of corridors, hallways, passageways, and stairways. The non-English-speaking passengers had even a more difficult time trying to find their cabins since all the signs were in English.

Once settled, they met their cabinmates. Third-class accommodation consisted of a variety of rooms with ten, six, four, or two beds per cabin. In many ships during that era, there was some separation between nationalities, races, and religions in third class. This was not discrimination but a decision made by passengers. As a traveler (especially alone), one was more comfortable sharing a cabin with people who spoke the same language or shared the same religion or background. Therefore it was reasonable for Jews to share a cabin. Today we know only of one case where two Jews who shared a third-class cabin: David Livshin from Latvia and Harry Corn from Russia. The two were from different countries yet had a lot in common. Harry Corn had a wife and two little children. David Livshin had a pregnant wife. Both Harry and David left their wives behind and traveled alone in order to settle in America, raise money, and eventually bring their families over. It was unlikely that the two of them were randomly bunked together. Each man probably requested a Jewish roommate.

There was another type of separation among the third-class passengers. Third-class cabins were in three different sections of the ship. Single men were sent to the bow section. Single women were in the stern section. Married couples and families were in the center of the ship. The third-class public rooms, dining rooms, and general rooms were open to all third-class passengers during the day.

First-class Jewish passenger Samuel Goldenberg. Courtesy: Bill Wormstedt

After the passengers found their cabins and arranged their bags, many went out to the open decks and watched the crowd that had gathered to wave good-bye. At 12:15 the *Titanic* started moving. Moments later the *Titanic* nearly collided with the *New York*, but thanks to quick action, the *Titanic* managed to avoid the collision. It took the *Titanic* more than four hours to reach Cherbourg, France. The ship was so large that it could not dock at the wharf. The *Titanic* dropped anchor in the harbor, and two tenders ferried the passengers from the docks to the *Titanic*.

The White Star Line separated the third-class passengers from the rest. The *Nomadic* carried first- and second-class passengers, while the *Traffic* carried third-class passengers. Before the third-class passengers boarded, they went through a medical checkup and questioning similar to the passengers in Southampton.[66] In third class at least two Jewish passengers joined the ship in Cherbourg: sixteen-year-old Usher (Asher) Pulner and thirty-seven-year-old Aaron Weller. Both were from Russia. Weller was a friend of Pulner's parents and was escorting him to Chicago. Boarding second class in Cherbourg were Samuel (born 1882 in Russia) and Hannah Abelson (born 1884 in Odessa, daughter of Michael and Diana) on a trip to America to visit relatives in New York. Their second class ticket cost them 24£.

Several Jewish businessmen joined first class. Among them were clothing manufacturer Martin Rothschild and his Catholic wife, Elizabeth. Another mixed couple was Jewish passenger Samuel Goldenberg and his Catholic wife, Nella. Samuel was a show dog judge and had worked at a dog show in Berlin. Their ticket cost them 89£ 2s, and they were accommodated in stateroom C92.

Also boarded in Cherbourg were ostrich feather importer George Rosenshine and his Catholic mistress, Mabelle Thorne.[67] George Rosenshine was friends with Jewish theatrical couple René and Henry Harris, also on the *Titanic*. As mentioned, many of the Jewish passengers were friends, acquaintances, and business partners. George Rosenshine was not the only Jewish passenger who traveled with a mistress. Benjamin Guggenheim (who also boarded in Cherbourg) traveled with his young French mistress, Ninette Aubart.

The *Titanic* left France after nightfall and sailed south. The ship bypassed the British Islands and anchored in Queenstown Harbor in Ireland. In Queenstown,

as in Cherbourg, the docks were not big enough for the *Titanic*, so the passengers were ferried by two tender boats, the *Amerika* and the *Ireland*. Most of the passengers that joined the *Titanic* at Queenstown were Irish and included no known Jews. A few sacks of mail were sent ashore, and many passengers took this chance to write and send letters to relatives and friends in England using White Star Line stationery. Among the passengers to do so was Jewish chemist Adolphe Saalfeld from first class who wrote a couple of letters to his wife, Gertrude, in Manchester about his experience on the *Titanic*. He wrote about how he strolled along the Promenade Deck for a whole hour and how he enjoyed

First-class Jewish passenger Adolphe Saalfeld in a visit to Granada, Spain. Courtesy: Astra Burka Collection

the pleasant air. He described the lavish meal he had for dinner, a meal full of exotic foods. He told his wife about his accommodations.[68] He wrote:

> I just had an hour's roaming about on this wonderful boat. I like my cabin very much; it is like a bed-sitting room and rather large. They are still busy to finish the last things on board.[69]

He also told her that he missed her and wished she would join him on his next voyage. In his letter, he also described the near collision with the *New York* in Southampton.[70]

After the tenders dropped off the passengers and collected the mail, the new passengers settled in their staterooms and cabins. The *Titanic* was anchored in Queenstown for over two hours. The *Titanic* started steaming away at 13:40 on April 11. She headed west toward New York with the hopes and dreams of many passengers and crew. On board were over two thousand souls, and at least eighty of them were Jews. The *Titanic* was never seen from land again.

5

EATING KOSHER ON
THE ATLANTIC ROUTE

Gershon (Gus) Cohen was born in London to an observant Jewish family. His parents were Israel and Rachel Cohen. Gershon had three brothers: Abraham, Mark, and Hyman, and he worked in a print shop to help support the family. In 1912, at age eighteen and unemployed, he decided to try his luck in America. He did not have enough money for the trip, so he borrowed some from a friend. His initial plan was to sail at the beginning of April, but his father forbade him to sail during Passover. His parents insisted that he would stay with the family in England for the Jewish holiday, especially for the *Seder*.[71]

Third-class Jewish passenger Gershon Cohen. Source: Titanic-Titanic.com

The first available ship that sailed from Southampton after Passover was the *Titanic*. Gershon purchased a third-class ticket, which cost him 8£ 1s, and took a train to Southampton. His father escorted him to the ship. Gershon Cohen was an observant Jew. During the trip, he could eat only kosher products. Could he eat on the *Titanic*?

The *Titanic* was a luxury ship. One of the most important features of this luxurious ocean liner was the exotic food. During the voyage, a bugler would announce the upcoming meals. Breakfast was served at 08:30, lunch was served at 13:00, and dinner was served at 18:00. Every meal lasted for an hour and a half.

In the center of the ship, on C Deck , was the first-class dining room, a very large room that spread out the entire width of the ship. It was, in fact, not only the largest room on the *Titanic*, but the largest room on any ship of the day. More than five hundred passengers could eat there together. The first- and second-class kitchens were next to the first-class dining room, toward the stern. Adjoining the kitchens was the second-class dining room. The third-class kitchen and dining room were on F Deck.

Third-class dining saloon of the Olympic. The Titanic *had identical facilities. Source: Wikimedia Commons*

Sixty chefs and assistants cooked for and served the passengers, who enjoyed meals that were incomparable to any other ship. Second-class meals were just as luxurious as any first-class meal on other ships, and even steerage passengers enjoyed good food. First-class dinners consisted of eleven servings. The third-class breakfast included Quaker oats and milk, smoked herring, jacket potatoes, boiled eggs, liver and bacon, fresh bread and butter, and tea and coffee. Third-class passengers were even served fresh fruit.[72]

The meals were for all passengers without discrimination of race or religion. To determine if observant Jewish passengers were served kosher food, it is necessary to examine the changes that were made in the shipping business regarding the availability of kosher food during the Atlantic crossings from Europe to the United States as immigration increased.

In late nineteenth century and beginning of the twentieth century, the journey to America was long and exhausting. Many of the ships that crossed the Atlantic Ocean were old, rickety sailboats. Conditions for steerage passengers were awful. Their bathrooms were nowhere near the sleeping areas, and the passengers had to cross the ship to reach the reeking toilets. Rats, bugs, and cockroaches were everywhere. Steerage passengers ate at tables in the public rooms, and the sleeping areas were large open spaces without any privacy for the poor travelers.

In several ships there was some sort of separation between people of different races, nationalities, and religions, but any separation applied only to the sleeping areas. Observant Jews did not have their own separate area for kosher food. The crossing was hard for all steerage passengers, but it was even harder for observant Jews who had to cope with horrendous conditions and handle the challenge of kosher food. Shipping companies did not always supply kosher food. Jewish passengers had to eat whatever they brought with them, usually dry bread and herring.

Eating kosher on the Atlantic route was not easy, and not all the passengers survived the voyage. Some died during the Atlantic crossing. In 1909 a young Jewish immigrant named Gisella Greiner starved to death in a hospital in Ellis Island. Apparently kosher food was not available during the voyage, and she chose not to eat for the entire crossing.[73]

The transfer from sailboats to steamships shortened the voyage across the Atlantic. The steamships crossed from Europe to America in a week and a half. The older ships did it in three weeks. Nevertheless, the voyage was still difficult and wearying, especially for observant Jews.

As the years went by, there was an improvement in the conditions of steerage passengers. As the ships became larger, the shipping companies started to make an effort to improve conditions. Over several decades, millions of immigrants crossed from Europe to the United States, and the shipping companies competed amongst themselves to accommodate the endless stream of passengers. This was expressed by better conditions and service. Third-class passengers on board the *Titanic* enjoyed amenities that were unavailable on any other ship. They had fresh food and clean sheets. The White Star Line decided to offer the third-class passengers service from stewards.

During this period a Jewish businessman named Albert Ballin (1857–1918) started to supply his ships with kosher food for the Jewish passengers. He was a successful businessman in the shipping business and the managing director of the Hamburg America Line, one of the largest shipping companies serving the North Atlantic at the time. In addition his father ran an organization that aided Jewish immigrants and assisted them in the immigration process. Albert Ballin knew that many Jewish passengers were observant, and they kept kosher. He realized that supplying kosher food in his ships would bring more customers to his company.[74]

Jewish businessman and shipbuilder Albert Ballin.
Source: *Library of Congress*

The first evidence of supplying kosher food for passengers on the North Atlantic route was in 1904. In June that year, a Yiddish newspaper based in Poland (*Hazfira*) announced that the Hamburg America Line supplied all their ships with kosher meals for Jews traveling to New York. It also announced that their ships would provide a room for a synagogue. Later that year a notice was published in Trenton, New Jersey, that an American shipping company would supply kosher meals for Jewish passengers. The notice also stated that Jewish passengers would have a separate dining room and their own sleeping area separate from other passengers. In 1905 kosher meals were supplied on board the *SS Philadelphia*.[75] During the same time period, kosher meals were also supplied for Jewish passengers crossing the Mediterranean Sea from Europe to Jaffa Port, especially for observant Jews traveling to the Holy Land.

Typical Yiddish advertisement for availability of kosher food for Jewish passengers, Hamburg American Line (1906-1910). Source: Historical Jewish Press

In 1909 the United States Immigration Commission published a report about conditions for immigrants traveling from Europe to America. The report gave an account of a shipping company (conveniently the name of the company was removed from the report) that had been investigated. According to the report the company employed a chef working under rabbinical supervision to be responsible for taking care of the interests and needs of Jewish immigrants who traveled on the company's vessels and to care for their welfare. The report noted that this man was a pioneer and that no other shipping company supplied this service. Until then kosher kitchens and chefs onboard ships were a private initiative, and the kosher chefs were not part of the ship's crew. This man had to prevent discrimination toward the Jewish passengers and provide kosher meals on all the company's ships. Among his duties was ensuring adequate sleeping arrangements for Jewish passengers and making sure that their conditions were not inferior to other passengers. The report mentioned that this man had a team of chefs with rabbinical supervision to work on the various company ships.[76]

By 1910 the trend was quite common. Some ships sailing the North Atlantic route would sail with a kosher kitchen, a separate dining room, and even a synagogue. On many ships kosher meals were available for passengers of all classes. By 1912 many shipping companies were serving kosher meals to Jewish passengers on their ships. The ships had separate sets of dishes for dairy and meat products.

When the *Olympic* and *Titanic* were being built, the White Star Line decided that the two new ships would supply kosher food for third-class passengers. In 1911, the third-class menu was published. The menu included all items to be served for every meal. On the bottom of the menu,

WHITE STAR LINE
Specimen Third Class Bill of Fare
Subject to Alteration as Circumstances Require

	Sunday	Monday	Tuesday	Wednesday	Thursday	Friday	Saturday
Breakfast	Quaker Oats and Milk Smoked Herrings and Jacket Potatoes Boiled Eggs Fresh Bread and Butter Marmalade, Swedish Bread Tea and Coffee	Oatmeal Porridge and Milk Irish Stew Broiled Sausages Fresh Bread and Butter Marmalade, Swedish Bread Tea and Coffee	Oatmeal Porridge and Milk Ling Fish, Egg Sauce Fried Tripe and Onions Jacket Potatoes Fresh Bread and Butter Marmalade, Swedish Bread Tea and Coffee	Quaker Oats and Milk Smoked Herrings Beefsteak and Onions Jacket Potatoes Fresh Bread and Butter Marmalade, Swedish Bread Tea and Coffee	Oatmeal Porridge and Milk Liver and Bacon Irish Stew Fresh Bread and Butter Marmalade, Swedish Bread Tea and Coffee	Quaker Oats and Milk Smoked Herrings Jacket Potatoes Curried Beef and Rice Fresh Bread and Butter Marmalade, Swedish Bread Tea and Coffee	Oatmeal Porridge and Milk Vegetable Stew, Fried Tripe and Onions Fresh Bread and Butter Marmalade, Swedish Bread Tea and Coffee
Dinner . .	Vegetable Soup Roast Pork, Sage and Onions Green Peas Boiled Potatoes Cabin Biscuits, Fresh Bread Plum Pudding, Sweet Sauce Oranges	Barley Broth Beefsteak and Kidney Pie Carrots and Turnips Boiled Potatoes Cabin Biscuits, Fresh Bread Stewed Apples and Rice	Pea Soup Fricassee Rabbit and Bacon Lima Beans, Boiled Potatoes Cabin Biscuits, Fresh Bread Semolina Pudding	Rice Soup Corned Beef and Cabbage Boiled Potatoes Cabin Biscuits, Fresh Bread Peaches and Rice	Vegetable Soup Boiled Mutton and Caper Sauce Green Peas, Boiled Potatoes Cabin Biscuits, Fresh Bread Plum Pudding, Sweet Sauce	Pea Soup Ling Fish, Egg Sauce Cold Beef and Pickles Cabbage, Boiled Potatoes Cabin Biscuits, Fresh Bread Cornflour Pudding Oranges	Bouillie Soup Meat Pie and Brown Potatoes Boiled Potatoes Cabin Biscuits, Fresh Bread Fruits and Rice
Tea	Ragout of Beef, Potatoes and Pickles Apricots Fresh Bread and Butter Currant Buns Tea	Curried Mutton and Rice Cheese and Pickles Fresh Bread and Butter Damson Jam Swedish Bread Tea	Haricot Mutton Pickles Prunes and Rice Fresh Bread and Butter Swedish Bread Tea	Brawn Cheese and Pickles Fresh Bread and Butter Rhubarb Jam Currant Buns Tea	Sausage and Mashed Potatoes Dry Hash Apples and Rice Fresh Bread and Butter Swedish Bread Tea	Cod Fish Cakes Cheese and Pickles Fresh Bread and Butter Plum and Apple Jam Swedish Bread Tea	Rabbit Pie Baked Potatoes Cheese and Pickles Fresh Bread and Butter Rhubarb and Ginger Jam Swedish Bread Tea

SUPPER—Every Day.—Cabin Biscuits and Cheese.   Gruel, Coffee.   Fresh Fish served as substitute for Salt Fish as opportunity offers

Kosher Meat Supplied and Cooked for Jewish Passengers as desired

Olympic's third-class menu (1911). Kosher meat supplied and cooked for Jewish passengers as desired (on bottom of menu). Source: Smithsonian Institution

the following comment was written: "Kosher meat supplied and cooked for Jewish passengers as desired."[77]

An equivalent document for the *Titanic* was never found in any archive. The fact that the *Titanic* sunk with everything on it and the disappearance of most of her documents make research difficult. Nevertheless the 1911 menu for *Olympic* third-class passengers is proof that kosher meals were served on the *Titanic* as well.

According to White Star Line policy, all linens, souvenirs, envelopes,

[Kashruth under the direct supervision of the London Jewish Ecclesiastical Authorities, headed by the Very Rev. Dr. J. H. Hertz, Chief Rabbi of the British Empire. Supervising Representative at Southampton—The Rev. M. L. Gordon.]

STRICTLY KOSHER MENU

R.M.S. "QUEEN MARY"   Monday, June 8, 1936

Dinner

Iced Tomato Juice
Fillet of Anchovies   Green Olives   Sardines in Oil
Herrings in Tomato   Salted Cucumbers   Roll Mops
Radishes   Smoked Salmon

Boiled Fresh Salmon and Cucumber
Fried Haddock and Lemon

Creamed Potato and Celery Soup

Eggs Various—to order

To Order—Plain, Spanish and Savoury Omelettes

Corn on Cob   Buttered Spinach
French Fried and Baked Jacket Potatoes

Salads—Lettuce, Tomatoes and Vegetable
French and Russian Dressing

Assorted French Pastry

Milk Rice Pudding

Pineapple and Raspberry Ice Cream and Wafers

Cake

Chocolate Creams   Baked Apples

Oranges   Bananas   Apples
Tea   Matzos   Coffee

Authorised Shomer on board: Mr. D. JACHIMOWITZ

Kosher menu for Jewish passengers, Queen Mary, *1936. Source: Historical Jewish Press.*

writing pads, and other objects had the White Star Line name or symbol implanted on them, but not the name of the ship. The items were interchangeable, which made things easier for the White Star Line. No dishes, crockery, silverware, plates, serving utensils, decanters, or cutlery had the *Titanic's* name on them. That is how we know what the kosher dishes from the *Titanic* looked like although none of the dishes from the *Titanic* were ever found. Where did the kosher food come from? Who supplied the kosher meat?

At the beginning of the twentieth century, there was a small Jewish community in Southampton. The mostly Orthodox community had a rabbi who also served as the *shohet* (butcher). When the shipping companies decided to provide kosher meat for Jewish passengers traveling from Southampton, this rabbi was responsible for supplying kosher meat for the ships. At first all kosher meat was supplied by the Jewish community in Southampton, but as the demand grew, other Jewish communities in England started to supply kosher meat as well. Over two million Jews immigrated from Europe, and Southampton was a major embarkation port.

The supplier of kosher meat for the *Titanic* was P. Galkoff's Family Butchers in Liverpool. Once on board, the meat was stored along with the other meats on G Deck, toward the stern of the ship. Galkoff's butcher shop continued to supply kosher meat for ships sailing from Southampton until it closed in 1979. The building was abandoned for some years. In 2013 the building eventually became part of a medical center complex. Discussions are currently underway about how to preserve Galkoff's shop.[78] On board the *Titanic* there was a chef who was in charge of the kosher food.

SPECIMEN THIRD CLASS BILL OF FARE.		
SUBJECT TO ALTERATION AS CIRCUMSTANCES REQUIRE.		

Availability of kosher meat for Jewish passengers, White Star Line, 1913.

The White Star Line employed Charles Kennel, born in Cape Town, South Africa, to be the kosher cook on the *Titanic*. His last registered place of residence was Southampton. Charles Kennel served the White Star Line for several years. Before joining the *Titanic*, he served on the *Olympic* for nine months and was paid 4£ a month. He was thirty years old when he boarded the *Titanic*.[79] On the *Titanic's* crew list, he is listed as a Jewish cook. Sometimes he is referred to as a Hebrew cook or kosher cook, and in some places he is listed as a "chef" instead of "cook," but basically they all mean the same thing.*

The position of a kosher cook on a passenger ship raises many questions. Was the kosher cook Jewish? Does the kosher cook have to be Jewish? Was there a kosher kitchen on the *Titanic*? Who served the kosher food to the Jewish passengers? Did Charles Kennel have a Jewish staff with him? Was there a rabbi on board to supervise? What about other kosher foods, such as dairy products? What about *Sabbath* wine? Was kosher food available to all three classes? Was Charles Kennel in charge of supplying all the needs of the Jewish passengers, such as a place to pray? Was there a synagogue on the *Titanic*? Many of these questions will forever remain unanswered, but from the information available, some questions actually do have answers.

Charles Kennel was the one who supplied the kosher meat to the Jewish

---

There is an interesting misprint regarding the Hebrew cook. In The Wall Chart of the Titanic *(Tom McCluskie, 1998), there is a list of the ship's crew. Among the cooks and chefs, there is an interesting mistake regarding Charles Kennel. Under his name is the title "Herb cook." Charles Kennel was not charged with the responsibility of taking care of the herbs on the ship; he was a Hebrew cook. It is possible that the mistake was of shortening the word* Hebrew *to* Heb *and somehow became* Herb.

passengers on board the *Titanic*. Unfortunately, the information about the *Titanic's* kosher cook is very little. It is not easy to determine if he was a Jew himself. Some *Titanic* researchers, including Charlie Haas and John Eaton, believe that he was not Jewish.

According to *Halacha* (Jewish law), a person who does not follow Jewish law cannot supervise the preparation of kosher food. Therefore such a person cannot be responsible for making sure other Jews follow Jewish law. This principle goes back to the time of the *Mishnah* (200 CE). A Jew who is an *Am Haaretz* (uneducated Jew/person) is not reliable on *Halachic* matters. This principle is one of the foundations of the *Kashrut* issue. *Kashrut* is one of the most complex issues in Judaism, and specifically in this field, trust is extremely important.

If the person who is responsible for cooking kosher food is not Jewish, there is a need for rabbinical supervision. That is why if Charles Kennel was not Jewish, it would have been necessary for a rabbi to be on board the *Titanic* to supervise him. The White Star Line did employ a rabbi to supervise over Jewish affairs on the ships, but he was not on the vessels during the voyages. The kosher cooks were his representatives, and if they were not Jewish, the food might be questionable. If the rabbi of the White Star Line had followed the trustworthy principle, all the kosher cooks on the company's ships would have been Jewish – and Charles Kennel among them.

Therefore a non-Jew or a non-observant Jew might not take Jewish law seriously, thus causing a *Halachic* mishap or make the food (or dishes) *treif* (non-kosher), either on purpose or by mistake.

To avoid the necessity of cooking kosher food on the *Titanic*, it is possible that the meat was precooked or that only smoked meat was served. That possibility is not likely, however, because meat was actually cooked on the *Titanic*. Throughout the voyage, passengers enjoyed a variety of cooked meat, fresh fruit, and fresh bread during the meals.

The kosher kitchen was located on F Deck alongside the third-class kitchens. The kosher kitchen was very small and crowded, with barely enough room to hold an oven and a surface area. All kosher food was prepared on board, including dairy products and bread.

Why should the Jewish passengers be served stale bread, precooked meat, and a smaller selection of food products? The shipping companies had gone beyond the era where Jews could not eat during the voyages. Jews no longer had to eat whatever they brought with them. In addition, if all the kosher food was precooked and prepared in advance, there would not be a need of a kosher cook, but only a kosher waiter. Charles Kennel was not a waiter. He was a cook, a kosher cook. He cooked and prepared the kosher meat (and other kosher food products) for the Jewish passengers onboard the *Titanic*. The Jewish passengers enjoyed fresh meals with food that was just as good as the other passengers. Charles Kennel was probably Jewish.

Most of the Jews on board the *Titanic* who asked for kosher food were from third class. That is why the White Star Line advertised that kosher food would be supplied specifically on the third-class menu and not on the menus of the other two classes. That is why the kosher kitchen was located in the third-class kitchen area. There is no evidence of supplying kosher meals for first-class or second-class passengers. Most first-class Jewish passengers were not observant and ate non-kosher food. Adolphe Saalfeld, for example, ate exotic non-kosher foods and described the meals in a letter to his wife. It is known that Benjamin Guggenheim did not keep kosher, and Isidor Straus was not religious either.

If there was a first-class Jewish passenger on board the *Titanic* who might have asked for a kosher meal, it was the Polish-born diamond dealer Jacob Birnbaum. Birnbaum was the son of an Orthodox family. His family immigrated from Warsaw to Antwerp and established a diamond business. Birnbaum, age twenty-five, was single and probably one of the youngest first-class Jews on board the *Titanic*. Both his parents were observant Jews, and Birnbaum kept a kosher diet.

First-class Jewish passenger Jacob Birnbaum. Photo credit: Branton Family Trust

Unfortunately there is no evidence of any kind for a Jewish section in the first-class or second-class dining rooms or kitchens. In 1933 the only existing photo of the kosher kitchen on the *Olympic* was published. In the photo two people are seen. The man on the left with the tall chef's hat is the kosher cook; his name is unknown. The man on the right is Rabbi M. L. Gordon, a representative of the Jewish community in Southampton. He was the rabbinical supervisor over the *kashrut* matters for the White Star Line at the time. In the background, it is clearly seen that the kosher kitchen is extremely small and can barely fit an

Rabbi M. L. Gordon and White Star Line chef at the kosher kitchen of the Olympic, Titanic's *sister-ship, 1933.*
Source: Titanic *International Society Archives*

oven and a working station. Above the entrance of the kosher kitchen is a sign in English and in Yiddish that reads: "Kosher Kitchen."

Karen Kamuda from the *Titanic* Historical Society stated that all the kosher dishes – including plates, silverware, and serving utensils – were marked with the word *kosher* in English and Hebrew (or Yiddish) and were differentiated as *Fleishik* (meat) and *Milchik* (milk). She also claimed that there were kosher dishes for Jewish passengers from all three classes, not only third-class Jews. In addition the White Star Line gave rabbinical authorities permission to inspect the kosher dishes from time to time. It seems that the White Star Line took the *kashrut* issue very seriously and hired the proper personnel to take care of the needs of the Jewish passengers.[80]

On the other hand, *Titanic* researcher John Eaton stated that there is difficulty in determining that there were kosher dishes on the *Titanic*. Eaton said that today we have precise lists of all the items the White Star Line supplied the *Titanic* with, and nowhere on the list is there any mention of kosher dishes. Eaton has said the original *Titanic* blueprints show that there was a small room reserved as a kosher kitchen, and he claims the room was very tiny. Unfortunately, those original blueprints have been lost. It is possible that there was not just one room for the kosher cooking but several rooms for different functions, such as cooking, baking, meal prep, a room for the kosher dishes, and several rooms for storage.[81]

Kosher plate used by the White Star Line. Courtesy: National Museum, Liverpool

Titanic researcher Charles Hass has located the sleeping quarters of the *Titanic's* kosher cook. His room was on F Deck on the port side adjoining the third-class dining room. Charles Kennel shared a room with seven other cooks.[82]

Another aspect that needs to be taken in to account is the language barrier. Most of the Jews who fled Eastern Europe did not speak English, and it would have been inefficient if the person responsible for the benefit of the Jewish immigrants could not understand a language that they could speak, such as Yiddish. Therefore it is only reasonable that Charles Kennel spoke Yiddish, or at least understood Yiddish, to be able to communicate with his "clients." Who else would have assisted the Jewish passengers if not the kosher cook?

In 1935 when the *Olympic* was taken out of service, all furnishings and fittings were sold at auction. All kosher pieces of equipment were scattered and sold to private collectors. Unfortunately only a small number of kosher dishes can be found in museums today. The rest of the equipment is scattered all over England.

In 1987, two years after the *Titanic* was found, a new era began for the ship's legacy. Artifacts were salvaged from the bottom of the ocean. Thousands of items from

White Star Line kosher set of dishes.
Courtesy: National Museum, Liverpool

the wreck and debris field were raised, including bottles, light fixtures, luggage, coal, personal belongings, and even pieces of the hull. Many dishes were found and salvaged. None of the dishes were from the kosher kitchen.

In the Merseyside Maritime Museum in Liverpool, a set of White Star Line kosher dishes is on display. The kosher dishes were actually manufactured in the middle of the 1920s, more than a decade after the *Titanic* sunk. In the center of each dish, the word *kosher* in Hebrew is inscribed, and on some of the dishes the words *milk* in English and *Milchik* in Yiddish is inscribed, while inscribed on others are the words *meat* in English and *Fleishik* Yiddish. On the outer rim there is an adornment and the words *White Star Line*. As mentioned earlier, the ship's name does not appear on the dishes. The dishes were made of white porcelain and are in excellent condition.

Today many replicas of White Star Line dishes are sold in museums and in souvenir shops, especially in England and America. Occasionally someone sells a dish as an "original" from the *Titanic* to try to get a higher price. Any real *Titanic* artifact is illegal to sell, however. Most White Star Line artifacts were manufactured years after the *Titanic* sank. The kosher dishes used by the White Star Line are so rare today that anyone who would try to sell such an item is most likely a con trying to sell a replica for a high price to

take advantage of *Titanic* collectors. In 2012, in close proximity to the one hundredth year anniversary of the sinking, someone from England tried to sell a dish described as an original *Titanic* kosher platter. The oval-shaped platter was made of metal, and engraved on the platter was the White Star Line flag along with the words *kasher* and *Milchik* in Yiddish and the word *kosher* in English. The man eventually sold the platter for the astronomical price of 226£.

Kosher plate used by the White Star Line, possibly a replica. Source: unknown

In 2015 someone from the United Kingdom sold a replica saucer on eBay for 328£. It was listed as: "White Star Line RMS *Olympic Titanic*-period rare kosher service saucer." Authentic White Star Line dishes with similar decorations were manufactured in the 1920s to 1930s. It is well known among *Titanic* researchers that none of the kosher dishes on the *Titanic* have been found. Therefore this platter was not a *Titanic* artifact. Furthermore, none of the White Star Line kosher dishes on display in museums are from the *Titanic*.

From the life story of the Jewish passengers on the *Titanic*, and from the little we know regarding some of the Jews in third class, we know their *Kashrut* habits. Some were born to observant Jewish families. Gershon Cohen was one, and so were David Livshin and Leah Aks. Other observant Jews in *Titanic's* third class included Abraham Joseph Hyman, Shimon Maisner, and Sarah Roth. Another one of the observant Jewish passengers was twenty-five-year-old Jennie Dropkin (sometimes spelled Drapkin). She came from Belarus and was immigrating to America. To her delight she was able to eat the kosher meals that were served throughout the voyage. She and many other Jews sailing the *Titanic* believed they could enjoy a pleasant voyage.

6

PLEASURE CRUISE

Besides the lavish meals, the *Titanic* offered a lot of activities for a pleasant, relaxing voyage. Second-class passenger Eva Hart, age seven, was enthusiastic about everything on the ship. Eva's mother, Esther, was frightened that something bad might happen to the ship and was not happy sailing on such a huge vessel. On the first night she could not sleep. Eva's father, Benjamin, on the other hand, was just as excited as Eva. He did not socialize much, preferring to keep Esther and Eva company. On the night of April 14, Benjamin Hart went to sleep early.[83]

Second-class Jewish passenger Benjamin Hart with his wife, Esther, and daughter, Eva. Source: Wikimedia Commons

In addition to the smoking rooms, the lounge, the reading room, the café, and the promenade, first-class passengers used the gym equipment, which simulated cycling and rowing. The gymnasium was located on the starboard side of the Boat Deck near the first-class promenade. The *Titanic* and the *Olympic* were the first ships to have an indoor swimming pool (for

$1 a ticket) and a Turkish bath (for ¢25). The swimming pool and the Turkish bath were located on the starboard side on F Deck and were reserved for first-class passengers only. Another first-class attraction was the squash court, located on G Deck.[84]

Second-class attractions included a reading room, a smoking room, and a promenade. Second-class passengers socialized while playing cards, dominoes, or chess.[85]

Passengers, especially from first class, sent telegrams from the wireless radio room. The *Titanic* had strong telegraph equipment and could send telegrams to quite a distance. Passengers enjoyed sending and receiving greetings to their friends on other ships in the area and even directly to America.

One telegram was from Ida and Isidor Straus. The couple enjoyed strolling on the promenade. One of their sons was on the *America* on its way from New York to Europe, so they sent him a telegram. Later that day they received an answer from him when the two ships were in close range.[86] Other Jewish passengers sending telegrams included Edger Mayer, René Harris, and Benjamin Guggenheim.

Passengers spent hours relaxing on the deck chairs and reading books in the open air. Nobody on board ever thought that the lifeboats taking up so much space on deck would be needed. During the day the air was pleasant, but at night the temperature dropped and passengers stayed indoors.

Third-class passengers enjoyed the outdoors on open spaces reserved for them. One was the third-class Promenade Deck at the stern and the other was the third-class open space at the bow. Third-class passengers also had public rooms where they played cards and socialized. For all three classes, the *Titanic* was a pleasure cruise.

Meals (especially for first class) were served in a formal manner, and fashion stylist Edith Rosenbaum described them as being rigid. She also described the social interactions as being artificial. In a letter she sent before leaving Queenstown, Edith wrote:

> It is a monster and I can't say I like it. . . To say that it is wonderful is unquestionable. Am going to take my very much needed rest on this trip, but I cannot get over my feeling of depression and premonition of trouble.

The *Titanic* was a ship of dreams. Every passenger found a preferred and most enjoyable activity. Every person found a way to pass the time on the great and luxurious ocean liner. The women on board enjoyed nice, quiet afternoons in the reading room.

One of the most favored activities among the first- and second-class men was sitting in the smoking room and playing cards. They spent time developing business skills, smoking expensive cigars, gossiping, and discussing politics. One of the Jewish passengers who spent an awful lot of time playing cards in the smoking room was William (Bertram) Greenfield, a furrier, who was traveling with his mother, Blanche. The two boarded the *Titanic* at Cherbourg. They occupied staterooms D10 and D12, and their ticket cost them 63£ 7s.

After dinner steerage passengers would gather in the general room and sing, play music, and dance while imagining a better life in America.[87]

Jewish passengers socialized with business associates. Isidor Straus met

EMILE BRANDEIS, 1884,
J. L. BRANDEIS & SONS, MERCHANTS AND BANKERS.
OMAHA.

First-class passenger Emil Brandeis.
Source: Library of Congress

with historian Colonel Archibald Gracie, an expert on the American Civil War, and the two discussed American history. The colonel had written a book about the Civil War and wanted Isidor's opinion on it. Isidor also knew several of the Jewish passengers and met with them, as well as with Benjamin Guggenheim, who was an old friend.[88]

Guggenheim spent most of his time with his entourage in his suite. He also met with business associates but did not enjoy the company. He did take part in the fancy meals and met with the other wealthy passengers for business issues, but he usually kept to himself.[89]

Jewish businessman Emil Brandeis hosted business meetings in his stateroom. Brandeis was a friend of Isidor Straus, and the two men met during the voyage. Brandeis was also a good friend of Henry and René Harris and met with them several times during the voyage. Brandeis enjoyed the meals in the first-class dining room and described the exotic foods in a letter to his family.[90]

Back in third class, Leah Aks and Bella Moor (and many other young mothers) enjoyed a nice and relaxing voyage. They received luxury unavailable

Eli Moskowitz, grand staircase, Titanic *Exhibit, Tel Aviv, 2014. Photo credit: Reuven Kastro, Courtesy:* Makor Rishon

on other ships. It was the little but very important things such as easy access to a bathroom. The luxury and comfort designed for third-class passengers of the *Titanic* and *Olympic* is well portrayed in the official description of the White Star Line as reviewed in *Titanic: a Passenger's Guide*:

> The accommodation for third class passengers in these streamers is also of a very superior character, the public rooms being large, airy apartments, suitably furnished and in excellent positions, and the same applies to the third class staterooms and berths.

Although there were only two bathtubs in third class, there were plenty of toilets. That was a novelty. Other ships did not offer such comfort and pleasure. Bella's son, Meyer, age seven, enjoyed running around the third-class passageways and climbing up and down the stairways. He asked adults for empty cigarette packets that featured pictures of cowboys and Indians so he would have something to play with.[91]

As bunkmates, David Livshin and Harry Corn got to know each other and spent time together. The two of them probably met with other Jewish passengers and hung out with them as well. The observant Jewish passengers met during the meals and services. A synagogue was not reserved specifically for Jews, but it was possible for a group of Jewish passengers to pray as a group without drawing attention from the other passengers.

Benjamin and Esther Hart ate meals in the second-class dining room. They were placed with other families and enjoyed their company. On Saturday night Esther could not sleep. She lay in bed fully dressed, staring at the ceiling. Suddenly she jumped up; she felt some kind of turbulence, as if something in the ship's movement changed. She asked Benjamin to go out to the deck and check to see if everything was all right. Benjamin assured her that everything was fine. Nevertheless, eventually he went to investigate, returning to say that everything was okay. The ship was moving at an unchanging speed, and there was absolutely nothing to fear. The next day during breakfast, they shared the experience with some of their fellow passengers. One of the passengers tried to explain to Esther that the sound she heard and the turbulence she felt were probably caused by the friction of the machinery, as it was a new ship and the machines were new. The

First-class Jewish passenger René Harris. Source: Washington Times, 17 April 1912

explanation did not lessen her fears. Esther remained frightened and still believed something bad might happen to the ship. On Sunday night Benjamin felt the drop in the temperature and told Esther that it was colder, but he did not mention icebergs. Esther's fear increased daily. She did not like the ship before they boarded, and she did not like the ship during the voyage.[92]

No one expected a disaster. On Sunday morning, April 14, third-class passenger Gershon Cohen won a guessing contest regarding the daily speed of the ship. Later that day he played a game of chess with a passenger he did not know. He noticed that the air was very cold, and he told his partner he thought they were near icebergs. His playing partner and nearby passengers ridiculed him and said it was his imagination.[93]

One of the most bizarre events that happened to a Jewish passenger during the voyage was the accident and injury of René Harris. René and her husband, Henry, loved playing cards with friends. On Sunday morning she was asked to join a card game in one of the first-class suites. After winning ninety dollars, she went to her room, and when she returned to the game, she slipped on a grease spot left on the grand staircase by what is believed to have been a tea cake. (It was the same famous staircase where Jack and Rose met after their joint first-class dinner in the 1997 blockbuster film). René fell and broke her arm.[94]

Dr. Henry Frauenthal, a Jewish orthopedic surgeon, treated her, bandaged her, and put her arm in a sling. Dr. Frauenthal, his wife, Clara, and his brother Gerald (Isaac) were returning to New York after a vacation in France. After her accident, René did not return to the card game, but instead retired to her stateroom to recuperate after the startling ordeal.

Evening fell over the *Titanic*. The ship continued its course toward New York. During the day several ice warnings were sent to the *Titanic*. Only some were given to the bridge. The temperature dropped below zero. Only a handful of passengers were brave enough to stroll on the Promenade Deck.

Those who wanted to keep warm by exercising could have gone to the gymnasium. It would have been impossible to believe that in a few short hours the gymnasium would turn into a temporary shelter during the upcoming evacuation of the ship.

Many of the passengers were in the smoking rooms, playing cards and smoking. The lights went out at 22:00 in the third-class public rooms, and the steerage passengers were told to return to their cabins.[95]

At 23:30 most of the people on board the *Titanic* were in bed. Only a handful of first-class passengers were still in the smoking room. William Greenfield was one of them. Adolphe Saalfeld was also in the smoking room at the time. René Harris was in her stateroom, still aching from her injury. Benjamin Hart was in bed, and so were the Strauses, the Moors, the Akses, and most of the other passengers. The *Titanic* sailed on in the freezing water. The passengers had no clue that the *Titanic* was heading toward her destiny.

7

DISASTER

Toward midnight, Charles Stengel rolled over in bed. He had trouble falling asleep. Stengel, whose full name was Charles Emil Henry Stengel, was the son of Jewish immigrants from Germany. He was a businessman and worked in the leather trade. He and his wife, Annie May, were returning to New Jersey after a vacation in France. They joined the *Titanic* at Cherbourg and occupied stateroom C116, not far from the first-class entrance on C Deck. Their ticket cost them 55£ 8s. The time was 23:39, it was very dark outside and very cold, but Charles Stengel was in his warm bed. Nevertheless, he just could not fall asleep.[96]

At that very moment, the lookouts were in the crow's nest, gazing into the distance. Frederick Fleet, one of the lookouts, noticed something. A few seconds later, he realized it was an iceberg. Immediately he rang the bell and telephoned the bridge. When the phone was answered, all Fleet did was yell: "Iceberg right ahead!" First Officer William Murdoch sent an order to the engine room to turn the ship around and shut off the engines. He then pressed the buttons to close the doors between the watertight compartments.

It was too late. Thirty-seven seconds later, when the ship was turning and it seemed as though the *Titanic* would not hit, the iceberg swiped against the starboard side of the ship. There was no need to call Captain Smith. As soon as the *Titanic* hit, he rushed to the bridge. A few moments later Thomas Andrews, the ship's designer, arrived too, and the two men examined the extent of the damage. Within a few minutes, it was clear to the captain that the boiler rooms and mailrooms were flooded and the ship would sink. Andrews told Captain Smith that the ship would be underwater in an hour or two. Captain Smith ordered the crew to prepare the lifeboats.[97]

It took a very long time for the passengers and the crew to realize that a disaster had occurred. The *Titanic* seemed much safer than the little lifeboats. The first-class passengers were ordered to put on life vests and head toward the Boat Deck. At first many did, but after a while, most went back indoors due to the cold. First-class stairways were crowded with passengers wearing life vests. There was no alarm or panic. Almost an hour after the collision, the lifeboats were still empty. Eventually people were practically forced back to the Boat Deck and into the lifeboats.

The first lifeboat to leave the ship was Lifeboat 7. Nineteen lucky people were saved in this lifeboat, including Jewish fur trader William Greenfield and his mother, Blanche. Lifeboat 7 was launched at 00:45, almost an hour after the *Titanic* hit the iceberg. An hour earlier, William Greenfield had been in the first-class smoking room playing cards. Even after the collision, they continued playing. When they asked a steward what was going on, the steward replied that everything was fine and there was no reason to panic. The steward, like most people on board, had no idea what was going on. William Greenfield and his friends kept playing until they were ordered to put on life vests and head toward the Boat Deck. The occupants of Lifeboat 7 were all first-class passengers and crew.[98]

First-class Jewish passengers William Greenfield and Blanche Greenfield, with Williams daughter Anne. Source: Encyclopedia Titanica, photo credit: Nell Greenfield

At 00:55, over an hour after the collision, the second lifeboat was launched. This time it was Lifeboat 5 with forty-one first-class passengers and crew. Several Jews were in Lifeboat 5, including Annie Stengel. When the ship hit the iceberg, she and her husband, Charles, were awake but did not think anything terrible had happened. Charles believed the noise came from propeller blades. The couple noticed that the engines had stopped. Charles went to the Boat Deck to investigate, and Annie joined him. On their way to the Boat Deck the couple ran into Captain Smith. Without saying a word, they understood that something terrible had happened. They saw the despair in his eyes. After they were ordered to put on life vests, they understood that the worst had happened. They returned to their stateroom, Charles put his life vest on, helped his wife with hers, and the couple returned to the Boat Deck. While waiting near the lifeboats, they were told that everything was under control and the whole issue was a safety precaution. Eventually Annie was asked to enter the lifeboat. Charles helped her into the lifeboat and then went back a few steps and remained on the cold deck.

Dr. Henry Frauenthal, his wife, Clara, and his brother, Isaac, were also among the first-class Jews who were saved in Lifeboat 5. Henry helped his wife into the lifeboat, but at first did not enter himself. As the lifeboat was lowered into the water, the two brothers leaped into it. First Isaac jumped and landed safely. Henry jumped and landed right on top of Annie Stengel, breaking several of her ribs. Ironically, the same man who assisted the injured René Harris a few hours earlier was the one to injure Annie while attempting to rescue himself.

Several more Jews were helped into Lifeboat 5. Those included: Samuel Goldenberg (and his Catholic wife, Nella) and Ruth Dodge and her son, Washington Dodge Jr. Ruth's husband escaped in Lifeboat 13.

First-class Jewish passengers Dr. Henry and Clara Frauenthal. Source: unknown

On the port side, Lifeboat 6 was launched at 00:55 with twenty-eight people, including one Jewish passenger. On the cold deck stood Edgar (Josef) Meyer, a mechanical engineer, who helped women into the lifeboat. His wife, Leah, stood beside him. The two had gone to the Boat Deck as soon as they realized that something was wrong. At first, Leah refused to enter a lifeboat without her husband. Edgar tried to convince her to enter the lifeboat, but in vain. The couple felt uncomfortable arguing in public, so they returned to their stateroom, where Edgar finally was able to convince Leah to enter a lifeboat. He reminded her about their daughter waiting in New York. They returned to the Boat Deck, and Edgar helped Leah into the lifeboat. Leah continued to beg her husband to join her, but he, like most of the men, was prevented. Leah Meyer had to sit in the lifeboat and watch her husband standing near the rail of the ship. As the lifeboat was lowered, Edgar disappeared from her sight. His body, if recovered, was never identified.[99]

Lifeboat 3 on the starboard side was launched at 01:00 with thirty survivors. Among them was Jewish chemist Adolphe Saalfeld, who was in the first-class smoking room during the collision. He ran outside and saw the iceberg as it sideswiped the ship. When the lifeboats were being lowered, he was standing near Lifeboat 3 and asked if he could get in it. One of the officers told him he could, so he did. As the lifeboat was being lowered, he remembered that he had forgotten his leather bag with his perfume samples in his stateroom. The bag and the samples went down with the ship.[100]

The most controversial lifeboat was Lifeboat 1, which was launched with only twelve survivors: five passengers and seven crew members. After Charles Stengel assisted his wife, Annie, into Lifeboat 5, he strolled along the Boat Deck and noticed that Lifeboat 1 was almost empty. He asked First Officer William Murdoch if he could enter it. Murdoch approved, but as the lifeboat was already being launched and was below the deck, Charles Stengel had to roll himself into the lifeboat. Another Jewish passenger who escaped in Lifeboat 1 was Abraham Salomon, who was returning to New York after a business trip to Europe. Salomon was in luck because he was standing on the right side of the ship. Although Captain Smith gave the order "women and children first," William Murdoch, the officer in charge of the starboard side, enabled men to enter the lifeboats as long as there was room. On the port side Second Officer Charles Lightoller, who was in charge, insisted on "women and children only" even if there was room in the lifeboat. Salomon was standing on the starboard side, so Murdoch let him into the lifeboat. Most men were not that lucky.[101]

First-class Jewish passenger Charles Stengel.
Source: Encyclopedia Titanica

Lifeboat 8 was launched at 01:10 with twenty-eight people, two of them Jewish. First-class passenger Emil Taussig helped his wife, Tillie, and their daughter, Ruth, into the lifeboat but then was told to move back. No men were allowed into Lifeboat 8. Tillie and Ruth Taussig survived; Emil's body, if recovered, was never identified.

Ida Straus was almost saved in Lifeboat 8. Isidor and Ida Straus went to the Boat Deck as instructed. They stood near the lifeboat and watched as their maid, Ellen Bird, was helped in. Ida handed her a scarf and told her she would not need it anymore. After the disaster, Ellen tried to return the scarf to the family, but Sara, Ida's daughter, said she could keep it as a souvenir.[102]

When the officers told Ida to enter the lifeboat, she refused to leave her husband. In an exceptional gesture, Second Officer Lightoller offered Isidor a seat in the lifeboat. Lightoller told Isidor that he was an esteemed gentleman and there was room in the lifeboat for such a respected person. To everybody's surprise Isidor rejected the offer and announced that he would not enter a lifeboat before the other men. Isidor continued to try to persuade Ida to enter the lifeboat without him. Ida refused and said: "We have been living together for many years. Where you go, I go."

To the crewmen she said, "I will not leave without my husband. I will stand by him until the last moment. In life we were together, and so we will be in death."

Eventually Lifeboat 8 was lowered without the noble couple. Ida and Isidor stood by the rail together. Many witnesses saw and heard Ida and Isidor Straus during those moments. One of them was Charles Stengel who later said in an interview to the *Globe:*

> Mrs. Straus clung to her aged husband. An officer seized her and tried
> to carry her to a waiting boat, but she would not go. Then the sailors
> strove to tear her from the man whose life partner she had been for
> more than a score of years, but she clung desperately to him.[103]

Another version of the story was told by a passenger of the *Carpathia.* His name was John Badenoch, a good friend of the Straus family, and he heard the story from *Titanic* survivors while on the *Carpathia.* Later that year he recorded the story as he heard it and gave it to Straus family members. He also described his attempts to find Isidor and Ida amongst the survivors on the *Carpathia* but in vain.[104]

According to his story, soon after the *Titanic* hit the iceberg, Ida and Isidor went to the Boat Deck. They were just as surprised as the rest of the passengers. As the lifeboats were being filled, the crewmen urged Ida to enter a lifeboat. Isidor tried persuading her to enter a lifeboat. After their maid, Ellen Bird, entered Lifeboat 8, Ida moved away from the lifeboats. Isidor continued with his persuading, but she insisted on staying with him or leaving with him. She would not go without him. Eventually, after the two moved to the other side of the ship, Isidor convinced her to enter a lifeboat. She put one foot in a lifeboat but when she noticed that Isidor would not follow her into the lifeboat, she retreated to the Boat Deck. She wrapped her arms around him, and that was the end of that. The couple stood calmly as the rest of the lifeboats were launched and chaos surrounded them. The two did not make any other attempt to try to save themselves.

According to what John Badenoch understood, Isidor was not allowed to enter a lifeboat although he was an esteemed gentleman and one of the oldest passengers. Ida's body, if recovered, was never identified. Isidor's body was recovered a few days later, identified, and taken ashore for burial.[105]

Benjamin Guggenheim did not wake from the collision. His valet woke him up after midnight and convinced him to dress and go to the Boat Deck. Guggenheim, without any enthusiasm, put his life vest over his suit but then changed his mind and went to the Boat Deck without the life vest. Guggenheim, followed by his entourage, went to the cold, open deck. His mistress was put into a lifeboat, and Guggenheim told her that there was absolutely nothing to worry about. He assured her that they would meet again soon. Guggenheim, at this point, probably did not understand yet the seriousness of the situation and that the ship would sink. When he realized that the *Titanic* was sinking, he returned to his stateroom and dressed in a good suit. Guggenheim returned to the Boat Deck, gave a short message to a man nearby and asked him to please give the message to his wife, Florette, in New York if he survived:

> I played the game out straight and to the end. No woman shall be left aboard the ship because Ben Guggenheim was a coward. Tell her my last thoughts were of her and of our girls.

He also said to tell his wife that he did all he could to fulfill his duties. Guggenheim then went to the first-class grand staircase with his valet. When approached by a steward, he refused to wear the life vest again and announced: "We are dressed in our best and ready to die as gentlemen."[106]

Legend says that he asked for a glass of brandy and a cigar. The last time he was seen, he was sitting on a chair near the first-class grand staircase, watching as the water level rose. Benjamin Guggenheim, the richest Jew on the *Titanic*, died and his body, if recovered, was never identified.

Edith Rosenbaum was getting ready for bed when she felt the collision. She noticed the shadow of the iceberg as it passed by her stateroom window. She realized that something was wrong, so she got dressed and went to the first-class promenade on A Deck, where she saw a few people playing with some chunks of ice. She joined them for a while but it was too cold for her, so she went back to her stateroom. A few minutes later a friend knocked on her door and advised her to put her life vest on. He assured Edith that she should not worry and soon she would return. Before she left she locked every window, every door, and every trunk in her three-room suite. She carried all nineteen keys with her to the Boat Deck.

At first she refused to enter any lifeboat. While standing on the deck, near Lifeboat 11, she remembered that her toy pig was still in her stateroom, so she sent one of the stewards to bring it to her. After that she still refused to enter the lifeboat because she was afraid she would fall between the lifeboat and the side of the ship. The little lifeboat was rocking from side to side, and it frightened her. In order to enter the lifeboat she had to jump. She said that she could not; she was not an acrobat. Finally one of the crewmen threw her into the lifeboat. He thought that the toy pig was a baby. Edith Rosenbaum was saved.[107] She left the *Titanic* in Lifeboat 11 at 01:35. Lifeboat 11 was the most crowded, with seventy people.

René Harris could have been saved in one of the first lifeboats, but she refused to leave without her husband, Henry. At the time of the collision, the two were in their stateroom. They did not feel the collision, but they did notice that the engines had stopped and the ship was still. Henry went to the Boat Deck to investigate. When he returned he told René that he was told they should wear life vests and go to the Boat Deck. Henry put René's jewelry in his pockets. When the couple reached the Boat Deck, they were led to Lifeboat 4. While standing near the lifeboat, they met John Jacob Astor, the richest man on the *Titanic,* who was helping his pregnant wife, Madeleine, into the lifeboat. René refused to enter the lifeboat without Henry. Lifeboat 4 left the *Titanic* without her. Time went by, and the lifeboats were being launched one after the other, and René was still on board. Even Captain Smith noticed René, scolded her, and ordered her to enter a lifeboat. She still refused to leave without her husband.[108]

A few minutes later, René and Henry Harris noticed Ida and Isidor Straus. The two women talked, and Ida tried to convince René to try to get into a lifeboat. Ida told René that she was old and ready to face death, while René was still young. Isidor also tried to convince René. He told her that she was young and that she should choose this opportunity to live. As last he

First-class Jewish passenger Henry Harris. Source: Encyclopedia Titanica

said: "Go! And may God be with you!" Apparently Isidor succeeded and René agreed at last to try to save herself. Henry helped her into collapsible Lifeboat D, the last lifeboat to be launched safely from the *Titanic*. As the lifeboat was being lowered, Henry threw a blanket toward René to keep her warm. A friend of Henry's, Emil Brandeis, was with him and also helped.

Earlier, as they were standing on the Boat Deck, one of the officers approached René, Henry, and Emil, said that everything was under control, and told them to wait in their rooms for further orders. Another officer approached them and told them to wear their life vests and wait. Emil Brandeis went back to his stateroom, put on his life vest, and returned to be with the René and Henry. At this point, the listing of the ship was so steep that it was very difficult to stand. The three were wearing their life vests when finally Emil and Henry assisted René into the lifeboat. After that, Emil and Henry stayed on the Boat Deck and waited.[109]

Among the first-class Jewish passengers, René Harris was the last to leave the ship. Collapsible Lifeboat D was launched with great difficulty at 02:05, only fifteen minutes before the *Titanic* was lost forever. Henry Harris died, and his body was never identified.

There are contradictory stories about the final moments of Emil Brandeis. According to one version, he tried to escape dressed as a woman. Most witnesses said that that was not true. Others saw him standing near the band. The *Titanic* was at a very steep tilt, and it was nearly impossible to stand any more. Eventually he either fell off the ship or jumped. Emil's body was recovered a few days later, identified, and taken for burial.[110]

Four first-class women and one hundred first-class men died in the disaster. Among the Jewish passengers who died was Benjamin Forman. Several Jewish survivors saw him that night. Edith Rosenbaum saw him in the first-class library an hour or two before the collision. Abraham Salomon saw him after the collision and offered to join him and go to the Boat Deck, but Forman, who was already wearing his life vest, insisted on staying indoors. Samuel Goldenberg also testified that he met Forman that night. Benjamin Forman died, and his body, if recovered, was never identified.[111]

Jacob Birnbaum went to the Boat Deck but was not permitted to enter a lifeboat. He was still on the *Titanic* when the ship broke in two. That was when he eventually jumped off and tried swimming away in order to reach one of the lifeboats. He was sucked under the freezing water and was swamped when one of the four funnels collapsed. His body was recovered a few days later, identified, and taken ashore for burial.

George Rosenshine helped his mistress, Mabelle Thorne, into a lifeboat but was not permitted to follow her. His body was recovered a few days later, identified, and taken for burial. Other first-class Jewish passengers who died included Erwin Lewy, John Baumann, Herman Klaber, Herman Klaber, Solomon Banewe, and Martin Rothschild. Their bodies, if recovered, were never identified.

Many second-class passengers were lucky. Eight of the lifeboats were on the second-class promenade on the stern section of the Boat Deck, and many second-class passengers had easy access to the lifeboats. The rest of the lifeboats were on the bow section reserved for first-class passengers. A short while after midnight, second-class passengers were told to put on life vests and head toward the Boat Deck. When Captain Smith gave the order to evacuate the passengers, the crewmen started filling the lifeboats on the bow section, and only when those lifeboats were launched could the crewmen start evacuating the second-class passengers in the lifeboats on the stern section. That is why the first lifeboats to leave the *Titanic* were only half full and their occupants were mostly first-class passengers. The lifeboats with the second-class passengers were launched later. The first lifeboat from the stern section was launched at 01:20.

At this time, most of the rescued first-class passengers were already in lifeboats, but an hour and a half after the collision, most of the lifeboats were not yet launched. The *Titanic* was still fairly safe, and the tilt was not too steep. No one was panicking. The air was extremely cold, and most passengers preferred to stay indoors. The lifeboats were still being launched half full. The first lifeboat to be relatively full was Lifeboat 10, launched at 01:20 with fifty-five survivors. Among them was Hanna (Henya) Abelson, who was immigrating with her husband, Samuel, to New York where he had a brother. Hanna and Samuel were born in Odessa, fled Russian anti-

Semitism, and boarded the *Titanic* in Cherbourg. Samuel put his wife into the lifeboat but was not permitted to join her. His body, if recovered, was never identified.

Seven-year-old Eva Hart was asleep when the *Titanic* hit the iceberg. Her mother Esther was in bed but again had trouble sleeping. When the *Titanic* hit, she felt the vibration of the iceberg swiping against the hull. Later she said it felt as if a train had pulled into the station. As soon as she felt the vibration, she leaped out of bed. She had done the same thing the night before and had woken her husband because of "noises" she heard. This time she woke him again and said she thought something bad had happened. "This time I am sure of it," she said. She practically begged Benjamin to go outside and investigate. He got dressed and went to the upper deck. When he returned, he told Esther that Captain Smith had ordered an evacuation drill. Esther insisted that such drills would not be done so late at night.

Esther and Benjamin dressed in warm clothes and prepared to leave the room. Eva was asleep the whole time. Her parents woke her, dressed her, wrapped her in a blanket, and carried her. On their way to the Boat Deck, they ran into a stewardess whom they recognized. She could not answer any questions as she did not understand the gravity of the situation. Her body language showed that something terrible had happened, but she did not have any information.[112]

When Benjamin, Esther, and Eva reached the Boat Deck, they realized their lives were in danger. The tilt was quite noticeable and many people were screaming. Benjamin realized that lifeboats were being prepared to be filled with women and children, and he understood that he might die. He withdrew to the side and prayed. Esther saw him, yet she did not know what he prayed. When Esther recalled the incident, she said that he "prayed a Jewish prayer."[113] A crewman approached and said that women and children had to get into the lifeboats. He led Benjamin, Esther, and Eva from one lifeboat to another and eventually found room in Lifeboat 14. Benjamin placed Eva into the lifeboat and then helped Esther. He was told to move back, for men were not allowed into the lifeboats.

At that moment a man jumped into the lifeboat but was forcibly removed by several crewmen. One officer took out a revolver and fired into the air. He warned the men that whoever tried to jump into a lifeboat would be shot. His exact words were: "I will shoot him like a dog."

Benjamin stepped back to avoid the commotion and called to Eva. He told her to be brave and watch over her mother. Poor little Eva cried and begged the officer: "Please do not shoot my daddy." The lifeboat was launched at 01:25 with sixty survivors (the full capacity was sixty-five people). As the lifeboat was lowered, Benjamin waved to his wife and daughter until they were out of sight. Many women and children in the lifeboat were sobbing, and an officer yelled at them to be quiet. After the lifeboat reached the water, Eva heard the men on deck shouting. Esther noticed that at first there wasn't any panic, but as time went by and lifeboats were being lowered and the tilt was becoming more noticeable, passengers on board started to scream in terror. Esther and Eva Hart were saved, yet Benjamin's body, if recovered, was never identified.

At 01:30 Lifeboat 9 was launched with fifty-six survivors; many were second-class women and children, including Rosa Pinsky who was Jewish. At the same time, Lifeboat 12 was launched with forty survivors, including Amy Frances Jacobsohn, her sister, Rachel Juli Cohen, and their mother, Alice Frances Cohen Christy. Amy's husband, Sydney (Samuel) Jacobsohn, helped the three women into the lifeboat but was not permitted to join them. His body, if recovered, was never identified.

Another Jewish woman who made it into Lifeboat 12 was Miriam Kantor. Her husband Sinai's body was recovered a few days later, identified, and taken ashore for burial.

In second class seventy-eight out of ninety-two women survived, including all the Jewish women. Only fifteen of the 157 second-class male passengers survived. Not a single Jewish man in second class survived, including Leopold Weisz and Samuel Greenberg, whose bodies were recovered a few days later, identified, and taken ashore for burial.

Second-class passenger Dr. René Jacques (Jacob) Lévy could have been saved. He went to the Boat Deck and helped load women in the lifeboats. When he was inside Lifeboat 11, he saw that it was full and that there were women standing on the Boat Deck, so he returned to the ship and made room for one more woman. René Lévy's body, if recovered, was never identified.

Second-class passengers Israel Nesson and Moses Aaron Troupiansky also lost their lives in the disaster. Their bodies, if recovered, were never identified.

Things in third-class were much worse. First-class and second-class passengers were helped into lifeboats. They were told where to go and how to get there. Third-class passengers were on their own. The "lucky" ones who were on the starboard side of the bow heard the unfamiliar grinding noise and felt the unexpected vibration of the collision with the iceberg. Within minutes, ice water began penetrating the cabins. The passengers woke in fright, leaped out of bed, and stepped into freezing water. For many long minutes, the passengers wandered the passageways without knowing what to do or where to go.[114]

Third-class stewards were just as confused as the passengers were. Eventually Captain Smith gave the order to wake all the passengers in third class and instruct them to wear life vests. The stewards went from room to room, knocked on doors, and woke everybody up. They ordered the passengers to put on their life vests and wait for further instructions. Many passengers did not speak English and could not understand the stewards. Others did not understand what the commotion was about, and no one was able to explain what was happening. With all the running around, the yelling, the rumors, and the confusion, it was mayhem.

Third-class passengers did not have access to the Boat Deck and the lifeboats. The third-class open space was one deck lower than where the lifeboats were, and the upper decks were locked. To reach the Boat Deck, third-class passengers had to climb over closed gates. There was no standard policy about separating third-class passengers from the other two classes in an emergency. Some gates were deliberately locked to prevent the passengers from going to the upper decks while wealthy first-class passengers were lowered in the lifeboats. Some gates were open. Some were locked, then opened, then locked again. After the disaster, the surviving officers testified that there was no separation between the classes during the evacuation, yet the statistics of the casualties and survivors say otherwise.

In first class, only one child died. In second class, every child survived. In third class, fifty-three of the seventy-six children died. The situation for the men was even worse. Almost all the third-class men died. In first class, a third of the men survived.

When the third-class passengers finally broke through the gates and when some stewards finally led passengers to the Boat Deck, most lifeboats were gone. The *Titanic* was on an angle, and the tilt was steep. The stern was rising out of the water. The bow was submerged. The lifeboats were now launched at full capacity, and some were launched beyond capacity. With the arrival of the hundreds of third-class passengers, things became worse. The crew locked arms and formed a barrier to prevent men from rushing to lifeboats being filled with women and children.

As mentioned, there was no set policy. Several third-class stewards helped passengers to the Boat Deck. Some allowed only women and children to pass through the gates, while others did not distinguish between passengers. People got lost in unfamiliar first-class passageways. A few stewards personally led women and children through the endless labyrinth of passageways and stairways and escorted them to lifeboats.

One lucky third-class woman who was escorted to the Boat Deck was Bella Moor and her son, Meyer. They were with a group of women and children led by a steward who unlocked a gate, guided them through first class, and led them to the lifeboats. Bella and Meyer were helped into Lifeboat 14. Bella left her cabin with only the clothes she was wearing and her immigration papers. She was worried that she would be deported if she arrived at Ellis Island without the documents. Meyer wanted to return to the cabin to get the cigarette covers he had collected. The crewmen did not pay attention to his request and lowered the lifeboat. Amongst the third-class Jewish passengers, Bella Moor and Meyer were the first to leave the ship. Eva and Esther Hart were in the same lifeboat.

Leah Aks and her son, Frank, ten months old, were also helped by stewards. Leah Aks was told to put on a life vest and go to the deck. She reached one of the gates that separated third class from second class, but it was locked. She yelled for help, and a steward came over, lifted Frank, and passed him over the gate. He then helped Leah climb over the gate. Leah took Frank and started wandering until she met a group of third-class women being led by a steward. She joined them and eventually reached the Boat Deck. As she was waiting to enter a lifeboat, she found herself standing next to Madeleine Astor, the pregnant wife of John Jacob Astor. The richest woman on the *Titanic* and a steerage woman with a baby in her arms stood side by side. Madeleine Astor noticed poor little Frank shivering from the freezing cold, so she wrapped him with her shawl. With teeth shaking from the cold, Leah thanked her without knowing who her savior was.

As they were standing there, a man tried forcing his way into the lifeboat. The crewmen dragged him out of the lifeboat and told him that only women and children could enter the lifeboats. The man approached Leah and said, "Women and children first? I will show you women and children first!" He then snatched Frank out of Leah's arms and threw the baby overboard.[115] Leah, trying desperately to find her son, moved toward the lifeboat, but the crewmen blocked her way, thinking she was rushing the crowded lifeboat. She was pushed back, and the lifeboat was lowered without her.[116]

Leah searched for her son from the deck, but eventually, still in shock, she was pushed into another lifeboat. The other women in the lifeboat tried to cheer her up, but in vain.*

Lifeboat 13 was launched with sixty-four survivors, almost at full capacity, at 01:40. Among them were several Jews, including Jennie Dropkin from third class and five-year-old Virginia Ethel Emanuel, also from third class. After reaching the water and before disconnecting the ropes, the lifeboat was almost crushed by Lifeboat 15, which was being lowered as well. Only the screams of the occupants and the quick action of the crewmen prevented a catastrophe from happening. The crewmen cut the ropes in time and rowed the lifeboat to safety.[117]

Because of the "women and children first" rule (and in many cases "women and children only"), some third-class women were assisted and escorted. Nobody assisted the third-class men. Many of them were stopped by locked gates. Others were blocked by stewards. The men who wished to live had to find their own way out of third class and into the lifeboats.

Gershon Cohen was one of those men. He was sleeping at the time of the collision. He woke up from the impact but did not think much of it and went back to sleep. He woke up again from the commotion of his cabinmates. He immediately went to the Poop Deck but found there were no lifeboats there. He saw chunks of the iceberg that had crashed onto the deck. He returned to his cabin, but when he got there, the floor was flooded. He heard stewards ordering third-class passengers to wear life vests and wait for instructions. After waiting a while with many of the impatient passengers, he realized there would not be any instructions and that the crew did not have a plan. People still believed that the *Titanic* would not sink, but when a steward said it would, Cohen decided to save himself. Wearing his life vest, he went back to the Poop Deck. He saw that the lifeboats were not there and he would have to climb to the higher decks to reach them. He climbed over the rail and found himself on the second-class open deck (the Boat Deck). He noticed that the band was playing cheerful tunes and rockets were being fired every

---

Some researchers claim Leah Aks was rescued in Lifeboat 13, but others, including Don Lynch, claim she was actually rescued in Lifeboat 4.

few minutes. A seaman called to him and invited him to enter Lifeboat 12. By the time Cohen reached the seaman, the lifeboat was already being lowered. He jumped toward the hanging ropes, slid down, and headed for the lifeboat. He was wearing leather gloves so his hands were safe from rope burns. He missed the lifeboat, fell into the water, but was pulled into the lifeboat at 01:30. Cohen was one of the only men in the lifeboat, so he helped with the rowing.[118] He shared the lifeboat with second-class passengers Miriam Kantor and Amy Frances Jacobsohn, her sister, Rachel Juli, and their mother, Alice Frances Cohen Christy. Gershon Cohen was one of the very few lucky third-class Jewish men who survived.

But Cohen was not the only one. Berk Trembisky (Picard) woke from the collision, went with a group of third-class men, got lost, split from the group, and found a door leading to second class. He reached the second-class promenade on Boat Deck, climbed over to the first-class promenade, and entered Lifeboat 9 as it was being lowered at 01:30. Second-class passenger Rosa Pinsky was in this lifeboat too.

Another Jew who had to act on his own was Abraham Joseph Hyman. During the commotion in the third-class public room, Hyman tried to pass the closed gates but was violently blocked by stewards. He went from gate to gate until he found one that was opened and finally escaped third class. He made it to the Boat Deck after most of the lifeboats were already gone. It was over two hours since the collision. He made his way to collapsible Lifeboat C. When he got there, a ring of crewmen blocked the men from approaching the lifeboat. A few shots were fired in order to stop the hundreds of men from reaching and swamping the lifeboat. Hyman saw that collapsible Lifeboat C was the only lifeboat around. The *Titanic's* list was very noticeable, and there was a lot of screaming and panicking at this time. Hyman found a way around the human blockade and reached the lifeboat. He assisted several women into the lifeboat and then entered it too. After settling in the lifeboat, the crewmen stopped others from entering.[119]

Hyman was not the only Jewish survivor in the lifeboat. Twenty-

Third-class Jewish passenger Abraham Josef Hyman with wife Esther. Photo credit: J. A. Hyman Titanics Ltd.

six-year-old Sarah Roth was one of the third-class women who had reached the Boat Deck and was allowed into the lifeboat. Collapsible Lifeboat C was launched with much difficulty at 02:00 and was one of the last lifeboats to leave the sinking ship. In the lifeboat was the managing director of the White Star Line, Bruce Ismay. Hyman was one of the only men in the lifeboat, and he had to help row. By this time, the ship was sinking fast, and the people in the lifeboat were scared that the ship would cause suction and overturn the lifeboat. They decided to row toward the lights in the far distance. As it turned out, those lights were of the *Californian* about fifteen kilometers away. Although the crew of the *Californian* saw the *Titanic* and vice versa, the *Californian* never came to the aid of the sinking *Titanic* and none of the lifeboats ever reached the *Californian*.

All the accessible lifeboats were gone. The only lifeboats left were the two small collapsible lifeboats that were stored on the roof of the officer's quarters. The only way to launch them was to climb onto the roof, untie them, and try to connect them to the davits. The entire bow section of the *Titanic* was already underwater. The captain was nowhere to be seen. The list was nearly impossible to withstand. The desperate men who were trying to release the two collapsible lifeboats were struggling. The water was reaching the windows of the officer's quarters. At last collapsible Lifeboat A was released, but it was washed away by a huge wave that threw everyone into the water at 02:20. Collapsible Lifeboat A was filling with water, but about twenty people were able to hold on to it and climb in. Some of them died in the next two hours due to the freezing cold.[120]

The last lifeboat to leave the *Titanic* was collapsible Lifeboat B. Actually it was the other way around: collapsible Lifeboat B did not leave the *Titanic*; the *Titanic* left the lifeboat. As the men were desperately struggling with the ropes, the ship vanished beneath them, and the lifeboat drifted away, still upside down. This happened at 02:20. Over thirty people tried to climb onto the lifeboat. Among them were Second Officer Charles Lightoller (the highest-ranking survivor), Harold Bride (the junior wireless operator) and Colonel Archibald Gracie (a good friend of Isidor Straus). One Jew made it to collapsible Lifeboat B. Third-class passenger David Livshin somehow found his way from third class to the Boat Deck and managed to hold on until the last minute. The poor, drenched survivors who climbed onto collapsible Lifeboat B had to spend the night trying not to slip off the overturned lifeboat.[121]

Third-class Jewish passenger David Livshin. Courtesy: Rachel Mines

One Jewish passenger tried his luck in escaping the sinking ship a different way. Third-class passenger Eliezer (Leslie) Gilinski reached the third-class open deck (the Poop Deck). Instead of climbing over to the Boat Deck, he jumped into the freezing water and swam to a piece of ice that was floating nearby. The little iceberg was large enough for several others as well. Eventually almost twenty people made it to that little piece of ice. They spend the night calling for help and trying not to die from the cold.[122]

Most third-class men did not have a chance. From the time of the collision until the last moments, most men in third class were held back. When the *Titanic* sank, many of them were trapped and could not escape. Among them were many Jews: Harry Sadowitz, Aaron Weller, Leo Zimmerman, Simon Kutsher, Zalman Slocovski, Jacob Cook, Woolf Spector, Nathan Goldsmith, Shimon Maisner, Maurice Moshe Sirota, Harry Cornblatt, Asher Pulner, and probably many others. Their bodies, if recovered, were never identified.

Information about many victims is scarce. Very little is known about most third-class Jews. Aaron Weller, for example, born in 1875 in Russia, was a tailor, married, and had three children. All that is known about Leo Zimmerman is that he was born in 1883 in Germany, was a farmer, and was single.

The whereabouts of Typkia Friedberg and her husband are unknown. As a woman, Typkia should have been rescued. As a third-class passenger, though, her chances were low. Did she refuse to leave third class without her husband? Did she make it to the Boat Deck? Typkia Friedberg was the only known third-class Jewish women to die in the disaster along with her husband. Their bodies, if recovered, were never identified.

Compared to the first and second classes, the percentage of third-class survivors was extremely low. Fewer than ninety women (less than half) survived. Only twenty-five children (less than a third) survived. Thirteen percent of third-class men survived (fewer than sixty out of 440).

Among the third-class Jewish women and children, all survived except Typkia Friedberg. Among the third-class Jewish men, only three survived.

From the beginning, the crewmen acted gallantly and set a good example for the passengers. While lowering the lifeboats, Captain Smith ordered Officers Lightoller and Murdoch to make sure that every lifeboat would have enough seamen to row and take care of the passengers. The mortality of the crew was catastrophic. Many crewmen on the *Titanic* did not have a good chance of

Sinking of the Titanic. *Photo credit: Willy Stöwer, die Gartenlaube, 1912*

survival, and most perished. Of 890 crewmen, fewer than two hundred survived. Among the female crew members, three died and twenty survived. Both known Jewish crewmen (second-class barber Herbert Klein and kosher cook Charles Kennel) died. Their bodies, if recovered, were never identified.[123]

The last moments of the great *Titanic* were intense. At 02:00, all the lifeboats were gone. The bow was submerged. The firemen and the stokers could no longer keep the electricity going, and all the lights went out. The *Titanic* was doomed. People were rushing to the stern, but it was so steep that people slipped and fell into the water. Boilers and other heavy machinery crushed people to death. Hundreds of passengers jumped desperately into the water. People threw deck chairs into the water and tried building tiny rafts. The forward funnel collapsed into the water, crushing dozens of people. The stress on the hull was extremely immense. As the bow sank underwater and the stern rose higher and higher into the air, the pressure caused the hull to crack and then to break. The bow plunged to the bottom of the Atlantic, and the stern leveled and wobbled in the water for a few more minutes like a huge cork. The few who were still holding onto the stern were trying to grip the rail. Most lost their strength and fell into the water. The interior of the ship moved about and crashed. The beds, the boilers, the dishes – anything that could detach from its place did, with a huge roar. The noise was deafening. Anyone in the lifeboats who had the courage to watch was terrified. Most turned their heads away. The stern wobbled in the water for a few moments and then started sinking until it disappeared completely. The *Titanic* was gone.

Abraham Hyman in collapsible Lifeboat C heard the sound of the great ocean liner breaking in two, but it was too dark and he could not see exactly what was going on. Meyer in Lifeboat 14 pointed toward the *Titanic* and told his mother that the lights went out and the ship was disappearing. His mother, Bella, was too terrified to look, but she saw the dozens of swimmers who tried to call for help. Even when she closed her eyes, she could still hear the screaming of the dying people in the water. She was sure that she would die too. She guessed that there weren't any ships nearby and that her lifeboat would drift away and everyone would die.

Seven hundred and twelve survivors, among them thirty-five Jews, crowded together in the lifeboats and waited. Many of the survivors heard the screaming of the hundreds of desperate people in the water. As the minutes went by, the screams became weaker and weaker and eventually ceased altogether.

The long night was unbearable for Annie Stengel. She was in Lifeboat 5 and had been injured during the evacuation. Several of her ribs were broken, and she was in great pain. To make things worse for her, she believed that she had lost her husband. She did not know yet that Charles had survived. She cried with the other women. So many women became widows that night! René Harris in collapsible Lifeboat D wept for her husband, Henry. Hanna Abelson in Lifeboat 10 cried for her husband, Samuel. Esther Hart in Lifeboat 14 cried for her husband, Benjamin. Tillie Taussig in Lifeboat 8 wept for her husband, Emil. No one wept like Leah Aks, though. She sat in Lifeboat 13 and wept for the loss of her baby, Frank. She was traumatized. Her baby had been snatched out of her arms and thrown overboard. What would she tell her husband, Samuel, when she arrived in America? How would she tell him about his son he had never seen?

In Lifeboat 11 Edith Rosenbaum tried to cheer up some children by winding up the tail of her toy pig and playing the tune. Gershon Cohen in Lifeboat 12 spent most of the night rowing. He too heard the screams of the dying. Those sounds haunted him for the rest of his life, but during those dark hours, he could not think about them. He was helping the seamen in the lifeboat. They were trying to reach the other lifeboats that were wobbling about in the freezing Atlantic. Eventually Lifeboat 12 joined Lifeboat 14 and later also joined collapsible Lifeboat B. Several of the women were asked to assist with the rowing. Leah Mayer helped with the rowing in Lifeboat 6.

Some of the lifeboats were overcrowded, and water was penetrating them. Esther Hart was asked to get rid of some of the water. She did not have anything to use, so she tried with her bare hands. The water was freezing.

After Lifeboats 12 and 14 were tied together, some of the survivors were transferred from one lifeboat to another. Seven-year-old Eva Hart was transferred from Lifeboat 14 to Lifeboat 12 and temporarily separated from her mother. In the distance, she noticed the screams of the dying and then the silence.

Of all the lifeboats, the survivors who tried to hold on to Collapsible Lifeboat B had the worst time. The lifeboat was overturned, and it was nearly impossible to climb onto its back. David Livshin spent a very long time in the cold water until he was able to climb on to the lifeboat. By the time the overturned lifeboat joined Lifeboats 12 and 14, he froze to death.[124]

Eliezer Gilinski waited in vain to be rescued from the floating ice. He was not able to survive the freezing air and died during the night. His body was found on the ice several days later.[125]

At 03:30 some of the survivors thought that they noticed rockets being fired in the distance. It was an approaching ship. It was the *Carpathia,* and it was coming to the rescue.[126]

When the dawn broke, the approaching ship was visible to many survivors. One by one, the lifeboats started rowing toward the rescue ship. The longest night of their lives was over.

8

ON BOARD THE *CARPATHIA*

Captain Arthur Rostron was the captain of the Cunard ocean liner *Carpathia*. The *Carpathia* could not have made it to the scene in time to save all the passengers and the crew of the *Titanic*. She sailed at her top speed but had to maneuver around the many icebergs on her way. In total, she bypassed at least six large icebergs and many other smaller ones. When she finally arrived at the scene, she picked up all 712 survivors.[127]

The *Carpathia* was a passenger ship. The Cunard ocean liner could accommodate over two thousand passengers, but that night she was carrying fewer than eight hundred passengers. She had sailed from New York on April 11 and was on her way to the Mediterranean Sea via the Straits of Gibraltar. During the crucial night of April 14, she was east of the *Titanic*. She turned around and sailed west toward the *Titanic* as soon as the captain received the desperate call for help. There were other ships in the area, but of the ones who heard the *Titanic* calling for help, she was the closest. The *Californian* was much closer and even visible during the night, but her radio operator was sleeping and the captain only heard of the disaster in the morning when it was too late.[128] The second ship to arrive near the scene was the *Olympic,* but she was advised not to come too close; the sight of the sister ship would surely cause panic and depression among the survivors.[129] From the moment the *Carpathia* was visible, it took over four hours to complete the rescue and board all the survivors. The last survivors boarded the *Carpathia* after 08:30.[130]

When day broke, it seemed as if the survivors in the lifeboats were surrounded by an army of large sailboats. The sunlight shone on the "sailboats" in a thousand colors. It was a spectacular vision. The large objects

Collapsible Lifeboat D approaches the Carpathia *on the morning after the disaster. Among the survivors in the lifeboat is first-class Jewish passenger René Harris. Source: Wikimedia Commons*

were not sailboats, but actually icebergs in many shapes and sizes. Some of the survivors noticed that one of the icebergs was larger than the others and believed that it was the iceberg that had felled the *Titanic*.

As the lifeboats approached the rescue ship, the crewmen on board the *Carpathia* opened several bays of the gangway doors and hung out ropes, ladders, and canvas bags. All the healthy men climbed ladders or ropes and boarded the ship. The children were placed in canvas bags and pulled on board. Not all the survivors were able to climb on their own. Some were too exhausted, too injured, or too overwhelmed. René Harris, who broke her arm several hours earlier and was still wearing a sling, was hoisted in a chair sling. Since most of the occupants of the lifeboat René was in were third-class women, she was mistaken for a third-class passenger and taken to the area designated for the third-class survivors. She demanded to be taken to the first-class area, the crew of the *Carpathia* apologized, and hours later she finally was transferred to the first-class area.

Seven-year-old Eva Hart, who had been separated from her mother during the night, found her hours later. She stood on deck and watched as many of the women waited in vain for their husbands until they were led away in tears.

As the survivors boarded the *Carpathia*, they were sorted into three groups according to class, similar to the arrangement on the *Titanic*. The passengers were asked for their names and class and then escorted to the appropriate area that had been defined in advance. Class was firmly enforced, and even the poor, overwhelmed survivors could not escape segregation. The strict customs and the uncompromising rules were in effect even for those who lost their loved ones, all their belongings, and suffered through the hardest night of their lives. Some first-class survivors (especially the women) were housed in the *Carpathia's* officers' quarters and *Carpathia's* first-class quarters. Some second-class survivors were also housed in cabins. Third-class survivors were housed in the *Carpathia's* public and dining rooms. The survivors were separated also by gender. The first day on board the *Carpathia*, most of the women were anxious because they did not know their husbands' fates. They wanted to send telegrams to other ships to see if there were other survivors.

That afternoon Captain Rostron gathered all the first-class survivors in the main dining room. He held a short memorial for the victims and offered a prayer of thanks for the survivors. He did the same with second- and then third-class survivors. Crewmen circulated among the survivors and wrote down their names. Attempts were made to compose a list of survivors and a separate list of victims. Both lists were inaccurate with numerous mistakes. The official lists were based on what the survivors said, but the exact number of survivors and their names is still unknown.

One interesting mistake made it to the *New York Herald*. The list of first class survivors included Mr. and Mrs. Henry Frauenthal and Mr. and Mrs. J. G. Frauenthal. Although Henry was married to Clara, and both survived, Gerald (Isaac) Frauenthal was single.

All the survivors were questioned on the *Carpathia* at the request of the United States Ministry of Immigration. They were asked for their name, age, destination, and occupation. One of the more interesting questions the survivors were asked was for their nationality or ethnic group. Most Jewish survivors gave their country of birth for nationality but several identified themselves as Jews. Among them were Leah Aks, Gershon Cohen, Jennie Dropkin, and Rose Pinsky. When asked for their nationality, they all answered that they were Jewish. Others, such as Abraham Hyman, identified themselves as "Hebrew."

Surviving crewmen gathered together for a memorial in honor of their friends. They shared experiences, compared personal views of the events, and supported each other.

That same day three victims were buried at sea. The three died during the night while in the lifeboats but had been brought onto the *Carpathia*. One victim was David Livshin, who was able to climb onto the overturned collapsible Lifeboat B and was transferred to Lifeboat 12 during the night. When the *Carpathia* picked up the survivors, he was among the dead. His body was pulled onto the *Carpathia* with the survivors. He and two more victims were buried at sea after a short memorial funeral. A Catholic priest and a Protestant minister led the ceremony. On Livshin's body were documents with his alias name, Abraham Harmer. With that name, he was listed on the *Carpathia*. If only his true identity had been known, and if only his religion had been known, perhaps Livshin would have been granted a Jewish ceremony.

The weather was calm during most of the journey to New York, but two days after picking up the survivors, a storm broke out and it started raining. Most survivors did not write their memories of the disaster or share their traumatic experience with each other during the voyage. Instead most survivors kept to themselves. There was not much communication between the survivors and the *Carpathia's* passengers. Captain Rostron's policy was that the *Titanic* survivors were not to mingle with the *Carpathia* passengers. However, the passengers welcomed the survivors with warmth, opened their cabins, and shared clothes with them.

Many survivors were in mourning. Esther Hart mourned for Benjamin while

Group photo of Lifeboat 1 survivors on board the Carpathia. *Standing second to the right (in white cap) is Jewish survivor Abraham Salomon. Charles Stengel is not in the frame. Source:* Daily Mirror

taking care of Eva. Annie Stengel was treated by the *Carpathia's* doctor for the ribs that broke when Henry Frauenthal landed on her in the lifeboat. To add to her anguish and sorrow, she was in mourning over her husband, Charles. Little did she know that he was alive and well. While Charles was searching for her, he happened to bump into George Brayton, the card conman. The two men had met on board the *Titanic* a few days earlier during a card game and Brayton figured that it would be easy to lure Stengel into illegal activity. While on board the *Carpathia*, Brayton approached Stengel and told him that he lost all his belongings in the disaster. He believed that Stengel would give him money. Stengel did not fall for the trap and suggested that Brayton sue the White Star Line for his loss and gain his money back. Brayton also invited Stengel to join him in a horse racing scam. Stengel refused and went on searching for his wife. What a surprise it was for her when he found her and they were reunited! Most other women were not as lucky.

Another Jewish survivor who wept for the loss of a loved one was Leah Aks. The last memory of her ten-month-old baby was when he was snatched out of her arms. She turned down any attempt of consolation. After being pulled on board the *Carpathia*, she searched the decks for her lost son in vain. For two days she secluded herself in a room. She could not sleep or eat. During the storm most passengers stayed indoors, but when the weather was better many went out on deck. Leah was convinced by another survivor to go on deck and get some fresh air. Leah strolled along the open deck for a while, when suddenly she heard a baby crying. She imagined that she heard her son, Frank. She noticed that a baby was in the arms of a woman she did not know.* Leah became convinced that this baby was actually her own. Leah approached the woman and demanded that she return the baby to her. Both women began arguing and started a commotion. Crewmen rushed to the scene and were amazed to see two women arguing over a baby. None of the crewmen knew who the rightful mother was, so they escorted both women to Captain Rostron to decide what to do.

Captain Rostron found himself in the role of King Solomon and had to determine who the real mother was and who was not. Both women claimed the baby. He requested that both women come to his quarters to state their claims.

Even today, the women's identity is unknown. She might have been an Italian immigrant named Argene Del Carlo who was pregnant at the time and had lost her husband in the disaster. It is possible, though, that she was an Englishwoman named Elizabeth Ramell from second class who was traveling alone. This is another unsolved mystery.

He asked the women if the baby had special characteristic. After a few moments of silence, Leah said, "I am Jewish and so is my son. He is circumcised." A quick check revealed the truth. As it turned out, during the evacuation when Frank was tossed overboard, he landed in one of the lifeboats. The woman holding the baby told Captain Rostron that she was sitting in the lifeboat and someone handed the baby to her. After the *Titanic* sank, she believed that the baby was a heavenly compensation for the loss of her husband. The explanation was not satisfactory, and Frank Aks was rightfully returned to his mother Leah.[131]

Meanwhile the survivors of Lifeboat 1 posed for series of group photos, some of which were published. In one photo Abraham Salomon stands next to the Duff Gordons. Charles Stengel had been cropped out of the photo by the newspapers.

During the late hours of the morning of April 15, the *Californian* arrived at the scene and offered to assist in any way. The *Californian* was fifteen kilometers from the site where the *Titanic* sank. Her wireless operator was asleep during the dramatic night. Only when he woke and turned on his equipment did he realize what had happened during the night. Only then did Captain Stanley Lord, captain

Jewish survivor Gershon Cohen (in center, sitting in a deckchair, his head leaning down) on board the Carpathia. *Source:* New York Journal

of the *Californian,* grasp the fatal errors of his crew. The watchmen on board the *Californian* saw a ship in the distance and rockets being fired. They woke the captain and told him, yet no one suggested waking up the telegraph operator.

Many survivors wanted to send telegrams from the *Carpathia* to inform people of their survival. Second-class passenger Amy Frances Jacobsohn, whose husband had died, sent a message that she was safe and did not know what happened to her husband, Sydney. She wrote:

Do not be alarmed Sydney may be on another boat

First-class passenger René Harris, whose husband Henry died, sent a telegram to her father-in-law. In the message she wrote:

Am safe praying that Henry has been picked up by another streamer. Arrive Carpathia

First-class passenger Abraham Salomon wrote:

Safe and well. Arrive Thursday afternoon. Cunard Steamer Carpathia

Second-class passenger Hanna Abelson, who had lost her husband, Samuel, wrote a telegram as well, but because of the heavy traffic in the wireless room, her message was never sent. Her message was only two words:

Saved. Carpathia.

Third-class passenger Gershon Cohen did not write or send a telegram from the *Carpathia.* Instead he wrote some letters describing the events.In one letter he wrote, he mentioned the number of Jews on board the *Titanic.* He wrote that he noticed that there were over forty Jews in third class. Forty-two Jews in his section of third class, to be exact. He concludes the topic with the words:

Five only remained. One man two married women one single and myself. So I must be considered lucky. *

His letters are on display in museums in England and the United States.

While the *Carpathia* was sailing toward New York, the world was anxiously waiting for news. Anything that was sent by the wireless was published around the globe. During the voyage to New York, a rumor started that five dogs and one pig had survived the *Titanic* disaster. The fact is that some of the dogs on board the *Titanic* were actually saved, but they got the story with the pig all wrong. The pig that was saved was actually Edith Rosenbaum's toy pig, which played a tune that relaxed the children during the long night in the lifeboat. Somehow, someone on board the *Carpathia* started a rumor that there was a live pig onboard.[132]

Only when the *Carpathia* docked would it be known how many people had died and how many survived – who lived and who perished.

In the meanwhile, the world was anxious to receive information about the disaster.

9

REACTION OF THE JEWISH PRESS

While the *Carpathia* was sailing toward New York, news of the disaster made its way too. In an era in which the fastest means of communication was the telegram, the only way to send reports about the disaster was from the small wireless room on board the *Carpathia*.

באסטאן , ס׳איז דערהאלטמען גע־
וואָרען א ידיעה , אז די שיף ,קאר־
פאטיא' געהט קײן ניו־יאָרק מיט 868
פאסאזשירען , וואָס זענען נערατטעוωעט
געוואָרען בײ דער שרעקליכער קאטאס־
טראָפע מיט דער שיף „טיטאאָניק".
וואָס ס׳איז געוואָרען מיט די איבּריגע
פאסאזשירען איז פאַרלוֹיפָיָג אונבּע־
וואוסט , נאָר מ׳רעכענט , אז זײ זענען
אלע דערטרונקען געוואָרען .

A notice about the Carpathia *on her way to New York (in Yiddish). Source:* Der Mament, *April 17, 1912*

In the newspapers of April 15, the description was optimistic. The headlines on both sides of the Atlantic Ocean said that the *Titanic* had sunk but all on board had survived. In the *Evening Sun* (New York), the headline on April 15 was: "All *Titanic* passengers are safe." The report was that all survived and boarded the *Carpathia* and the *Parisian*. The article added that the *Titanic* was being towed to New York by the *Virginian*. Other newspapers that day wrote in a similar way. The headline in *The World* (Vancouver) was: "*Titanic* sinking: no lives lost." The headline in the *Daily Mail* (London) was similar.

Only the next day, April 16, did the world media understand the unbelievable dimensions of the catastrophe. The *New York Tribune* reported that there were around 1,340 casualties and 866 survivors. The *New York American* wrote that the number of casualties was between 1,500 and 1,800. It took most newspapers a long time before they reported the correct numbers of victims and survivors. Even the survivors did not know that they were the only survivors and that no passengers had been rescued by other ships.

One who eventually reported the full account of the disaster of the *Titanic* even before the *Carpathia* reached New York was David Sarnoff, a young Jewish radio operator. Sarnoff was the lucky one who was at the right place at the right time. He was operating his radio on the roof of a New York building. For three days he listened to the reports from the *Carpathia* and passed on the news to the local newspapers and from there to the rest of the world.[133]

Sarnoff was born in 1891 in Uzlyany, a small Belarusian shtetl near Minsk. His parents were observant Jews. His father, Abraham, immigrated alone to New York before the turn of the century. His mother, Leah, raised David and his four siblings by herself. David studied the Torah and other Jewish studies at the small Jewish school, the *cheider*. Leah and the children immigrated to New York in 1900, and the family lived on the Lower East Side like most Jews during that era. To help support his family, David began working at age nine only two days after arriving in America, selling Yiddish newspapers. At age fifteen, his father died, and David became the breadwinner. He left school to work in the field of communications. He was fascinated by the telegraph and bought himself a mini-telegraph machine. He taught himself how to use it and send messages via Morse code. David was fired when he refused to work on Rosh Hashanah and Yom Kippur. Sarnoff then found work as a radio operator for the new Marconi Radio Company, sending and receiving wireless messages to and from ships at sea.

By 1912 David Sarnoff was a permanent employee of the Marconi Radio Company. He worked from a radio station on a New York rooftop. His radio was very powerful and could reach a great distance. On the night of April 14, he was at his station, listening to the traffic of the radio at sea when suddenly he heard wireless messages regarding a ship in distress. He tuned in and followed the messages from several ships in the North Atlantic. He also heard radio messages from the *Olympic*.[134] Sarnoff was one of the few people to receive all the news from the disaster and relay it to the media in New York. On April 15 he heard radio signals from the *Carpathia* and worked nonstop to record all the information being sent from this ship. He compiled (inaccurate) lists of survivors and victims while sitting at his station for three consecutive days until the *Carpathia* arrived in New York. As the *Carpathia* approached the East Coast, more radio operators were able to catch signals, but Sarnoff was definitely one of the first and the most influential. By the time the rescue ship reached New York, the world knew the dimensions of the tragedy.

In an interview with the *Saturday Evening Post* in August 1926, Sarnoff said that he received radio messages regarding the *Titanic* disaster from the *Olympic*. In the interview, he said that after hearing the first messages, he listened to the radio for three consecutive days. During that time the phone in his small station did not stop ringing. Everybody wanted to know what happened to the *Titanic*. There was so much radio traffic that there were telecommunication problems. Sarnoff also said that the traffic was so heavy

Jewish radio operator David Sarnoff at his radio station in New York. Source: Hagley Museum and Library

that President Taft ordered all other radio stations in the area to shut down in order to allow Sarnoff to communicate with the *Carpathia*.

As the hours went by, the station was mobbed by journalists, reporters, and relatives of *Titanic* passengers. An officer was sent to secure the station. Very few visitors were allowed in, including two relatives of Isidor Straus. The two stood behind Sarnoff as he worked the wireless and watched while he wrote the names of the survivors as delivered by the radio operator on board the *Carpathia*. Sarnoff later told his interviewer that deep in his heart he wished that Isidor and Ida Straus would be among the ones saved only to get rid of the two relatives. When it was apparent that Isidor and Ida had not survived, the relatives were escorted out of his station. When the list of survivors was complete, he started working on the list of victims. After working for three straight days, he took off his earphones, turned off the radio equipment, and slept for twenty-four hours straight.

On board the *Carpathia*, the lone radio operator had a lot on his hands. Since one radio operator could not handle all the traffic, he was assisted by *Titanic's* radio operator, who suffered from exposure to the freezing water. Together the two of them worked around the clock to send messages regarding survivors and victims, and messages from the survivors to relatives in the United States and Europe.[135]

One of the people who waited anxiously was Edward Frauenthal. He was in the large mob outside the offices of the White Star Line in New York. When the first list of survivors was posted outside the office, he read the names, and when he saw that both his brothers were on the list he ran to the nearest phone to tell his wife the good news. He was so excited that he got dizzy and dropped the receiver.[136]

Within days, every newspaper in America and Europe reported the news of the *Titanic* tragedy. The reaction of the Jewish press was just as confusing at first. Many Jewish newspapers reported the news. At first the reports were optimistic but misleading. As time went by the reports were more accurate but still had many mistakes. There were problems with translation and misspelling of peoples' names. Many Jewish newspapers took a special interest in the Jewish victims and survivors and emphasized the deaths of Isidor and Ida Straus as well as Benjamin Guggenheim. One paper in Jerusalem said: "Sixty thousand Jews in *Eretz Yisrael* went into mourning when hearing about the disaster."[137]

At the time, Israel was under Ottoman rule. Most Jewish newspapers were in Hebrew and Yiddish. In Europe the Jewish press was in local languages (Polish, Russian, French, and so on) as well as Hebrew and Yiddish. In America, Jewish newspapers were published in English, Hebrew, Yiddish, and even Ladino.

A week after the disaster, *Herut* (Jerusalem) published a collection of reports in Hebrew about the sinking of the *Titanic*. The reports were copied from other newspapers and translated to Hebrew by the editors. The reports were confusing and misleading. For example: "No loss of lives. Latest report: great loss of life." The confusion in the media lasted for many weeks. Another report contained a partial list of survivors and victims in Hebrew.

One of the Hebrew correspondents was Itamar Ben-Avi (1882–1943) who lived in Paris. He was a journalist and worked for several newspapers including

Herut and *Hazvi*. Ben-Avi was also active in the Zionist movement. He heard the terrible news and telegraphed a report to newspapers in Israel. He translated and described the details of the tragedy as reported by the French media. He portrayed the general feeling of the French, of newspaper boys standing in the streets and yelling their headlines to sell more copies.

In *Hazvi* (Jaffa) Ben-Avi dedicated an entire page to reporting the disaster. The reports included condolences from the American public, from King George V of England, and from Wilhelm II, the German Kaiser.[138]

טביעתה של האניה טיטניק ואברותיה.

ניו יורק, 17 אפריל, מהאלפים, מהאלפים ומאתים איש שנמצאו
על האניה ,טיטניק, ושנטבעו כליל נצולו רק שש מאות חמשה
ושבעים, פרטים חסרים עוד.

גורלם של מיליונירים,

לונדון, 17 · אפריל, 675 מנוסעי הטיטניק ומאתים
מאנשיה, נצולו.

המיליונירים אסטור וגנדרבילם נטבעו.

הטיטניק היתה אחת האניות היותר גדולות, והכילה משא
של ששה וארבעים אלף טון.

בכל מעם מאשימים באסון זה את רב-חובלה של האניה
שאמו בכמת-מרוץ גדולה ביותר, בכדי לזכות בתואר שקצבה
לזה חברת האניות שלה היתה שיכת גם הטיטניק.
גם את חברת-האניות מאשימים בשביל זה שלא הכינה
באניה סירות הצלה כי אם בעד שמונה מאות איש, ונמצא
אמוא כי הנשארים הוכרחו להטבע.

איזידור שטרויס בין הנטבעים,

לונדון, 19 אפריל (ס. ע.) בין הקרבנות של האניה
הנטבעת ,טיטניק, גם נמצא גם הטיליוני׳ר ההנורי איזידור שטרויס
מהמשפחה המיליונירית שטורוס האמריוקנית, אחיו של נתן
שטרויס שהיה שהיה זה מקרוב בירושלם ומר שמה סכומים גדולים
למטרות של צדקה.

Telegrams (in Hebrew) regarding the sinking of the Titanic. *Source:* Moriah, *April 22, 1912*

The Hebrew newspaper *Moriah* (Jerusalem) contained quotes from telegrams from New York and London. One report said that there were only 605 survivors. Another report stated that the cause of the disaster was that the captain of the *Titanic* sailed the ship at an extreme speed in order to break a speed record. Another report blamed White Star Line for providing too few lifeboats that could save only 800 passengers while other passengers had no chance of surviving. *Moria* also mentioned that Isidor Straus had died and emphasized that he was the brother of Nathan Straus who had visited Jerusalem recently and donated generously for the welfare of the Jews in Jerusalem.

In the Jewish media in Europe, there were many reports about the disaster. *Hamizpe* (Krakow) published a detailed report in Hebrew about "the large British ship that sank with 1,700 souls." The report included fear for the life of the Jewish philanthropic millionaire Nathan Straus. The newspaper based the notice on reports from other newspapers that supposedly had simply stated: "The famous millionaire Straus is among the dead." A few days after the disaster, many prominent victims were announced, and the editors of *Hamizpe* apparently had confused Isidor with his brother Nathan. The editor probably thought that

בחוץ לארץ

נתן שטרויס על דבר נסיעתו לארץ ישראל.
ת הפדריציה הציונית בקליוולנד קבלה לפגירתה אספתה
ב מאת הפילנברום הבמפורסם המליונר נתן שטרויס
יי של המליונר איחדיור שטרויס, שנפל לקרבן בעת
ון של "טיטאניק") בדרבר נסיעתו האחרונה לארץ
אל.

"בעת בקורי האחרון בפלשתינה — מוהב שטרויס —
זוממתי לראות את ההתקדמות הגדולה של הארץ
ז להמצב שראיתי של הד"ר הרצל ושל האידיאל הגדיל
ועת הרוח הגדיל של הד"ר הרצל ושל האידיאל הגדיל
ר בקרב ישראל הצעיר. בשליחת הורחים האחרונים
ז כל ישותי מלאה במחשבה הציונית ולבי נלבי נלדי
ה הצעות למובת ארצנו הקדושה. אולם בגלל האסן
א (של "טיטאניק") הני עצבי מרונשים ולא יכולתי,
ת חפצי, להוציא מיד את מאיי אל הפועל. מטבה
י לי הידולח זת לדרך דברתה ולברה. וביו וביו

*Nathan Straus' apology for not
attending a Zionist meeting in Ohio
because of his brother Isidor's death
on board the* Titanic *(in Hebrew).
Source:* Hazfira, *August 4, 1912*

Nathan was on the *Titanic* and not Isidor. It is also possible that the confusion was because Nathan had just visited Jerusalem. The article in *Hamizpe* added that Nathan Straus had generously donated to deprived children in Jerusalem. The editor stated that the name Straus was among the dead and he feared that it was in fact Nathan. As we know, the victim was Isidor.[139]

The Hebrew newspaper *Hazman* (Vilna) published contradicting reports about the disaster. The reports were based on telegraph messages the newspaper received. One stated that all passengers survived. Another report said that there were fewer than seven hundred casualties. A third report, based on news from the agency in London, said that all female passengers had been saved. The reports also included notices about the collision and details about the evacuation.[140]

Hazman published a letter stating that the German parliament, the Reichstag, expressed "great sorrow in the name of Germany for the loss of 1,500 people from various nations." Two weeks after the disaster, *Hazman* published a notice about the deaths of Benjamin Guggenheim and Isidor Straus. Most notices in *Hazman* were copies of reports and translations of notices from other newspapers and reports supplied by Jewish sources such as Itamar Ben-Avi.[141]

Another Hebrew newspaper in Europe with details about the disaster

חדשות היום.

תמיכה לקרובי האובדים ב,טיטאניק'. דציר
ורוסי בלונדון מודיע, כי כל הקרובים של קרבנות
הקבבמרופה דמראה שעל ה,טיטאניק', הרוצים ליהנות
מכסף הנדבת שנקבצו למיבת הנגועים, יכולים לפגות
ללונדון על שם ראש העיר עד היום הי'ט באינינטם
למכפר דישן.

*Compensation notice by the Russian
consulate in London (in Hebrew).
Source:* Hazfira, *May 12, 1912*

An embarrassing (but amusing) mistake was made by the editors of this article. They accidently wrote that the Titanic *sunk in the Red Sea instead of the Atlantic Ocean. The mistake was probably an unintentional reference to the crossing of the Red Sea during the exodus of the Israelites from Egypt. The* Titanic *disaster took place less than a week after Passover, when it is traditional to celebrate the famous miracle of the Red Sea.*

למען התנפל עלינו בעלילות גמבוות. גם את האסן
הגדול והנורא של האניה ,טיטאניק", אשר לשמעו דאבה
כל נפש , דורש הוא כמ כסף ותמר בתוך ענין של יהודים,
והנדו שופך את מררתו על הנוסעים היהודים הרמעטים,
שנמעו במחלקה הראשונה ונמלטו מרדת מצולה, ובהמת
רצח הוא קורא: ,הביטו, מצרים, וראו, מי בראש, ומי
הם הנומעים תמיד במחלקה הראשונה? גם על אמץ
לבה של מרת ש ט ד ר ו ים וההבתת הגדולה והנאמנה
לאישה, שלא רצחה לעזוב ובחרה למות עמו שלובת-
דרע , ואשר כל העולם הנגאור ראה בעוברה זו את ספל
האהבה הנאמנה שבין איש ואשתו , — לועג הצורר
הפרא הוה , ובצהלת היה-טרף , ברהנפלה על מרפה ,

was the Orthodox newspaper *Machzike Hadas* from Lemberg (Lwów). One article reported thatthe cause of the disaster was the ship's speed. Another was about the *Titanic* recklessly sailing into an iceberg-infested area.[142] The writer asked if Bruce Ismay was responsible for the disaster.*

Jewish Response to anti-Semitic claims regarding the sinking of the Titanic *(in Hebrew).*
Source: Hazfira *May 12, 1912*

On May 12, there was a notice in *Hazfira* (Warsaw) in Hebrew. The notice said that relatives of the victims could address the mayor of London and request compensation from the Russian consulate.

On July 27, there was a notice in *Hazfira* about Jewish victims whose whereabouts were unknown. Among the names were twenty-six-year-old Israel Nesson and twenty-four-year-old Moses Aaron Troupiansky. Both were from Russia and second-class passengers.[143]

The *Hazfira* also wrote about the anti-Semitic claims involving the

נשארו בשביל זה בלי כל משען לחם או ברשימת הנצולים מאנית טיטאניק
שנתפרסמה עתה בלונדון וניוארק נמצאו אלה השמות שהובם בודאי יהודים וגם
השאר נראה שיהודים הם אלא שאין לדעת על ברור , האיל ואין שואלים את
הנוסעים לאמונתם ודתם, ומהם בודאי ישנם גם מארצנו רוסיא , האיל וכבר הודיעו
שמעיר מאהליעוו נמעו באני' ההיא , ואלה הם הנצולים אבעלסאאהן העניא, אברהטמאן
אינגמט, בארואוויטש ג., בארואויטש ה., נאלדענבערג שמואל ואשתו
הערטמאן ושתי בנותיה, היימאן אברהם, ועבעד פאסיא , טוסיג (אשה) , שייסן נערה,
טרענטשינסקי בערקא, כהן ג., לעהמאן (אשה), טייער (אשה), מאם א, סיאלאמאן ע. ל.
עליאם ג., ראזענבוים נערה, ,דאט שרה', ראהטשילד ט. אשה טא אתמזל יצאה

List of Jewish survivors (in Hebrew). Source: Hamodia, *May 2, 1912*

behavior of some of the Jewish passengers during the evacuation. Apparently there were anti-Semitic articles in several newspapers around Europe that used the *Titanic* disaster to arouse anger toward Jews, describing them as cowards. The *Hazfira* wrote against such claims:

> Observe Christians and see who was in the front. Who were the passengers in first class![144]

Headline: Great Tragedy of the Titanic *(in Yiddish).*
Source: Forward, *April 16, 1912*

The article stated that most steerage passengers, who were Jewish, died. The *Hazfira* also protested the violent inciting and mocking in anti-Semitic newspapers by reporting the heroic behavior of Ida Straus.

On May 2, the Orthodox newspaper, *Hamodia* (Poltava, Ukraine) published an interesting article. This newspaper was an Orthodox paper with Yiddish and Hebrew editions in its Hebrew edition. The article included a list of Jewish survivors from all three classes. The list had many mistakes. Some survivors, including Abraham Hyman, Gershon Cohen, Samuel Goldenberg, and Sarah Roth, were Jewish. Others were not, such as Bertha Herman and Samuel Goldenberg's Catholic wife, Nella.

What makes it even more interesting is that some names on the list in *Hamodia* do not appear on the *Titanic's* passengers list whatsoever. Those names include Trantinsky Bercka, Barawitch George, and Barawitch Marian. These names are not on the *Titanic* passengers list, but appeared in an unofficial list of survivors recorded by the *Carpathia* crew. Who these people were remains a mystery.* It is possible that they were Jews who sailed with assumed names or that these names were mistakenly added to the list. However, *Hamodia* added a clarification:

> Most of them are Jewish, but we cannot be sure because the passengers were not asked about their religion or their beliefs.

The list contained a total of twenty-four names. Of those, only ten were really Jewish.

Many Yiddish newspapers reported the disaster. On May 2, the headline in *Der Mament* (Warsaw) was: "A large ship = catastrophe!"[145]

Der Mament published several reports in April and May. The Yiddish

---

Robin Gardiner points out in his book The Titanic Conspiracy *(1995) that there is a gap between the official survivors list and the list received by the* Carpathia. *That gap became a "list of survivors picked up by the* Carpathia *but do not appear on the passenger list." More than a hundred names appear on this new list, the Barawitch family among them.*

version of *Hamodia* also published several reports. The *Forward* (New York) published numerous reports and even exclusive interviews with several Jewish survivors.

The Jewish media in English also referred to the disaster. The *Jewish Chronicle* (London) published a comprehensive article several days after the disaster about the Jewish point of view of the disaster. The article spoke about the masses of Jewish immigrants who fled Europe to America and added that there were many Jewish victims on board the *Titanic*. The article mentioned what a loss to the Jewish people the death of Isidor Straus was and sent condolences to his brothers, Nathan and Oscar.[146]

Several articles and editorials were published in the *Sentinel* (Chicago). On April 19, the *Sentinel* published a large report about the *Titanic* disaster from a Jewish point of view. The reporter wrote about concern for Isidor and Ida Straus, concern for Henry Harris, and included a quote from his wife, René, from the telegram she sent from the *Carpathia*. The article also mentioned Erwin Lewy.[147]

The *Sentinel* also published a list of Jewish passengers in third class. The list was composed by information received from Liverpool and did not differentiate between victims and survivors. The list had twenty-two names but only half of them were actually Jewish. The list included Leah Aks and her baby, Frank (both misspelled Oks),* Gershon Cohen, Harry Sadowitz (misspelled Sabowitz), Wolf Spector, Maurice Sirota (misspelled Serota), Harry Corn, Nathan Goldsmith, Sarah Roth, and Leo Zimmerman. The list also included Abraham Harmer (the assumed name of David Livshin). The rest of the names on the list in the *Sentinel* were either not Jewish or were not on the *Titanic* passengers list.[148]

Again, such mistakes were commonly made and added to the confusion. Among the names on this list that do not appear on the passengers list were Sucha Holman, Herman Badman, and Fishel Eberhart. Were these Jewish passengers traveling under assumed names? Did they survive? What were their true names? We will never know.

In the Jewish newspaper *Bnai Brith Messenger* (Los Angeles) there was yet another list of Jews. The report begins with the words: "The following Jews were on board the *Titanic*."

In the New York Herald, the list of third class survivors, include the names Leak Aksaks and Filly Aksaks, who are no other than Leah and Filly Aks.

First-class passengers on the list in *Bnai Brith Messenger* were Benjamin Guggenheim, Henry and René Harris, Herman Klaber, Edger Lewy, Emil Taussig, Edith Rosenbaum, Isidor and Ida Straus, and Adolphe Saalfeld. Mistakes include the Catholic wives of Martin Rothschild and Samuel Goldenberg. The list in *Bnai Brith Messenger* added second-class passengers Samuel and Hannah Abelson, Samuel Greenberg, Benjamin Hart, René Lévy, Leopold Weisz, and the Jacobsohn family. Also on this list there were several names of non-Jews.

The *Bnai Brith Messenger* also refers to third-class passengers:

> It was known that there was a large number of Jews among the 710 steerage passengers and it is feared that all of them went down when the ship sank.[149]

An editorial by Abram Hirschberg in the *Sentinel* on April 26 was about the courage of Ida Straus. He called her an *Esheth Chayil** and responded to anti-Semitic claims against Jews:

> What a silencing answer have they given to the scoffers, who have scornfully questioned the bravery and heroism of the Jew! Will the Anti-Semite still contend that the Jew is a craven and a coward in the face of such overwhelming evidence to the contrary?

The editorial concluded:

> What an aureole also wreathes itself around the form of Mrs. Straus as we see her standing there, the very incarnation of *Esheth Chayil*, gently, yet persistently, refusing even death to sever the indissoluble tie of love that bound her in life so strongly and tenderly to her husband.[150]

Jewish names were mentioned in the general media in Europe and the United States. The last words of Benjamin Guggenheim ("Tell them no woman died because I was a coward") were published in the *Washington Times*.[151]

---

* The Hebrew expression Esheth Chayil *(also spelled* Eshet Hayil*) is a biblical phrase from Proverbs (chapter 31). It literally translates to "woman of valor." The phrase/praise is a biblical definition of the "perfect wife."*

> The last words of Benjamin Guggenheim—his dying message to his wife—were brought to her by a room steward:
> "Tell her I played the game out straight and to the end. No woman shall be left aboard the ship because Ben Guggenheim was a coward. Tell her my last thoughts were of her and of our girls."

Benjamin Guggenheim's last words. Source: Oakland Tribune, *April 20, 1912*

The *New York Times* published many articles about Isidor Straus in April and May. The *Humeston New Era* (Humeston, Iowa) lauded Ida's heroism.[152] A week after the disaster, the French newspaper *Excelsior* published a drawing showing Isidor and Ida Straus holding each other and waiting for death. The headline in the *Denver Post* was: "Mr. and Mrs. Straus go down with arms entwined." And the *New York Herald* described Henry Harris as "one of the best known theatrical managers in the country."

Sarah Gitel Gilinski received the notice of the death of her son, Eliezer, while she was riding a train on her way home from Vilna. She recognized his name on the list of victims in the newspaper she was holding.[153]

One notice from the *Aberdare Leader* was interesting because it mentioned Eliezer Gilinski and refers to him as "Hebrew." Abercynon is a small

Illustrated description of the Strauses' final moments. Source: Excelsior, *April 20, 1912*

village in Wales and is where Gilinski lived for a while. Aberdare is a larger town nearby:

> An Abercynon Victim: Amongst the bodies of the *Titanic* victims that have been recovered is that of a young Hebrew youth from Abercynon, named Galinsky, who had only recently come over from

the Continent to see his brother. He was a most amiable young man, and his death has caused his brother and family deep grief.

Florette Guggenheim was in a New York hotel when she received the news from her brother-in-law, Solomon Guggenheim. He had a copy of a newspaper whose headline was: "Extra! Extra! The *Titanic* Sinks!" In that newspaper, Benjamin's name was listed among the dead. Florette rushed to the White Star Line offices to receive more details.[154]

A week after the disaster a notice was written about the death of Nathan Goldsmith. The notice was published in the *Evening Bulletin* in Philadelphia. The notice ended with information about a relief fund for his widow.[155]

Relatives of victims were anxious about their loved ones. Harry Sadowitz was one of the Jewish victims from third class. His father, Solomon, published a notice in the *Evening News* (Rhode Island) about his concern for his son and asked for information about his fate. He was not the only one. Many published notices about their missing relatives. Relatives of Emil Brandeis published a notice in the *New York Times*.[156] Simon Guggenheim was interviewed about his fear that his brother Benjamin was among the dead.[157] Relatives of Nathan Goldsmith published a notice in a local newspaper in Lithuania.[158]

Finding the dead bodies of the victims was another problem. The White Star Line sent several ships from Canada to the disaster area to search for the bodies. The first to arrive at the scene was the *Mackay-Bennett*. She left Halifax on April 17. She arrived and started to collect bodies on April 20. Several ships joined in the gruesome task. All the bodies that were identified were brought to Halifax for burial.

10

BURIAL OF THE VICTIMS

Toward the end of the nineteenth century, as the Jewish community in Halifax grew, a cemetery was needed. Jewish Baron Moshe (Maurice) De Hirsch donated money to purchase a plot to develop a cemetery near the Christian one. In July 1893 Rabbi Shimon Schwartz dedicated the plot, and it became known as the Baron De Hirsch Jewish Cemetery.[159]

View of Halifax Harbor, where the Titanic *victims were taken. Source: Library of Congress*

Not a single person, Jewish or not, thought in 1893 that one day the small Jewish cemetery along with the entire Jewish community would play an important role in an historical world incident.

On April 30, 1912, the cable ship *Mackay-Bennett* arrived at the Halifax harbor, carrying 190 bodies of the *Titanic* victims. In total the *Mackay-Bennett* recovered 306 bodies, but 116 victims were buried at sea. After registration and identification, the bodies were prepared for burial. Even in death there was class separation. First-class victims were placed in wooden coffins, while the others were wrapped in canvas bags. Most third-class victims were buried at sea. All the bodies were numbered and tagged. Of the bodies shipped to Halifax and identified, fifty-nine were claimed by relatives and buried in cemeteries across America and Europe, mainly in England. All remaining bodies were buried in Halifax. To prepare for the burial of the victims, all the bodies were temporarily kept at the Mayflower Curling Rink. Rabbi Jacob Walter from the local Jewish community in Halifax was asked

Titanic victims on their way to the morgue, Halifax.

to help identify Jewish victims. That night he found eight bodies he claimed were Jewish. Those were separated from the rest in order to transfer them for burial in the Baron De Hirsch Jewish Cemetery. None of the eight bodies were recognized by name, but Rabbi Walter claimed they were all Jews.[160]

The next day Rabbi Walter returned to the curling rink to identify more victims. He found ten more bodies he claimed were Jewish. Volunteers from the Jewish community transferred the ten bodies to the Jewish cemetery. It was a Friday, and the Jewish community wanted to bury all eighteen victims before the Sabbath. The rabbi, with the assistance of the local *chevra kadisha* (Jewish burial organization), dedicated a new section of the cemetery for the Jewish *Titanic* victims and quickly dug eighteen graves. As they were about to bury the bodies, they noticed that ten bodies were missing. The Canadian authorities had returned ten of the bodies to the curling rink. As the Sabbath

Rabbi Jacob Walter (center) at the Titanic *section in the Baron de Hirsch Jewish Cemetery, Halifax Canada. Photo credit: Russ Lownds via the John P. Eaton/Charles A. Haas* Titanic *Photograph Archive*

drew near, the remaining eight bodies were buried in the Jewish cemetery, none of whom were identified by name.[161]

After more bodies arrived in Halifax by other cable ships, Rabbi Walter located two more unidentified Jewish victims. The two were buried alongside the original eight. The ten bodies that were returned to the curling rink were buried as unidentified Christians in one of the two Christian cemeteries in Halifax.[162] Over the next few weeks, more bodies were brought to Halifax. Burying the victims was an exhausting process. In addition to the ten victims

Titanic *section of the Baron De Hirsch Jewish Cemetery, Halifax, today. Courtesy: Deanna Ryan-Meister*

already buried, Rabbi Walter claimed there were forty-four Jews among the remaining bodies. The authorities in Halifax did not rely on his judgment and refused to transfer any other bodies to the Jewish cemetery. Of those forty-four bodies, several were later identified by relatives, and none of them were Jewish. The authorities did not trust Rabbi Walter and forbid him from further searching for more Jewish victims. The unidentified bodies Rabbi Walter wanted were buried as unknown in the Christian cemeteries. Every unknown body was photographed and carefully documented for future identification.[163] Not a single one of them has ever been identified as Jewish.

In total, 328 bodies were recovered, and over 120 were buried at sea. One hundred and fifty bodies were buried in the three cemeteries in Halifax. Ten were buried in the Baron De Hirsch Jewish Cemetery. Twenty victims were buried in the Catholic Mount Olivet Cemetery, and 100 victims were interned in the Protestant Fairview Cemetery.

The Baron De Hirsch Jewish Cemetery is still in use by *Beth Israel* Jewish Congregation in Halifax. Recently the cemetery was renovated, with a new sidewalk and restoration of old graves. The *Titanic* section is usually closed for visitors.[164]

With the fiasco regarding the burials of Rabbi Walter's unidentified bodies, how many Jews are really buried in the *Titanic* section in the Jewish cemetery in Halifax? We know that dozens of Jews died when the *Titanic* sunk, but ironically not a single Jew is buried in the Jewish Cemetery in Halifax. Of the ten bodies buried there, only two were eventually identified. Neither of them were Jewish, nor were the other unidentified eight.

After the collision, second-class passenger Michel Navratil (sailing under the assumed name of Louis Hoffman) dressed his two sons, aged two and three, and took them to the Boat Deck. Navratil had kidnapped his sons from their mother and was fleeing with them to America. On deck he was blocked by crewmen who did not allow male passengers near the last few lifeboats. He convinced the crewmen to allow him to save his two young sons. A steward handed the boys to women in collapsible Lifeboat D, which was one of the last lifeboats to be launched from the sinking ship.[165] As the lifeboat was launched, he called to his sons:

> When your mother comes for you, as she surely will, tell her that I loved her dearly and still do. Tell her I expected her to follow us, so that we might all live happily together in the peace and freedom of the New World.

The two little children were rescued, but their father died. Michel Navratil was one of the first bodies found by the *Mackay-Bennett,* and the body was recognized by his assumed name, Louis Hoffman, recorded in documents found on him along with a loaded revolver. When his body was in the curling rink, Rabbi Walter assumed that Louis Hoffman was Jewish and had the body transferred to the Jewish cemetery.

For a long while, the boys' true names were unknown. Their story and photographs were reported worldwide, and their mother recognized them in the French newspapers.[166] She was brought to America, reunited with her two sons, and returned with them to France. Years later the family was offered the opportunity to remove Michel Navratil's body from the Jewish cemetery to a Christian one, but the family decided to leave the body where it was.

Another non-Jew buried in the Jewish cemetery whose identity was confirmed was crew member Henry Frederick Wormald. Wormald, born in 1867, was married and worked as a first-class saloon steward. He was a White Star Line employee who served on other ships and had been transferred to the *Titanic* on April 4. During the evacuation he wore a life vest but could not enter a lifeboat.

His body was found by the *Mackay-Bennett* and taken to Halifax. He was wearing a steward's uniform and an overcoat embroidered with his name, along with personal items including a set of keys, a gold watch, and a knife. During the confusion at the curling rink, his body was mistakenly identified by Rabbi Walter and taken to the Jewish cemetery for burial. The next day the mistake was realized, but Wormald's family decided to leave the body there.

Tombstone of Titanic *victim Leopold Weisz, Jewish cemetery, Montreal Canada. Source:* the Canadian Jewish News, *April 1, 2012*

Eight other bodies were buried in the Baron De Hirsch Cemetery, including seven crewmen, none Jewish. Some bodies had tattoos with symbols of the sea such as anchors and sailors. They wore uniforms and carried room keys. After registering the unknown bodies, identification attempts were made, but none were ever identified. Two of them were probably stewards, three were probably firemen or trimmers, one was probably a porter, and one was probably a cook. The tenth grave is of a *Titanic* passenger whose identification is unknown even today. He, too, is not Jewish. He wore several layers of clothes but did not have any documents. It is important to note that all ten victims buried in the Baron De Hirsch Jewish Cemetery were male.

What about the rest of the victims? Were any of them identified as Jewish passengers?

In the process of identifying the victims, every detail was registered, including estimated age, hair color, height, condition of teeth, clothing, and personal items. Many bodies were identified by names sewn on their clothes.

Trying to identify Jewish victims should have been an easy task, especially male victims who were all circumcised. Unfortunately none of the unidentified male bodies were registered as circumcised. Even the Jewish victims, who were eventually identified without doubt, were not registered as circumcised. The process of the identification that Rabbi Walter was in charge of is strange. Why didn't he ever find and identify any actual Jewish victims? One may wonder why the other victims he claimed were Jewish were not buried in the Jewish cemetery and why the ten victims that were buried there were not Jewish. Also one may ask what happened to the other ten bodies Rabbi Walter thought were Jewish.

Were any Jewish victims identified? Where are they buried? At least forty of the Jewish passengers were lost with the *Titanic*. Most were never found or identified. In total only nine Jews were identified; two were buried at sea. David Livshin was taken on board the *Carpathia* and buried at sea the next day. Eliezer Gilinski was found by the *Mackay-Bennett* (body number 47). Although identified, he was buried at sea on April 21, probably because most third-class victims were buried at sea but perhaps because his body was decomposed and unfit for shipping to Halifax. He wore a gray coat, vest, pants, and a green shirt. His effects included pictures, a baggage insurance certificate, a five-dollar bill, and his boarding pass.[167]

All other seven identified Jewish victims were brought to Halifax. The bodies, all men and none from third class, were shipped to their families after identification. Authorities were eager to identify and bury the richer passengers. Of the seven Jewish bodies, one was buried in Europe, five in the United States, and one in Canada.

After the body of second-class passenger and Jewish architect Leopold Weisz was found by the *MacKay-Bennett* (body number 293) and identified, his family had it transferred to Montreal where his non-Jewish wife lived. He was buried at the Baron De Hirsch Jewish Cemetery, Montreal.* Rabbi Herman Abramowitz conducted the funeral.

His tombstone with the Star of David is inscribed in English. Even his Hebrew name, Aryeh Ben Avraham, is written in English. The Hebrew date of the *Titanic* disaster appears on the tombstone: 28 Nisan 5762.[168]

The bodies of Sinai Kantor, Emil Brandeis, George Rosenshine, Samuel Greenberg, and Isidor Straus were buried in the United States. Kantor and Rosenshine are buried in Queens, New York.

The body of Sinai Kantor was found by the *Mackay-Bennett* (body number 283) and identified. He wore a gray and green suit, a green overcoat, and a blue shirt. Personal items included a pocket telescope, a silver watch, a pocketbook, and several coins. The body was transferred

---

Not to be confused with the Baron De Hirsch Cemetery in Halifax.

Tombstone of Titanic *victim Sinai Kantor, Queens, New York. Source:* Western Queens Gazette; *Photo Jason D. Antos*

at his family's request to Miriam Kantor, his widow. She survived the disaster and temporarily stayed with relatives in Queens. Sinai Kantor was buried on May 5 (18th of Iyar) in Mount Zion Jewish Cemetery, Queens, New York. His tombstone is inscribed in English and Hebrew.[169]

The body of first-class Jewish passenger George Rosenshine was among the first to be found by the *Mackay-Bennett* (body number 16). He wore a gray overcoat, a black suit, and a pair of gloves. His clothes were marked with the letters G.R., and he had a gold watch, a pocketbook, and several documents. His name and address also appeared in his wallet. His body was sent by request to his brother in New York. George Rosenshine was buried in the family plot in Bayside Cemetery, Queens, New York.[170] In his will, he left contributions to several Jewish establishments, including Mount Sinai Jewish Hospital, the Hebrew Benevolent and Orphan Asylum, and the Montefiore Home.[171]

A notice from the *New York Times* after the disaster was related to the death of George Rosenshine:

Tombstone of Titanic *victim Emil Brandeis, Pleasant Hill Jewish Cemetery, Omaha Nebraska. Courtesy: Marta Dawes*

Died at sea, Steamer *Titanic*, on April 15, George Rosenshine, in the 46th year of his age. Prayers will be held at the residence of his brother, Albert Rosenshine, Hotel Ansonia, on Sunday, Monday, and Tuesday evenings, April 21, 22 and 23 at 6 o'clock. It is requested that no flowers be sent.[172]

The body of second-class passenger and South African Jewish businessman Samuel Greenberg was also among the first to be found by the *Mackay-Bennett* (body number 19) and identified. He wore a dressing gown, a gray coat, and a pair of blue pants. He was found with two watches and some American money. His body was transferred by his widow's request to New York and buried in a Jewish cemetery in the Bronx.[173]

The body of first-class passenger Jewish businessman Emil Brandeis was found by the *Mackay-Bennett* (body number 208) and identified. He wore a dark suit, a brown shirt, black shoes, and silk socks. His personal items included French and American money, a gold knife, a platinum and diamond watch chain, a gold pencil case, a gold ring, a gold cigarette case, and a gold matchbox. His body was transferred to his family in Douglas County, Nebraska, and buried in the family plot in Pleasant Hill Temple Israel Jewish Cemetery, Omaha, Nebraska. The cemetery is the oldest Jewish cemetery in Nebraska and is still active today. Several of his effects were donated to the Durham Museum in Omaha.[174]

The body of first-class Jewish passenger and diamond trader Jacob Birnbaum was found by the *Mackay-Bennett* (body number 148). He wore a light gray overcoat and a pair of blue pajamas. He had a gold ring with his initials (J.B.), a gold watch with a chain, a pocketknife, a memo book, a small bag, and several keys. After his body was brought to Halifax and identified, his

Tombstone of Titanic *victim Jacob Birnbaum, Machzikey Hadat Jewish Cemetery, Putte, Netherlands. Photo credit: Daniel Schechter*

Jacob Birnbaum's father wrote a few words in his calendar after the disaster. Source: unknown

family in Antwerp requested his transfer for burial. His father, Joachim Birnbaum, received the body in New York Harbor and brought it to Belgium. Jacob Birnbaum was buried on the day after *Shavuot* (the Jewish holiday of Pentecost) in the Netherlands. In fact Birnbaum is the only *Titanic* victim to be buried in the Netherlands.

Until the year 1910, Belgian Jews were buried in a Jewish cemetery in Antwerp. The cemetery was established in 1828 when there were only 150 Jews in Antwerp. In 1910 the local orthodox congregation *Machzikey Hadat* purchased a plot of land in a small Dutch town named Putte and dedicated it as a Jewish cemetery. From then on, Jews from Antwerp were buried in *Machzikey Hadat* Cemetery in Putte. Jews are not buried in Belgium because of a law that grants Belgian authorities the right to dig up graves and remove remains fifty years after burial. Jewish law forbids such a thing, so the Jewish community in Antwerp must bury their dead in the Netherlands. This Belgian law is still in effect, and even today the Jewish community in Antwerp uses the cemetery in Putte.

The top of Birnbaum's tombstone is shaped like a ship to resemble the *Titanic*. Birnbaum is the only *Titanic* victim whose tombstone is written entirely in Hebrew. The engraving includes the Hebrew date of the disaster (28 of Nissan), the date of the funeral (the day after *Shavuot*), and several quotes from Psalms.

The gold watch found on Birnbaum's body was donated to the National Maritime Museum in Greenwich. The watch is on display, along with several documents related to Jacob Birnbaum, in a new wing dedicated by Israeli philanthropist Sammy Offer.

The funeral of Isidor Straus was the one most covered by newspapers. His body was found by the *Mackay-Bennett* (body number 96). He wore a fur overcoat, a pair of gray pants, a coat, a striped shirt, brown boots, and black silk socks. He carried a pocketbook, a gold watch, a platinum and pearl chain, a gold pencil case, a silver flask, and some money.

The deaths of Isidor and Ida Straus caused grief and mourning among American Jewry, in particular Jews in New York. The story of Ida's refusal to leave without her husband became epic, and the couple was widely honored. Isidor's

Memorial plaque in honor of Ida and Isidor Straus, in Macy's department store, New York.
Photo credit: Dave Gardner

Straus Memorial Park, Broadway, New York. Courtesy: Dave Gardner

behavior during his final moments made him admired by Jews around the world, and the couple became a source of Jewish pride.

Although Isidor's body was found and identified, Ida's was never found. His body was brought to Halifax and transferred by train to New York. The family decided to wait several days before the funeral to see if Ida's body would be identified so the couple could be buried together. After some time it became clear that her body was not going to be found. Isidor was buried on Wednesday, May 8, in the family plot in Beth-El Jewish Cemetery, Brooklyn, New York. Isidor's brother, Nathan, was in Europe at the time after visiting Jerusalem. Rabbi Samuel Schulman led the ceremony, which was attended by over forty thousand

Straus Memorial dedication, 1915. Source: Library of Congress

people. The *World Evening Edition* reported that forty cars and five coaches followed the hearse. The paper stated:

Oscar Straus at the Straus Memorial dedication, 1915.
Source: Library of Congress

> Among those accompanying the remains to the grave were Mr. Straus' three sons and three daughters, his brother, Oscar Straus, with Mrs. Straus and their son, Roger Straus, Mrs. Edward Schaefer, Mrs. Robert Guggenheim, Mrs. Hochstadter and Supreme Justices Greenbaum and Lehman.

On May 13, a memorial for Isidor and Ida was held at the Educational Alliance Building. Over six thousand people attended to pay tribute to the couple. Thousands more stood outside.[175] William J. Gaynor, mayor of New York, delivered his eulogy. Zionist preacher Rabbi Zevi Hirsh Masliansky delivered his eulogy in Yiddish, saying:

> Their heroic death now becomes the inspiration of humanity in general and of Jewry in particular. For they have given to the world an example of Jewish heroism.[176]

In 1915 another memorial service was held to inaugurate Straus Memorial Square on Broadway. In 1928 at the request of the Straus family, Isidor Straus' remains were transferred to a private mausoleum at Woodlawn Cemetery in the Bronx. The engraving on the marble plaque includes a quote from the Song of Solomon:

Many Waters Cannot Quench Love,
Neither Can the Floods Drown It

Isidor's grave serves as a memorial for his devoted wife, Ida. In the city of New York there are several monuments to honor Isidor and Ida. At Macy's in Manhattan, once owned by the family, there is a memorial plaque in the couples' honor.

The Isidor and Ida Straus Memorial and Straus Park is located at Broadway and 107th street. The inscription includes a biblical quote from the Book of Samuel:

Lovely and pleasant they were in their lives,
and in death they were not divided.

A New York public school is named in their memory, and so is a dormitory at Harvard University in Cambridge, Massachusetts.

Most of the bodies from the *Titanic* disaster were never found. Of the 340 bodies found, about half were buried at sea. Over ninety bodies were buried as unknown. Although none of the records show any of the victims wearing Jewish clothes (*kippah*, *Tzitzit*, and so on), it does not prove that there weren't any Jewish victims among the unknown bodies found. One explanation is that, because the disaster happened late at night, many of the survivors barely had time to dress properly. Many of them escaped wearing pajamas. Jewish men, who usually wear prayer shawls during morning prayers, did not wear any that night. Even if there were many observant Jews on board the *Titanic*, it was not a custom then to wear Jewish items of clothing in public. Many observant Jews wore a *kippah* during meals and prayer, but not all day long. It is also possible that many of the observant Jews did not want to stand out among other passengers and wanted to avoid attention. In many Jewish communities it was a custom that only the head of the congregation, the rabbi, wore the traditional Jewish clothes. Otherwise it is odd that none of the unidentified victims had any Jewish clothes listed on their description. Still, the fact that none of the Jewish male bodies (even the ones that were identified) were registered as circumcised raises questions about the effort that was put into the identification attempt.

If Jewish victims were found, they were not identified, yet it is possible that several Jewish victims were buried in one of the two Christian cemeteries in Halifax.

11

THE *AGUNOT* ISSUE,
A RABBINICAL DILEMMA

Agunot are women whose husbands' whereabouts are unknown or whose husbands would not grant a *get* (a Jewish divorce document). An *agunah* cannot remarry. She is chained to her marriage. If she has children, while still considered married, the children are *mamzerim* (bastards by Jewish law). It is a very difficult situation.

One who depicted this awkward situation was Israeli writer and Nobel Prize winner Shmuel Yosef (Shai) Agnon (1888–1970) in his short story *And the Crooked Shall Be Made Straight*. His story is about Menashe Haim Hacohen, a young and penniless Jewish man from a *shtetl* of Buchach (in Eastern Ukraine) who was forced to wander from *shtetl* to *shtetl* to beg for alms. Before he left his home, his rabbi gave him a letter of recommendation to encourage other Jews to help him. After some time he sold the letter of recommendation to another beggar. The other beggar died, and the local Jews buried him. They noticed the letter and sent word to Menashe's wife to announce that her husband was dead. The rabbi of Buchach released her from her *agunah* status and granted her permission to remarry. Years later, Menashe returned to Buchach and saw that his wife had remarried and had a son from her new husband, making the boy a *mamzer*. Menashe realized that the mishap was because of the letter he sold. Menashe decided not to reveal the truth and lived the rest of his life at the Jewish cemetery. He befriended the undertaker and shared his secret only with him.

More than twenty married Jewish men died on the *Titanic*. According to Jewish law, their wives became *agunot*. As reflected in Agnon's story, a woman whose husband may be dead but his body's location is unknown is not permitted to remarry. The *Halachic* name for this phenomenon is *agunah*, which literally means "anchored." The woman is bound and tied to her marriage with a man but cannot terminate the marriage without a divorce. If it were proven that the husband is dead, the wife becomes a widow and can remarry. An *agunah* cannot remarry without definite proof that her husband is dead or if the husband is alive and he grants her the *get*.

In previous generations the discussion on the *agunot* issue was widened in *Halachic* literature.[177] One reason is the mass immigration from Eastern Europe to America that turned thousands of Jewish women into *agunot*. The problem troubled many rabbis both in Europe and the United States. Attempts were made to solve the problem using *Halachic* tools, such as giving the wife authorization to present the *get* to herself under rabbinical supervision. This solution was first suggested by Rabbi Yehuda Epstein, an American Conservative rabbi, after World War I. He suggested that a special clause should be added to the *Ketubah* (a Jewish marriage certificate) during the wedding ceremony. The clause would enable the wife, under certain conditions, to request the *Beth Din* (rabbinical court) to allow her to become divorced without her husband actually presenting her with the *get*. This way, the wife could escape from the fate of becoming an *agunah* for life and thus remarry. Rabbi Epstein's suggestion was welcomed widely by Conservative groups but was opposed with much intensity by Orthodox groups. The proposal created a large debate within the Jewish and rabbinical world in the United States, and eventually the suggestion was rejected by the Orthodox rabbinical court.[178]

The *agunah* issue is discussed in the *Mishnah*. One source for releasing *agunot* is in *Yevamot* (one of the *Talmudic* Tractates in *Seder Nashim*) and is as follows:

> If a women and her husband went to a country beyond the sea and at the time there was peace between him and her and also peace in the world, and she came back and said "my husband is dead" she may marry again.

Generations of rabbis have believed that if the woman is loyal and trustworthy, she can remarry in such a case, even without definite proof that her husband is dead. Rabbis believe that women would not make up such a thing and lie. If she lies, and her first husband returns, her children from her second marriage are bastards (*mamzerim*). That is why the *Mishnah* uses the phrase "peace between him and her," for there is no reason for her to claim that her husband is dead if she loves him. The *Mishnah* continues:

> If there was discord (dispute) between him and her and she came back and said "my husband is dead" she is not believed.

In other words, the nature of the relationship between the husband and wife before the disappearance of the husband, and the trustworthiness of the wife, is significant to determine if the rabbinical court can release the wife from her *agunah* status.

In the past, many cases of *agunot* were during wars. If the husband went to war, he may have returned. If the husband did not return, it is unknown if he was killed in the war, and he may still be alive. In World War I, hundreds of Jewish soldiers returned months after the war. In recent generations, rabbis did all they could to release *agunot*, but only within *Halachic* boundaries. To release *agunot* today, many rabbis use rabbinical digressions such as "evidence heard from the mouth of another witness" or "statements of a gentile made in the midst of conversation" or "invalid testimony" and others. Rabbi Shlomo Goren (1917–1994), who was the first Chief Rabbi of the Israel Defense Forces (IDF), had to treat numerous cases of *agunot*, such as the *agunot* of the Gush Etzion victims during the Israeli War of Independence, the *agunot* of the victims of the *INS Eilat* (an Israeli navy ship that was sunk in 1967 with forty-seven casualties), and the *agunot* of the victims of the *INS Dakar* (an Israeli submarine that disappeared in the Mediterranean Sea in 1968 with sixty-nine crewmen).[179] Rabbi Ovadia Yosef (1920–2014), the former Chief Rabbi of the State of Israel, assisted in releasing numerous *agunot* of Israeli victims of the Yom Kippur war (especially the wives of soldiers who were killed in the war and whose bodies were never found).

To understand the principle of *agunot*, there are two kinds of *agunot* in Jewish law. The more common cases of *agunot* are women who suffer from the unwilling disappearances of the husband such as disasters, wars, etc., but the lesser common cases of *agunot* are the women who suffer from husbands who refuse to grant the *get*, leave their wives but do not annul the marriage. In such a case the rabbinical authorities have no other choice but to force the husband to grant the *get*. In the era of the *Mishnah*, and later, during the Middle Ages, the Jewish communities were closed to the outer world and forcing husbands to grant the *get* was more effective. In later years, when Jews left their little *shtetls*, the rabbinical authorities lost much of their power over such insubordinate husbands. During the great immigration from Europe to the United States, many husbands left their wives in Europe and started a new life in America. Although the husbands' whereabouts were known, it was very difficult to force them to release the wives from their bonds of *agunah* status. Theoretically the *agunot* of unwilling disappearances of the husband is more complicated (is the husband dead or alive?), but it is easier to find ways to release the wives from their *agunah* status.

In such cases, rabbinical courts use *Halachic* tools to help the woman. Tools that usually are not accepted in other fields of rabbinical courts are accepted in the attempt to release an *agunah*. Usage of *Halachic* hypotheses, such as "water which has no end" versus "water which has an end," are widely accepted in the process of releasing *agunot* whose husbands' whereabouts are unknown, especially if the husband disappeared in a shipwreck or natural disaster. In the aftermath of huge disasters, the rabbinical courts depend on certified passenger lists, census lists, and official documents released by the governments, authorities, or shipping companies. For example, a formal document with an official list of victims is accepted in rabbinical courts as alternative legal proof that an individual lost his life even if the body was never found. After disasters with multiple casualties, there were attempts to release all the *agunot* with a collective solution rather than find a solution for every single *agunah*.

An excellent example would be World War I. After the war there were thousands of widows whose husbands never returned. Were they all really widows? Were any of the men still alive? After the war, there was a collective release of *agunot* conducted by rabbinical courts throughout Jewish communities in Europe and the United States. Yet some rabbis still preferred to study each case individually. Many rabbis were against collective releasing to avoid mistakes and future cases of remarrying and giving birth to *mamzerim*. One of their claims was that it had been proven that soldiers return home many months after the war and it is practically impossible to determine how long is needed to wait for a man's return before declaring that he was dead.

As noted, numerous men fled Europe under assumed names to avoid army service. Men paid bribes to change names and forge new identities. More extreme cases were those who forged death certificates to avoid enlistment. Agnon's story only proves the complexity of the matter.

As the wave of immigrants grew, so did the number of cases of *agunot* caused by shipwreck. More and more *agunot* approached rabbis and asked for assistance and a solution for their delicate problem. In the rabbinical ruling of *agunot* whose husbands were lost at sea, there was an explicit difference between disasters with survivors and disasters without any survivors.

Unfortunately, even in the twenty-first century, there were disasters that forced rabbis to deal with the *agunot* issue. At least eight *agunot* were reported after the terrorist attack on the World Trade Center on September 11, 2001, for example.

What about the *agunot* of the *Titanic*? The first reference to the issue was in a Hebrew article in *Hazman* (Vilna) on May 21, 1912. The article discusses the *agunot* of the *Titanic* in general, without specifically naming any widows. The discussion is a *Halachic* one, using *Talmudic* examples and Jewish ruling. The article refers to a debate held by rabbis in America in an attempt to release the *agunot* of the *Titanic* disaster.[180]

Only one *Titanic* widow is known to have approached a rabbi in order to be released from her *agunot* status. Immediately after the disaster Zvia Maisner sent her question to Rabbi Jacob Meskin. Maisner was the widow of third-class passenger Shimon Maisner. Shimon was born in Russia in 1878. He was a tailor who intended to immigrate to the United States and live in Massachusetts. Shimon and Zvia had three little children. The family decided that Shimon would travel first, and the rest of the family would go after Shimon got settled. He purchased a third-class ticket, which cost him 8£ 1s, and boarded the *Titanic* in Southampton.

Because he was not among the survivors and his body was never found, his wife, Zvia, did not know if she was considered a widow or not. Rabbi Meskin was the rabbi in the hometown of the Maisner family in Kherson (today in Ukraine). At first Rabbi Meskin decided not to recite the *Kaddish* over Shimon Maisner. Not reciting the *Kaddish* meant that Rabbi Meskin believed that Maisner was not dead. For Zvia, this meant that she was considered an *agunah* until told otherwise. Rabbi Meskin forwarded the widow's question to Rabbi Yaakov Yitzchak Rabinovitch (1854–1919). At the time, Rabbi Rabinovitch (also known as Jacob Isaac Rabinovitch) was the *Av Beth Din* (chief rabbi of the rabbinical court) in Panevėžys (Ponevezh), a large Jewish center in Lithuania. Both Rabbi Meskin and Rabbi Rabinovitch wanted to find a *Halachic* way to release Zvia from being an *agunah* and permit her to remarry. Rabbi Rabinovitch pondered the question and tried to reach a *Halachic* ruling. His ten-page answer was sent back to Rabbi Meskin.[181]

Rabbi Rabinovitch had to deal with several issues. First, he was required to consider the *Talmudic* discussion regarding the disappearance of a man at sea. He then quoted *Maimonides* (the *Rambam*):

> If a man was seen falling into the sea, even if he fell into the ocean, testimony should not be offered that the man died, because it is possible that he was cast away or escaped from the sea from an unseen place.

Rabbi Rabinovitch used the *Talmudic* distinction between "water which has no end," which is a large body of water like the ocean, and "water which has an end," which is a small body of water. Rabbi Rabinovitch used the principle of "water which has an end" from the *Talmudic* discussion in *Yevamot* and from the tale told by Rabbi Akiva:

> I was once travelling on board a ship when I observed a ship in distress and was much grieved on account of a scholar who was on it. When I subsequently landed in the province of Cappadocia he came to me and sat down and discussed matters of *Halacha* with me. "My son," I said to him, "who rescued you?" and he answered me: "One wave tossed me to another and the other to yet another until the sea cast me on the dry land." At that hour I exclaimed: "How significant are the words of the Sages who ruled that if a man fell into water which has a visible end, his wife is permitted to marry again but if he fell into water which has no visible end, she is forbidden."

If the boundaries of the body of water are seen (water which has an end) and the man does not escape, it is clear that he is dead, but if the boundaries of the body of water are not seen (water which has no end) and the man does not escape, it is unclear that the man is dead because he can escape from another place.

The next question Rabbi Rabinovitch answered was about the water in the *Titanic* itself. Was the water that penetrated the ship considered "water which has an end"? The hull of the ship was the boundary of the water. Was there any difference between a man who was trapped in the hull and disappeared with the ship and a man who escaped the sinking ship yet did not survive the night? Was a man trapped in the ship considered a man in "water which has an end"? Was a man who escaped the ship and jumped into the water considered a man in "water which has no end"? Rabbi Rabinovitch concluded that anyone trapped in the ship was considered dead because he was trapped in a body of water which has an end, but if a man was seen alive outside the ship (or on deck), he is not considered dead because he was in a body of water with no end – unless his body is found, in which case he is proven dead.

Rabbi Rabinovitch's next question was whether to accept the testimonies of the survivors who had witnessed the deaths of the victims. After learning about the disaster, he tried to rule that survivors were not reliable in that matter because they were terrified from the catastrophe, frightened, and could not have seen properly who died and who did not. Rabbi Rabinovitch also said that it was impossible for survivors to determine who was killed because the ship was so large that no one on board could see everything that was going on. Eventually he ruled that the survivors were reliable and in his opinion there was no reason to be harsh on the matter.

Rabbi Rabinovitch also dealt with the question of accepting the official testimonies of the White Star Line regarding the lists of survivors and victims published by English and Russian authorities. The *Halachic* problem with such lists and testimonies was that they were composed by non-Jews, usually unaccepted in rabbinical courts. Shimon Maisner was a Russian citizen, and his death notice was questionable because it was based on the Russian proclamation. Rabbi Rabinovitch based his decision on the ruling of the Rambam and of the sages of the *Talmud*. Although usually testimonies given by non-Jews are not accepted in rabbinical courts, Rabbi Rabinovitch ruled that in this case the testimony could fall under the category of the *Talmud* phrase of "statements of a gentile made in the midst of conversation." Therefore Shimon Maisner's death notice Zvia received from the Russian government was valid and acceptable and so was the list of victims composed by the White Star Line.

The conclusion of Rabbi Rabinovitch's ruling was without doubt. Although his body was never found, Shimon Maisner died in the *Titanic* disaster. Zvia Maisner could be released from her *agunah* status, recognized as a widow, and remarry. Rabbi Rabinovitch sent his long response back to Rabbi Meskin in October 1912, half a year after the disaster. Then Rabbi Meskin officially released Zvia Maisner. In addition Rabbi Meskin said that *Kaddish* should be recited over Shimon Maisner.

Several years after the disaster, Rabbi Meskin immigrated from Russia to Vermont. He became the rabbi of the Jewish community in Burlington and the rabbi of the *Chayei Adam* synagogue and congregation. In 1940 Rabbi Meskin published Zvia Maisner's *agunah* question, Rabbi Rabinovitch's reply, and his own ruling on the *agunah* issue in a book of questions and answers called *Bais Yaakov*.

It may be that the ruling in favor of releasing Zvia Maisner from her *agunah* status assisted other *agunot* of the *Titanic* to find a way to be released and continue their lives after the disaster. Without knowing the exact number of Jews who sailed on the *Titanic*, it is unknown how many Jewish women became *agunot* or asked rabbis for help. Some *Titanic* widows (Hannah Abelson, René Harris, and Leah Mayer, to name a few) were rescued by the *Carpathia* and certainly were overwhelmed after losing their husbands in the disaster.

12

Arrival of the Survivors in New York

While the *Carpathia* was sailing to America, New York authorities prepared to receive the survivors. Hospitals, shelters, and charity organizations prepared beds and food for the sick, wounded, or needy. Numerous organizations, including Jewish ones, declared that they would provide assistance. One of them was Mount Sinai Hospital that announced that they would be glad to assist and receive injured survivors.[182]

Jewish organizations sent delegations to the White Star Line pier to greet survivors, especially poor immigrants.[183] All major organizations lent a hand and cooperated without discrimination among survivors.

Jewish organizations received lists of Jewish passengers and prepared provisions for the survivors. On April 17, the Yiddish newspaper *Chicago Jewish Tribune* published twenty-two names of Jewish survivors from all three classes. The list, just as with other lists of Jewish passengers, was full of mistakes. Some names were not Jewish or were not on the passengers list. Some of them were in fact dead.[184]

On April 18, the *Forward* published the names of third-class Jewish passengers. The *Forward* also published a list of twenty-three Jews who were missing. Both lists contained misinformation.[185]

The survivors needed food, clothes, and money. Fortunately the publicity of the disaster caused many people and organizations to contribute funds. The National Council of Jewish Women (NCJW) sent a delegation, led by a Mrs. Perelman, to greet and assist survivors.

The NCJW was established in 1893, and by 1912 it had over 250 employees and volunteers. When the *Titanic* arrived in New York, the NCJW assisted several Jewish women survivors who were taken to a Jewish shelter named the Clara De Hirsch Home for Working Girls. The president of the institute was Sarah Straus, wife of Oscar Straus, brother of *Titanic* victim Isidor Straus. By the end of April, several Yiddish newspapers in New York wrote about the contributions of the NCJW to the survivors, but to respect the privacy of the women, the NCJW did not publicize their names. Jewish-owned factories and businesses donated clothes and food to the NCJW for survivors.[186]

Hadassah, the Women's Zionist Organization of America, an organization that was established in February 1912, also assisted survivors. The founder of Hadassah was Henrietta Szold (1860–1945), a good friend of Nathan Straus.[187]

After the disaster, Nathan was among the most generous contributors to Hadassah. Nathan and Henrietta agreed to collaborate in funding and establishing a new medical center in Jerusalem. Nathan Straus would fund the cost of building the establishment, and Henrietta Szold would provide payment for a nurse to travel from America to Jerusalem and work at the medical center. That is how the Nathan and Lina Straus Health Center in Jerusalem was established. The center is located on Straus Street (named after Nathan Straus). With the help of other contributors, there were enough funds to pay for two nurses.

As the years went by, Hadassah became one of the largest international Jewish organizations. Hadassah funded the creation of dozens of hospitals, medical centers, shelters, and other institutes. It would not be unrealistic to believe that Hadassah became what it became, over one hundred years after the *Titanic* sank, thanks to the contribution of Nathan Straus. It is also clear that his contribution to the organization was part of his way of paying respect to his brother, Isidor. Thousands of Jews, who were helped by Hadassah over the years, could thank Nathan Straus for his cooperation and friendship with Henrietta Szold.[188]

The *Carpathia* arrived at New York on the evening of April 18. She docked at the White Star Line pier and lowered the *Titanic's* lifeboats. She then continued to the Cunard Line pier. At 21:00 she docked, and the passengers started to disembark. The first to leave were the first-class passengers, followed by second class, then third, and finally the *Titanic's* crew.[189]

Before the third-class passengers disembarked, a small group of representatives of the United States Ministry of Immigration boarded the

Carpathia and questioned the passengers before they were allowed to enter the country. They were processed with medical checks and registration. The inquiries went quickly, and the passengers were released to leave the ship and enter the country.

Five-year-old Virginia Ethel Emanuel, a Jewish third-class passenger, was taken to her grandparent's home. Her grandfather, Samuel Weill, filed an insurance claim for $540 over the loss of Virginia's personal belongings.[190]

Many survivors had no place to go and were taken to orphanages, shelters, and hospitals. The Red Cross and other organizations provided shelter. One survivor who needed treatment was third-class passenger Sarah Roth. She was born in 1885 in Tarnow, Austria (today Poland), to a Jewish family and had one brother, Barnett. The family immigrated to Whitechapple, London, when Sarah was a child. When her father, Abraham, died, she went to live

Third-class Jewish survivor Sarah Roth (left) on her wedding day a week after the disaster. Source: New York Tribune

at the Jewish Hospital and Orphan Asylum in London.

As a young adult, Sarah became engaged to Daniel Iles, a Jewish man who immigrated to New York and worked in a department store. Sarah stayed in London and worked as a seamstress. After a few months Daniel sent for Sarah, so she bought a third-class ticket, which cost her 8£ 1s, and boarded the *Titanic* to join her fiancé. During the disaster she was able to reach the Boat Deck and enter a lifeboat. Among the things she lost was her wedding gown. In New York she was taken to the St. Vincent Hospital. A week later she married Daniel wearing a wedding gown donated by the Women's Relief Committee. Her maid of honor was a *Titanic* passenger whom she met and befriended during the voyage.[191]

Of all the Jewish organizations, volunteer groups, agencies, and shelters, the one that supported the largest group of Jewish survivors was the Hebrew Sheltering and Immigrant Aid Society (HIAS). Twenty-seven survivors, mostly Christian and Muslim and only a handful of Jews, were sent to the shelter run by HIAS. The shelter, located on the Lower East Side, had a dormitory, soup kitchen, and provided clothing for Jews in need. The society was founded at the end of the nineteenth century during the beginning of the huge wave of Jewish immigration. HIAS's goal was to provide immediate help to Jewish immigrants, and it ran a large shelter house in New York Harbor where Jewish volunteers gave food to immigrants and escorted them through the process at Ellis Island. This support included providing the landing fee, medical screening, and transportation services to New York City and even assistance with employment. HIAS also argued before the authorities to prevent deportations back to Europe. Many Jewish immigrants arrived famished after the long journey across the Atlantic Ocean. HIAS managed a huge kosher kitchen and ran a synagogue for Jewish passengers at Ellis Island.

After hearing about the *Titanic* disaster, in New York HIAS started preparing for the arrival of the survivors, especially those from third class. A committee was established, and Abe (Abraham) Cooper was appointed to head the delegation that received the survivors with two representatives of HIAS, Erving Livshitz and Samuel Masson. HIAS quickly raised over $2,350, which was distributed among the survivors who stayed several days at the shelter. HIAS announced that they would support and assist all survivors in need without regards to religion, race, or gender.[192]

During their stay at the shelter, the survivors were interviewed by the Jewish media. A team from Yiddish newspaper the *Forward* came to the shelter to interview Jewish survivors. In an article published later that month, survivors were described as exhausted, depressed, and weak.[193]

Among the Jewish survivors taken care of by HIAS were second-class passenger Hannah Abelson (who lost her husband, Samuel, in the disaster); third-class passengers Leah Aks and her son, Frank; Bella Moor and her son, Meyer; as well as Gershon Cohen and Berk Trembisky.

SURVIVORS OF THE TITANIC
In care of the Hebrew Sheltering and Immigrant Aid Society

די געראטעוועטע פון דער שיף טיטאניק

אונטער די אויפזעהונג פון די חברו שעלטערינג אין אימיגראנט אייד סאסייעטי

Photo by Ph. Karuda, 570 E. Houston St.

Titanic *survivors at the Hebrew Sheltering and Aid Society. In center: Bella Moor and son Meyer. To her right: Leah Aks holding her son Frank. Source: HIAS Photo Archive*

When interviewed by the *Forward,* Bella said that at first she thought she was going to die. During the evacuation she held Meyer tightly. She told her interviewer that she heard many people crying and calling for help and there was a lot of commotion, disorder, and chaos.[194] At the shelter Bella wrote several letters to relatives. She described her experiences and said that she was doing okay.

During his stay at the shelter, Gershon Cohen's relatives visited him. After a short time in New York, Cohen returned to England. He joined the British Army and fought against the Germans in World War I.[195]

Not all survivors at the Jewish shelter were Jews. In a photograph taken at the shelter, there are ten survivors, women with children; only Leah and Frank and Bella and Meyer were Jewish. Three women were third-class passengers from Lebanon (then part of Syria): Banoura Ayoub (age fourteen), who was immigrating to North America to join her family in Canada; Maria Al-Baclini (age five) who was immigrating to America with her family and eventually settled in New York; and Shawneene Whabee (age thirty-eight), who immigrated to America in 1906 and was returning to New York after visiting family in Lebanon.

Also in the photo were three second-class passengers from England: Jane Quick (age thirty-three) and her two daughters, Winifred (age eight) and Phyllis (age three), who were on their way to America to start a new life.

People, especially Jews, came to the Jewish shelter to meet the survivors. Some came to search for relatives and friends. Others came to show sympathy and to bring donations of food and clothes.

Other non-Jews who were assisted by Jewish organizations included Anna Maria Sinkkonen (age thirty) and Lyyli Silvén (age eighteen). Both from Finland and second-class passengers, they were housed at a Jewish Welcome Home located at 225 East 13th St., New York City.

After the disaster the American Red Cross collected donations to assist the survivors in need and for the relatives of some of the victims. One of them was Moses Aaron Troupiansky who died in the disaster. In the file of the report, Troupiansky was noted as a Russian Jew. The file includes the following:

> This young business man was lost while coming from South Africa to join his widowed mother and three sisters in New York and to establish himself in business here. He had been sending $20 a month to his mother. Two daughters were working; one was in an institution, a permanent invalid. Emergent needs were cared for by this Committee.

After recuperating, survivors started thinking about their future. Jewish survivor Miriam Kantor (who lost her husband, Sinai) went to relatives in Boston, Massachusetts, and then returned to her cousins in New York. A few days after the disaster, she was brought to the Ritz-Carlton Hotel to meet with the Russian consul. The meeting was arranged by wealthy first-class passenger Margaret (Molly) Brown, who attended the meeting and assisted Miriam Kantor throughout it. The two women met on the *Carpathia*. Miriam told the consul that she lost her husband in the disaster. She was very upset and distressed, and Molly Brown had to calm her down every few minutes. Miriam was described by Molly as a little, brown-eyed, baby-faced

Russian woman. When the meeting was over, the consul referred Miriam to the American Red Cross. A special Red Cross committee decided to help her by giving her fifty dollars every month for four years. Miriam Kantor hoped to learn to speak English and continue studying medicine as she did in Russia since she wanted to become a dentist. The Red Cross paid for her tuition. In total, she received over $2,500.[196]

In 1913 the Red Cross wrote a report about Sinai and Miriam Kantor. The report referred to Sinai as follows:

> The husband, about thirty years of age, was drowned. He was traveling with his wife, who was saved. He had been a commission merchant, earning about $2,500 a year, and was bringing to this country several trunks of valuable furs which he had expected to sell here. Both he and his wife were university graduates. He was ambitious to study medicine and planned to take night courses after he should get his business established in New York.

The money was transferred from the Red Cross to the National Council of Jewish Women (NCJW) who watched over Miriam. Such cooperation between the Jewish and non-Jewish organizations (NCJW and the Red Cross) is a testament to the good will of the various charities regardless of religion or race. After the *Titanic* sank, every organization was willing to help the survivors and did not care who they were or what their religion was. Jewish shelters gladly helped non-Jewish survivors, and for the same reason the Red Cross (and other organizations) helped Jewish survivors.

Hannah Abelson, who lost her husband, Samuel, in the disaster, also was aided by the Red Cross. The Red Cross report referred to her as well:

> Husband drowned, wife rescued. There are no children. He was a bookkeeper, 30 years of age. His wife, 28 years of age, is an expert dressmaker. She is living with her husband's brother in New York City. The wife suffered temporary disability due to exposure, but is now able to support herself by her trade. The property loss was more than $4,000. She received from relief sources other than the Red Cross, $1,928.

Most Jewish survivors stayed in New York City for a while and then returned to England or settled elsewhere in America.

Third-class passenger Abraham Hyman spent several months in the United States. Because of the disaster, his wife Esther did not want to cross the Atlantic Ocean, so he returned to England. First-class passenger Adolphe Saalfeld abandoned his dream to open a pharmacy in New York. He lost his perfume samples in the disaster and returned to his wife in England. For a while he continued to be a member of his synagogue in Manchester.[197]

Second-class passengers Alice Frances Cohen Christy and her two daughters, Amy Jacobsohn (who lost her husband Sydney) and Rachel Juli Cohen, stayed in the United States for a month. The three then returned to London and lived in England for the rest of their lives.

Before the survivors scattered around the world, the United States government, as well as the British authorities, wanted to investigate the *Titanic* disaster to try to prevent such catastrophes from happening again. The Americans started their investigation the day after the *Carpathia* arrived in New York.

13

INQUIRIES

The American inquiry officially titled "The United States Senate Inquiry into the Sinking of the RMS *Titanic*" opened on April 19 at the Waldorf Astoria Hotel in New York City. Later the inquiry moved to the Senate office building in Washington, D.C. More than eighteen witnesses and experts provided testimony during the eighteen-day inquiry. The man who established and led the inquiry was William Alden Smith (no relation to the *Titanic's* Captain Smith), an active Republican senator from Michigan. He was the main force behind the American inquiry, and one of his objectives was to review safety rules and regulations for transatlantic crossings. For Senator Smith, as for the entire committee, it was very important to hold the inquiry while the survivors recovered in New York, especially the British witnesses. Subpoenas were necessary in some cases.

The first to testify was Bruce Ismay. He had to explain to the Senate how he, a male and managing director of the White Star Line, was able to escape the sinking ship while so many women drowned. The American authorities did not want to hold him in the United States for long. Senator Smith handed Ismay the subpoena while the *Carpathia* was still docked in New York harbor. Another important witness was Second Officer Charles Lightoller, the highest-ranking survivor. Others who testified were Fredrick Fleet, the *Titanic's* lookout, and Harold Bride, *Titanic's* radio operator. Most of the surviving passengers who were called to testify were first-class passengers.[198]

Attending the Senate inquiry were ship captains, including the captain of the *Carpathia* (Arthur Rostron), captain of the *Californian* (Stanley Lord), captain of the *Olympic* (Herbert Haddock), members of the crews of the ships, and experts in navigation. Guglielmo Marconi, the inventor of the Marconi Radio Company, was invited to speak about the necessity of wireless radio on ocean liners. Topics discussed were regulations regarding ice warnings, the behavior of the crews and captains of the ships during the night (*Titanic*, *Carpathia*, *Californian*, and *Olympic*), and the inadequate number of lifeboats on board the *Titanic* (the *Titanic* carried twenty lifeboats, four more than required by the Board of Trade, yet had room for less than half the passengers and crew), the evacuation of the passengers into the lifeboats, the *Titanic's* speed during the voyage, and the means of rescue calls for help (radio, rockets, flares).

Senators visited the *Olympic* to lean about the structure of the sister ship. The inspection included the safety systems and mechanisms of the bulkheads dividing the ship into compartments.[199]

There were several bizarre moments during the days of the testimony. When one witness was asked what an iceberg is composed of, he responded, "Ice, I suppose, sir." At one point a witness was asked why none of the passengers tried to save themselves by entering the watertight compartments.

The inquiry proved that the *Titanic* did not have enough lifeboats and that the ship's crew did not know how to operate them or had practiced lowering them. The inquiry also proved that although the *Titanic* was warned over and over about the ice, the ship did not reduce speed while sailing into the ice zone. The committee condemned Captain Stanley Lord of the *Californian* for not coming to the aid of the *Titanic* even though the two ships were relatively close, about twenty kilometers apart. Several of the crew of the *Californian* even saw the rockets fired by the *Titanic* and tried to call her with a Morse lamp, but they failed to wake their radio operator who was off duty at the time. Captain Lord was accused of negligence and eventually became the scapegoat of the *Titanic* tragedy.

The following conclusions were reached:

Ships should reduce speed when entering an ice zone.
All officers on deck should be aware of the dangers.
Ships should carry enough lifeboats for all passengers and crew members.
Ships should operate the radio twenty-four hours a day.
Crews should hold lifeboat lowering drills.
All use of rockets at sea should indicate distress.

It was recommended that the President of the United States shall award Captain Rostron of the *Carpathia* the Congressional Gold Medal of Honor for his heroic actions, a recommendation which was gladly fulfilled.

One of the most disturbing questions the inquiry dealt with was the evacuation of the third-class passengers. Was there discrimination between the classes during the loading of the lifeboats? Were third-class passengers prevented from reaching the Boat Deck? Ironically, the Senate decided that there was no discrimination between the classes since passageways from steerage to the upper decks were open and third-class passengers were not forcefully held back. Unfortunately, the reality was that most third-class passengers died while many of the lifeboats left half-empty. The issue of discrimination between the classes and the low number of third-class survivors remain controversial.

The United States Senate concluded their inquiry on April 25, and the British inquiry began on May 2. The official name for the British inquiry was "The British Wreck Commissioner's Inquiry into the Sinking of the RMS *Titanic*," and it was held at the Scottish Drill Hall in London. The last few days of the inquiry were held at Caxton Hall in Westminster. Since the Americans and British had different agendas, the two nations did not hold a joint inquiry. The British inquiry was overseen by Sir John Bigham.

Attorney General Sir Rufus Daniel Isaacs (1860–1935) represented the Board of Trade and had the task of composing questions to witnesses. Sir Rufus was a Jewish barrister. His father was a fruit merchant, and young Isaacs entered the family business at the age of fifteen. In the mid-1880s he worked at the British Stock Exchange, but in the late 1880s he became a lawyer. Later he became a Parliament member and served in the British cabinet. He was knighted in 1910 and was the first Jew to serve as Lord Chief Justice of England and the first British Jew to

Sir Rufus Daniel Isaacs, British attorney general during the Titanic *inquiry. Source: Library of Congress*

become a marquess (1st marquise of Reading). Sir Isaacs was a Zionist, visited the Mandatory Palestine several times, and was the founding chairman of what became the Israel Electric Corporation. Israel's first turbine power plant, the Reading Power Station, located in Tel Aviv, is named after him. He also visited the hydroelectric power station in the Jordan Valley. Sir Isaacs died in 1935 and was buried in Hoop Lane Jewish Cemetery, in Golders Green, London.

Sir Rufus Daniel Isaacs composed a list of twenty-six questions concerning matters such as navigation, ice warnings, and the role of the *Californian*. Almost one hundred witnesses and experts testified over thirty-six days. Among the witnesses were representatives of the White Star Line, experts in international sailing laws, government officials, and ship builders. To help understand the tragedy, the inquiry presented a model of the *Titanic* that was used by witnesses to visualize the events.

Survivors who testified at the British inquiry included Second Officer Charles Lightoller, lookout Fredrick Fleet, radio operator Harold Bride, and chief baker Charles Joughin. Crewmen of the *Carpathia* and *Californian* also testified. One witness who drew a large crowd was Bruce Ismay. Another was Lucy Duff Gordon.

Other witnesses who drew attention were the crew of the *Californian*. Like the Americans, the British wanted to understand the strange behavior of the ship's crew that night and why they did not respond to the *Titanic's* distress rockets. One of the British conclusions condemned Captain Lord for not coming to the *Titanic's* rescue. Had the *Californian* sailed toward the *Titanic*, she could have saved many, if not all of the crew and passengers.

Both committees had many conclusions in common. Both agreed that the *Titanic* did not carry enough lifeboats although they fulfilled the laws by the Board of Trade. Both committees agreed that the ship's crew were not skilled in lowering the lifeboats and had not participated in lifeboat drills.

The British committee emphasized Captain Smith's role in the disaster, and although he sailed his ship into an ice zone without reducing speed, he was not condemned. Captain Smith died in the disaster and became a hero. The committee established the fact that the *Titanic* sank because she hit an iceberg and that by reducing speed as the ship entered the ice field, the collision could have been avoided.[200]

The British submitted their conclusions on June 30, 1912. Among their recommendations were changes in international sailing regulations and additional safety precautions for ships crossing the Atlantic Ocean. Because of the new regulations, not a single person has died as a result of a ship colliding with an iceberg.

Few third-class survivors testified at the inquiries. Only three testified at the American inquiry and none at the British inquiry. Of the three, one survivor was Jewish. His name was Berk Trembisky, and he testified on the fourteenth day of the inquiry, Saturday, May 4, 1912. His testimony was very important to the Senate in order to examine the claims of alleged discrimination between the classes during the evacuation and loading of the lifeboats.

Berk Trembisky was born in Warsaw, Poland, in 1878. He immigrated to France, where he changed his name to Benoît Picard (sometimes spelled Pickard). Later he moved to London and worked as a bag maker. He reverted to his former first name, Berk. In 1912 he decided to immigrate to San Francisco, California. At age thirty-two and single, he boarded the *Titanic* at Southampton. His ticket cost him 8£ 1s, and his cabin was number 10 on F Deck. After escaping the *Titanic*, he stayed for a few weeks at the Hebrew shelter (HIAS).

On the day of his testimony, he was brought to the Waldorf Astoria and sworn in by Senator Smith who asked him for his address. Since he did not have a permanent address, he gave the address of the shelter: no. 299 Hebrew Immigration Society. When asked for his name, he said:

> My name was Berk Trembisky. I was for a long time in France and I assumed a French name. As regards private business, I am Pickard.[201]

When asked for his occupation, he said that he was a leather worker, a bag maker. Then he was asked to share his experiences of his rescue from the *Titanic*.

Berk Trembisky told the Senate how he escaped. He described how he woke from the shock of the collision, which was not terrible but was noticeable. He and other passengers jumped out of bed, got dressed, and left their room at the stern on F Deck. He wanted to return to his room to take several items but was blocked by stewards. He was instructed to go forward toward the bow. He and the other passengers were not guided by the crew.

Trembisky explained to the Senate that passengers argued regarding the direction. Some said to go one way and others said to go another way. He decided to continue on his own and climbed up to a higher deck. He came across a door leading to second class. The door was not locked, and he entered and saw some passengers. From there he continued to climb to higher decks and eventually found his way into first class. When he reached the Boat Deck, he saw a few people, among them only two women. The women were being placed in the lifeboat. Noticing that there was room in the lifeboat, and without any more women in the area, he and several other men jumped into the lifeboat. Nobody stopped them, and nobody forced them out of the lifeboat. As the lifeboat was being lowered to the water he noticed the sheer size of the ship. He also noticed that the bow was sinking.

When asked for the number of his lifeboat, Trembisky apologized because he did not know and had not bothered to notice. (He was rescued in Lifeboat 9 which was lowered at 01:30 with over fifty survivors). Trembisky confessed to the Senate that as the lifeboat was being lowered, he was frightened and even told the seaman that he would rather return to the ship. The seaman laughed at him and said, "Do you not see we are sinking?"

Trembisky told the Senate that he noticed how deck after deck went underwater until the ship disappeared completely.

When he was asked about the discrimination or any attempt to prevent the third-class passengers from leaving the ship, he said over and over again that from his point of view there was no such attempt and that all the doors and gates leading from the third-class area were unlocked and open. All the barriers had been removed. When asked about the panic amongst the passengers, he said that there was no panic. Passengers felt no alarm or distress. Nobody felt the danger. The stewards kept reassuring the passengers that "nothing serious is the matter." When asked again about the assistance from the stewards, he said that he was instructed to take his life vest and leave the area.

Trembisky concluded his testimony with the words:

> That is all I know about it. I was one of the first to go. Of course, if
> I had stayed until a little bit later, I would have seen a little bit more.
> I was one of the luckiest ones, I think.[202]

Then he was excused from the stand.

Charles Stengel was the only other Jewish survivor called to testify at the

American inquiry. Stengel was called on the eleventh day of the inquiry, Tuesday, April 30, 1912. He was asked for his full name, address, and occupation. After giving his name he said that he lived in Newark, New Jersey, and was a leather manufacturer. He was asked to share his experiences of the disaster. He said that he had had trouble sleeping that night. His wife, Annie, woke him up to tell him he was hallucinating. At that very moment they felt the ship collide with the iceberg. Stengel described to the Senate how he assisted his wife to enter Lifeboat 5 and how he later walked over to Lifeboat 1. He asked if he could enter the lifeboat, which was mostly empty, and was granted permission. First Officer William Murdock, the officer in charge of the lifeboat, told him he could "jump in." Later in his testimony he mentioned Abraham Salomon, a Jewish man who also jumped into the lifeboat.

Stengel described to the Senate how he entered the lifeboat:

> I jumped onto the railing and rolled into it. The officer then said, "That is the funniest sight I have seen tonight," and he laughed quite heartily. That rather gave me some encouragement.[203]

Stengel was asked dozens of questions at the inquiry. Many questions were technical and dealt with the ship's speed, the height of the railing of the deck, the lights seen in the distance (the *Californian*), and the sounds the ship made as it went under. When asked if he knew of any passengers attempting to jump into the lifeboats, he mentioned the incident where two men (Dr. Henry Frauenthal and his brother, Isaac) jumped into Lifeboat 5, landed on his wife, and broke several of her ribs.

Stengel was asked to explain why his lifeboat left with so few survivors. He was also asked why the lifeboat did not return to the ship to pick up more survivors after it was lowered to the water. He said that the lifeboat was too far from the *Titanic* and the seamen in the lifeboat were scared it would be swamped and overturned by the other people or sucked in by the *Titanic*.

Senator Smith asked Stengel about the responsibility of the lifeboat. He asked him who took charge of the lifeboat once it was lowered to the water. Stengel told the senator that he shared responsibility with Sir Cosmo Duff Gordon because there were no officers in the lifeboat. He also told the Senate that he rowed during the night.[204]

Although the two men (Stengel and Trembisky) had probably never met and testified for different reasons, each contributed to the inquiry. While Trembisky's testimony was to debunk the alleged discrimination between the classes during the evacuation, Stengel was called to the stand in order to examine the ordeal of Lifeboat 1.

The Senate learned from Berk Trembisky that there was no discrimination between the classes. His answers about the unlocked barriers and the assistance received from the crew satisfied them. The Senate ruled that the crew acted properly and the third-class passengers were not held back. Berk Trembisky was living proof. The statistics prove otherwise, however.

The Senate learned from Charles Stengel all there was to know about Lifeboat 1, and his answers about his behavior and that of the Duff Gordons satisfied them. Eventually the Senate ruled that, although mostly empty, the lifeboat had to leave the *Titanic* because there were no women in the area while it was being loaded. Again, though, the American and British public opinion proved otherwise.

For many *Titanic* survivors, the publicity surrounding the disaster and inquiries started to fade with time. Yet the world was still thirsty for more.

14

EULOGIES, MEMORIALS, AND LAMENTATIONS

God, full of mercy, who dwells in the heights, provide a sure rest upon the wings of the Divine Presence, amongst the holy, pure, and glorious, who shine like the sky, to the people of the Titanic, who drowned in the sea and are gone to their eternal home…

The above quote is from the Jewish Prayer for the Dead, widely known as *El Malei Rachamim*. After the disaster, memorials and commemorations for the victims of the *Titanic* took place throughout the world. In many Jewish communities memorials were held for local Jewish victims. This particular *El Malei Rachamim* prayer was recited in April 1913, a year after the disaster. One of the greatest cantors at the time, Josef "Yossele" Rosenblatt (1882–1933), was given the honor of reciting the prayer at one of the main

Record of Titanic *Jewish prayer for the dead (El Malie, Rachamim) performed by Cantor Yossale Rosenblatt. Source: unknown*

memorials of the Jewish communities in New York. Rosenblatt, who was also a composer, recorded the prayer, sold the record, and refused to take the proceeds. Instead he donated the money to a fund for the families who lost loved ones on the *Titanic*.[205]

Cantors and rabbis all over the Jewish world reacted to the sinking. On the first *Sabbath* after the disaster (third of Iyar, April 20), dozens of rabbis in America referred to the tragedy in their weekly sermons. One of them was Rabbi Emil Hirsch of Chicago who said in his address:

The Jew knows how to live as is clearly shown all about us in this work a day world. It goes without saying he knows how to die. A moment like that which the world witnessed the other day, with many a home wreathed in sombre mourning and many a heart weighed down in sorrow, shows us that the Jew knows how to die.[206]

The Jewish community in New York, the largest in the United States, went into heavy mourning. The first *Sabbath* after the disaster, many arrived at synagogues to pray and hear comforting sermons and eulogies. One sermon was delivered at Temple *Beth-El* (Fifth Avenue and 76th Street), the synagogue where Isidor and Ida Straus had been members. Rabbi Samuel Schulman led the sermon.

TRIBUTE TO STRAUS PAID IN SYNAGOGUES

Family of Philanthropist Who Died on Titanic Present at Temple Beth-El.

SERMONS ON CATASTROPHE

Mrs. Benjamin Guggenheim, Made Widow by Wreck, at Temple Emanu-El—General Services To-day.

Services in the Jewish temples of the city yesterday were occasions of mourning for the dead in the Titanic disaster. At several of the synagogues the catastrophe was the subject of the sermon.

At Temple Beth-El, Fifth Avenue and Seventy-sixth Street, of which Mr. and Mrs. Isidor Straus, who died loyally together, were members, all the representatives of the Straus family now in the city were present. They were ex-Ambassador Oscar Straus, brother of the dead philan-

Tribute to Straus paid in synagogue. Source: New York Times, *April 21, 1912*

Services, sermons, and memorials were held at Temple Emanuel (43rd Street), the synagogue where several *Titanic* victims, including Benjamin Guggenheim and Edger Mayer, had been members. Guggenheim's widow, Florette, was present, and so was Leah, Edger's widow. *Titanic* survivor William Greenfield attended as well. Radio operator David Sarnoff was a member too. At Temple *Rodeph Shalom* (Lexington Avenue), the sermon was delivered by Rabbi Rudolf Grossman.[207]

The rabbis said words of tribute to the victims and words of comfort to the families. Before the disaster many rabbis saw the *Titanic* as a modern Tower of Babel, but after the disaster they talked about the end of the Babylonian rebel against God. Just as in the biblical story when mankind could not complete the construction of such a huge tower, with its peak in the sky, mankind had to be humble and not attempt to build such huge and "unsinkable" ships.

Besides the grief and mourning, there was a lot of pride in the noble behavior of the Jewish victims. Many cantors and rabbis mourned and honored the famous Straus couple. The rumor of Ida's gallant bravery was soon well known in Jewish communities around the world. One rabbi in Atlanta, Georgia, mentioned that there were several Jews among the wealthy passengers who perished, including Isidor Straus and Benjamin Guggenheim. He also said in his sermon: "The sinking of the *Titanic* is an event of great importance to the American Jewish community."[208]

Eulogies, memorials, and lamentations were held in synagogues all over the United States. In the Jewish community in Douglas, Nebraska, a special memorial was held in honor of Jewish victim Emil Brandeis. In Providence, Rhode Island, a memorial was held in honor of local Jewish victim Harry Sadowitz.

Memorials were also held in European synagogues in honor of *Titanic* victims. In the little Lithuanian *shtetl* of Ignalina, a memorial was held to honor local victim Eliezer Gilinski. In Antwerp, Belgium, the congregation gathered in synagogues to honor and remember local *Titanic* victim Jacob Birnbaum. Although the body of Herbert Klein (the second-class barber) was never found, the Jewish community in Leeds, England, went into deep mourning. Klein was a well-known member of the community and very beloved by his friends and neighbors. Sermons were held at the Great Orthodox Synagogue, also known as the Old Hebrew Congregation.[209] Southampton was hit the hardest. Hundreds of the *Titanic's* crewmen lived there. The Southampton Jewish community held a special memorial for Charles Kennel, the kosher cook.

Mayors, cantors, and public figures led memorial services for victims of all races. The tragedy of the sinking of the *Titanic* united people in mourning all over the world. One Yiddish paper wrote: "The sinking of the *Titanic* was a tragedy that left no heart untouched."[210]

Ida's famous last words were "Where you go, I go," and her wish to remain with her husband became an inevitable comparison to the biblical story of Ruth and Naomi, and Ruth's wish to remain with her mother-in-law as she expressed in the Book of Ruth:

> *Where you go, I will go and where you lodge I will lodge. Your people shall be my people and your God my God. Where you die, will I die, and there will I be buried.*

No wonder Ida Straus was nicknamed "Ruth of the *Titanic*." Ida's name and picture were in many newspapers, which praised her and wrote about her refusal to enter a lifeboat without Isidor and how Isidor refused to be saved before other men. Her heroic act made her one of the main tragic characters of the disaster. The fact that she was Jewish only added to the halo that surrounded her after her death.

Even pastors and priests praised Isidor Straus in their sermons. When Reverend Newell Dwight Hillis gave his eulogy in Plymouth he included a few words about the esteemed Jewish couple and referred to Isidor as a noble Jewish man:

> They have taught the young how to love and the old how to die... God bless the name of Straus henceforth.

Dr. Mason Clarke, a pastor of the First Presbyterian Church quoted Psalms in his sermon, and after praising many of the *Titanic's* victims, said:

> See those wives refusing to be torn from their husbands. See those venerable two . . . Hebrews in religion and race, son and daughter of the highest in devotion and character. See them standing by the rail clasped together . . . I can only wonder if the great words of their Hebrew scriptures did not flash across their minds in that great moment: "Love is strong than death, many waters cannot quench it neither can the floods drown it. Lovely and pleasant in their lives and in their death they were not divided."[212]

In 1917 when Rabbi Josef Meyer Levin published his book of sermons *To the House of David* (in Hebrew), he included a eulogy for the victims of the *Titanic*. His book contained various sermons for Passover, Rosh Hashanah, and other Jewish events. His *Titanic* eulogy is six pages long, and in it he reflected on his religious beliefs and his trust in God's

Victims of the Titanic *(in Yiddish). Source: Morris Rund, Yiddish Penny Song, 1912*

judgment. He pointed out that the *Titanic* sank with 1,600 souls, many of whom were "our brothers of the house of Israel" as he called the Jewish people. He described how beautiful the ship was, how she was the largest and most luxurious ocean liner ever built. He described how the angel of death, in the shape of an iceberg, collided with the ship, and how the people scrambled to the upper decks in horror. Rabbi Levin mentioned Isidor and Ida Straus and how Ida refused to be separated from her husband. Rabbi Levin also stated that Isidor Straus was a

Straus memorial pin.
Source: unknown

philanthropist who gave his wealth to charity for "our people." Rabbi Levin concluded his eulogy with a quote from the Book of Isaiah:

> *He will swallow up death for ever, and the Lord will wipe away tears from all faces.*[213]

Other rabbis who wrote sermons and eulogies about the *Titanic* include Rabbi Yehuda David Eisenstein, who wrote about the history of American Jews, and Rabbi Yitzhak Savitski, who wrote a sermon about the *Titanic* and how one should trust the Lord and his judgment. And there were many others.

Even in recent years rabbis have mentioned the *Titanic* disaster in their sermons. In 2003 a small booklet was published in Israel regarding the Space Shuttle *Columbia* disaster in which Israeli astronaut Ilan Ramon was among the seven victims. The sermon covered several disasters and dedicated an entire paragraph to the sinking of the *Titanic*. The message in the sermon was to accept the limits of mankind and be humble before the Lord.

In his poem on the *Titanic* disaster, German poet Hans Magnus Enzensberger wrote: "A gold mine for poets. A spectacular site in its beauty."[214] He was right since so many songs have been written about the *Titanic*. In fact, no other disaster had drawn so much attention in literature at the time. Already in 1912 songs about the *Titanic* were created. Over the years hundreds of melancholy songs, mostly ballads, have been composed. One song sung by Pete Seeger and other folk singers was called "The *Titanic* Song"; it was known for its chorus:

It was sad, it was sad,
It was sad when that great ship went down,
Husbands and wives and little children lost their lives,
It was sad when that great ship went down.

Jews found a path of mourning through Yiddish literature. Jewish composers and writers added their own work to the long list of *Titanic* ballads. The Jewish-American poet and composer Solomon Shmulewitz wrote his famous Yiddish lamentation: *Churbon Titanik, Oder Der Naser Keiver* (The *Titanic's* Destruction, the Watery Grave). American Jewry found consolation and comfort in their grief over Isidor and Ida Straus since the deaths of the esteemed couple touched their hearts. Shmulewitz merged those feelings of Ida's heroic act into his lamentation:

Man, you are no match,
For the cold ocean's power.
It is a wet and deep grave…
Shed tears for all the lives lost.
And for her noble courage.
All should honor and remember,
The name of Ida Straus.

Four years after the disaster, Russian-born Yiddish poet Aaron David Egoz who immigrated to America in 1869 wrote another memorial prayer in honor of the victims. The prayer was originally written in Yiddish in commemoration of those who died at sea.[215] One of the verses is as follows:

May God remember the divine souls of
Isidor Ben Rabbi Eliezer and Ida Bat Rabbi Nathan
The beloved couple,
Who carried out goodness in their lives,
Who walked hand in hand,
To help the poor and miserable
To defend the elderly, the sick and the weak.

Soon after the disaster, lamentations of the *Titanic* started to spread throughout Eastern European *shtetls*. The lamentations resembled the sorrow of other tragedies that accrued in the Jewish communities, such as pogroms and anti-Semitic persecutions. The lamentations about the *Titanic* reminded the community that leaving the *shtetls* and immigrating to America could have tragic consequences. Many young Jews left their families, went to America, and lost contact with family, friends, and Judaism itself. The *Titanic* tragedy reminded the families of the

The Titanic *disaster (in Yiddish). Composed by Solomon Shmulewitz. Photo credit: Hebrew Publishing Cooperation*

physical and spiritual dangers of moving to America.

Hundreds of poems, ballads, and songs were written about the *Titanic*. In fact, there were so many songs that the *New York Times* rejected many of the poems sent to the newspaper.[216] In 1912 over one hundred songs and ballads were written in the United States alone. Many had a strong connection to faith and glorified the passengers (mostly men) who had bravely faced death. Men who put their wives in lifeboats and died.

Many poems were written in Hebrew and Yiddish literature as well. In 1962 an article published in *Herut* (Tel Aviv) contained several examples. One of them was "Rivers of Tears," a poem written by the Yiddish poet Zalman Reizen published two months after the disaster.[217] The poem was originally in Hebrew:

Rivers of tears washed our eyes,
Titanic, for your miserable.
Our hearts torn to thousands of shreds,
For your orphans and widows.

But beyond the victims of the sea,
We wept, we wept over the two victims,
Isidor and Ida Straus.

The Hasidic writer and poet Yosef Zelig wrote a special poem for the Jewish holiday of *Shavuot* (Pentecost) to honor the victims. *Shavuot* was celebrated less than two months after the disaster while many Jews were still in shock and mourning. This unique poem was written in the style of the Aramaic liturgical poem *Akdamut* which is recited in synagogues on *Shavuot*. The structure of the poem is similar to the *Akdamut* in that every line ends with the syllable "Ta." The poem was originally written in Hebrew and is called *Te'avnu ve-Ta'inu ba-Titanik* (literally translates to "We Craved and Erred in the *Titanic*"). In his poem, Zelig criticizes the arrogance and condescension of the wealthy passengers of the *Titanic* who escaped the sinking ship while so many steerage passengers died.[218]

Zelig referred to the segregation, separation, and discrimination of the classes. He hinted at the fact that the first-class passengers had a chance to survive while so many immigrants from third class perished. In his poem he also accused the crew of assisting the wealthy first-class passengers while neglecting the poor immigrants of third class. He claimed that their way to the upper decks had been blocked.

Several weeks after the disaster, the Hebrew and Yiddish poet and writer Getzel Selikovitsch wrote the Hebrew poem *Masa Metzulot Yam* (literally translated as "The Burden of Depth of the Sea"). In his poem he accused the passengers of the *Titanic* of being overly confident, referring to the sinking of the unsinkable ship. His poem ends with a reference to the biblical Book of Lamentations (which describes the destruction of the First Temple in Jerusalem). The poem has an inevitable comparison between the disaster of the *Titanic* and the destruction of the First Temple.

Of all the songs, poem, ballads, and lamentations, the song that is most identified with the ship's sinking is a hymn written seventy years before the disaster. The song is "Nearer My God to Thee," its words loosely based on the biblical story of Jacob's dream. The motif of the song is calling to God for guidance in the dark hours. The words were written in 1841 and have absolutely nothing to do with the *Titanic*:

Nearer, my God, to Thee, nearer to Thee!
E'en though it be a cross,
That raiseth me,
Still all my song shall be,
Nearer, my God, to Thee,
Nearer, my God, to Thee, nearer to Thee,
Though like the wanderer, the sun gone down,
Darkness be over me, my rest a stone,
Yet in my dreams I'd be,
Nearer, my God, to Thee,
Nearer, my God, to Thee, nearer to Thee…

This hymn became part of the *Titanic* legacy after the disaster since many survivors claimed that this was one of the songs that the band played as the ship sank. Many survivors even claimed that "Nearer My God to Thee" was actually the last song that the band played when the water reached the upper deck, the ship was noticeably listing, and most of the lifeboats were gone. Several survivors claimed that they heard the hymn from the lifeboats. For decades historians and researchers have argued about the *Titanic's* last song. Walter Lord dedicated an entire chapter to the dispute in his book *The Night Lives On*. Although he was assisted by the testimonies and claims of many survivors, even he could not determine if the band actually played during those final moments, and if they did, what song they played.[219]

In the 1960s one of the Jewish survivors, Edith Rosenbaum (Russell) said in an interview to a British TV network: "I do not doubt that they were playing music. Other people heard it. But when people say that music was played as the ship went down, that is a ghastly horrible lie."[220] Another Jewish survivor insisted that "Nearer My God to Thee" was not *Titanic's* last song.

If "Nearer My God to Thee" was not the last song played, what was? Some claim that it was a tune by the name of *Songe d'Automne*, a waltz that was written in 1908 by Archibald Joyce. *Songe d'Automne* was in fact familiar to the band and passengers because it was part of the repertoire of the White Star Line. Other witnesses claim that it was another song with a similar name: "Autumn," a hymn written in 1785. Either way, there are those who claim (as Edith Rosenbaum pointed out) that the band could not have played anything during the *Titanic's* final hour. The ship was listing too steeply and it would have been nearly impossible for the band to stand steadily on the deck and play. Water was washing onto the deck. The band playing with water up their knees is only a myth. Moreover, the *Titanic* had two separate groups (a trio and a five-piece ensemble). The two groups did not mix during the voyage. In addition, one member of the band was a pianist and three were cellists, and it would have been impractical to drag the piano and cellos to the deck. Most *Titanic* researchers today believe that the eight band members did not play until the final moments. With all the contradicting testimonies and opinions, we will never know what the band played or what their final song was. Whatever the truth may be, "Nearer My God to Thee" will forever be associated with the sinking of the *Titanic* and has become one of the tragedy's symbols.[221]

The tragedy has been commemorated in song for over a century. New pieces were regularly added to the long list of songs, hymns, and ballads. Debbie Guzzi, a Jewish American poet, wrote a touching poem in the memory of an unknown third-class couple, the Friedbergs. Guzzi comments that Typkia is not a Jewish name, but Tikvah is a Hebrew women's name, and the word *tikvah* means hope. (Typkia and Tikvah do seem to be similar words). The husband's name is unknown. Guzzi also comments that survivors spoke about the couple. Guzzi suggests naming Typkia Tikvah and her husband Hershel. The poem was therefore entitled *Tikvah and Hershel.*[222] It has six stanzas and begins with the words:

> Gone I am. Sure as the sea rolls over the bones of the deep
> Gone is Tikvah, gone is hope, gone as so many Jewish brides
> From history in the guises placed upon them by gentiles.
> All who chose to remember at all, name me Typkia Friedberg.

The poem ends with the words:

> Up one level I made it, clothes in tatters, scratched and bleeding
> And then I too fell, under the boot heels of passengers.
> I do not rest beside my Hershel, yet with my last breath, I cried
> "Mother, mother you will never met him now."
> My dear, my heart, for before the *Titanic* ever sunk, we died.

15

FILM ADAPTATIONS

In a heavy *Ashkenazi* accent, a Jewish male recites a Hebrew prayer: "*Ve'ahavta et Adonay Eloheycha bechol levavcha…*" (Deuteronomy 6:5).

This Hebrew prayer (translated: "And thou shalt love the Lord, thy God, with all thy heart…") is part of the *Shema*, a prayer very familiar to religious Jews that is said during morning and evening prayers and is also part of the Jewish confession ritual before death. This particular Jewish worshiper does so during the final moments while the *Titanic* is disappearing from sight.

This is part of a scene from the 1958 film *A Night to Remember*, based on a book of that title by Walter Lord published in 1955. It is unclear if this Jewish passenger is sitting safely in a lifeboat or is standing on the stern of the ship and waiting for it to end. If a victim, he could have been any one of the dozens of Jewish victims. If he is a survivor, who is he? The first-class Jewish survivors were not observant, and there weren't any second-class Jewish male survivors. Only three Jewish men from third class survived: Abraham Hyman, Berk Trembisky, and Gershon Cohen.

Walter Lord, *Titanic* researcher, mentions in the acknowledgments for *A Night to Remember* that many survivors helped him with hsi research. He does not name them all, but he does mention Gershon Cohen, who he nicknames "Gus." He thanks him for "recreating the atmosphere that prevailed in steerage, [the] long-neglected side of the story."[223] Maybe Lord wanted to pay tribute to Cohen by giving his character the honor of reciting the *Shema* in his film.

Whether or not a Jewish passenger reciting the *Shema* was on board the sinking ship and not in a lifeboat, this scene honors Jewish passengers, both survivors and victims.

Many films about the *Titanic* were made. The first *Titanic* film was released in the United States on May 14, 1912, exactly a month after the disaster. It was a silent motion picture entitled *Saved from the Titanic* and starred Dorothy Gibson, a survivor. In the film, she wore the same clothes as she did during the disaster. Gibson also co-wrote the script. Today the film does not exist because all known copies were destroyed in a fire in 1914.

E D E N HALL, Jerusalem.
To-day at 6:45 and 9 p.m.
"ATLANTIC" — All English Talking
Film (The tragedy of the "Titanic")

Titanic *film (1929) in Jerusalem. Source:* Bulletin, *December 2, 1931*

Another *Titanic* film released in 1912 (in August) was a German film entitled *In Nacht und Eis* (*In Night and Ice*), also known as *Der Untergang der Titanic* (*The Sinking of the Titanic*).

This thirty-minute silent film describes the experiences of the passengers throughout the voyage, the collision with the iceberg, and the lowering of women and children into the lifeboats. The film also emphasizes the radio operator's heroic attempts to call for help.

In 1929 *Atlantic* was released, the first *Titanic* "talkie" (a non-silent film). Four versions of the film were made simultaneously: English, German, French, and one silent version. The plot is fiction and takes place on a large ocean liner named the *Atlantic* that collides with an iceberg and sinks. In the English version, there is a scene where an elderly woman named Mrs. Rool refuses to leave her husband, and she dies with her husband (the scene obviously imitates the story of Ida Straus). In the German version, the Jewish-German actor Fritz Kortner (1892–1970) played a leading role.* The film was successful and was played in Tel Aviv during the early 1930s.[224]

During World War II, Nazi Germany released a film about the *Titanic*. The film was directed and promoted by Nazi propaganda minister Josef Goebbels. The film was titled simply *Titanic*. The theme was not anti-Semitic but rather anti-American and anti-British. The film described the poor conduct of the British officers who eventually doomed the ship as if the greed of the British and Americans was responsible for the collision. The film also praised the heroic behavior of the "German" immigrants who chose to die as gentlemen and let their wives live as opposed to the cowardly first-class "British" male passengers who attempted to escape.

*After the Nazis came to power, Kortner, being Jewish, fled from Germany to the United States.

Whoever searches for a reference to Straus or Guggenheim in this film will be disappointed. Although Ida's heroic act was acknowledged and appreciated, her story did not suit the agenda of the film. Of course, no Jewish heroic act would be reenacted in a Nazi propaganda film. The absence of the Straus couple is noticeable, especially when the film is full of fictional characters. The tragic hero of the German film is a fictional German officer named Peterson who is the only German officer on the ship, while all other officers, including the captain, are British. In the film, during the voyage Peterson is accused by his fellow officers of deliberately trying to prevent the *Titanic* from winning a world speed record. The captain attempts to break the speed record held by a German ship. Therefore, Peterson's sincere concern for passengers is seen by the captain as sabotage. While this is being portrayed, the *Titanic* received wireless ice warnings.

Ida and Isidor are not mentioned, but there is a reference to a similar (yet fictional) story. As the lifeboats are lowered, a woman called Sigrid refuses to leave without her "male companion." Her male companion is (of all people) Officer Peterson, who says, "Sigrid, you must get into this lifeboat and leave the ship." But Sigrid replies, "No! I will go when you go," practically quoting Ida. As opposed to the true story of the Jewish elderly couple (Ida and Isidor), the German film illustrates the fictional story of the young and energetic Peterson (the hero of the film) and his "girlfriend," a wealthy woman who was traveling alone and fell for the officer. The ending of the "love story" is different too. As opposed to the true story, Peterson does not accept her refusal, orders her into the lifeboat, and she obeys.

Peterson performed other heroic acts. Toward the end of the film, he finds a weeping young girl, jumps into the water, and swims with her to a lifeboat. The film's message was clear. The only officer of the *Titanic* who acted with honor was the German one. The only officer with a human heart, compassionate, is the German one. To contrast Peterson's behavior, the film

Cinema RIMON
TEL AVIV
Sunday night and during the week:
The story of the great sea tragedy

"TITANIC"

With Fritz Kortner
and Francis Lederer.

In April, 1912, the greatest of all steamers, the leviathan of the seas, the glorious "Titanic" carrying 2,358 passengers went under. A moving story vividly reproduced on the screen
German speaking.
B.I P. London Production.

MATINEES:
Martha-Eggerth and Jan Kiepura in
"MY HEART IS CALLING YOU."

Titanic *film (1929) in Tel Aviv.* Source: *Palestine Post, May 14, 1937* showed the negative behavior of the British officers. In one scene, a British officer shoots aimlessly at a group of third-class German immigrants as they attempted to reach the higher decks of the ship.

Although he was the mastermind behind the making of the film, Goebbels banned it after a short run in German-occupied Europe. The film was a big hit in Europe, but Goebbels thought that the film weakened instead of strengthened German morale. The plot described many German casualties, "victims" of the disaster. There was fear that the film would gain support among British and American viewers.

While millions of Jews across Europe were murdered by the Nazis, the German adaptation of the *Titanic* story portrayed the fictional segregation of poor German immigrants locked below decks and prevented from escaping. In reality, as the *Titanic* was sinking, the stewards in third class called for "women and children first," but in the German film the steward tried to separate the men from the women by calling (in German) for "men on the starboard side, women and children on the port side," followed by a group of stewards who physically (and forcedly) separated the two genders. The pinnacle of the irony is when an officer whistles and yells: "*Schnell! Schneller!*" (Quick! Quicker!). It is a striking contrast to see the fictional yet cruel depiction of the crewmen while something real and much crueler was happening. When the film was produced, Nazis were gassing Jews in death camps. While a fictional crewmember was yelling "*Schnell!*" at a group of fictional Germans, real German officers were yelling "*Schnell!*" at real Jews as they were forced into gas chambers. To make things even more haunting, many of the extras used in the film were actual German soldiers.

As a German film with an anti-British agenda during World War II, the final scene is of the inquiry where the "Board of Trade" accused the British captain and crew for the disaster. The film ends with the following caption:

The deaths of 1,500 people remain unatoned for . . .
An eternal condemnation of England's quest for profit

Most of the film was shot on the *Cap Arcona*, a German ocean liner. She was the largest and fastest ocean liner on the German-South American route. Similar to the *Titanic*, the *Cap Arcona* held wealthy passengers in first class, many second-class passengers, and hundreds of immigrants in third class. In

1940 she was seized by the German navy, the *kriegsmarine*, and converted into a ship used as a floating barracks for German troops during the war.

Because she was one of the largest passenger ships in Germany, the *Cap Arcona* was seized in 1942 by the Ministry of Propaganda especially for the film.

Ironically Otto Wernicke, the German actor who played Captain Smith, was married to a Jewish woman and had to bribe the Nazi party for a special permit to be able to work in Nazi Germany.

After the film was completed, the *Cap Arcona* was used as an evacuation ship, and toward the end of the war it was used for the evacuation of over 25,000 German troops from East Prussia as the Soviet Army advanced on the eastern front. As the Allies closed in on the German Army, the *Cap Arcona* was converted into a prison ship and became part of a prison flotilla. Concentration camps were emptied, and thousands of prisoners were transferred to prison ships.

Tragically, the fates of the *Cap Arcona* and *Titanic* were not too different. On May 3, 1945, two years after the *Cap Arcona* was part of a film set, the British Royal Air Force attacked the flotilla in the Baltic Sea. On board the *Cap Arcona*

The Cap Arcona *ablaze after the British attack, 1944. Source: Wikimedia Commons*

were over 5,000 prisoners, many of them Jewish, who were to be executed by order of S.S. and Gestapo leader Heinrich Himmler. After the British war planes started the attack, many of the prisoners jumped into the water in an attempt to swim to shore. Most of them were murdered by the Germans who gunned them down. This was one of the largest number of deaths from an attack on a ship in World War II.* The *Cap Arcona* was sunk only three days

---

According to a 2012 History Channel documentary about the Nazi Titanic *film, the German army deliberately loaded the* Cap Arcona *with prisoners, knowing that the British Royal Air Force would attack the ship. This way the Germans could dispose the prisoners and put the blame on the British.*

after Hitler's suicide and one day before the official unconditional surrender of the German Army to the Allies. The death toll on the *Cap Arcona* was three times the *Titanic's*. Of all the *Titanic* film adaptations, the 1943 German epic was the most political and controversial.

In 1953, ten years after the Nazi film, a *Titanic* film was released by 20th Century Fox. Entitled simply *Titanic*, the plot depicts a (fictional) married couple. The woman kidnaps her two children (aged ten and eighteen) from their father and takes them on the *Titanic*. The father discovers this, buys a last-minute third-class ticket, and boards at Cherbourg.

This is the first *Titanic* film where Ida and Isidor Straus were mentioned by name. Their characters are referred to and appear several times in the film. Toward the end, as women are being lowered into lifeboats, Second Officer Lightoller offered Ida a seat. She refused, yet he persisted as it was the last lifeboat. She replied, "Please, sir, I am a very old lady. I have been with Mr. Straus most of my life, and I will not leave him now." Lightoller sighs and gives the order to lower the lifeboat. Ida and Isidor embrace and watch as the lifeboat was lowered.

Benjamin Guggenheim is also featured in the film, but his character is uncredited. In one of the first scenes, the purser sends off several bellhops with gifts and bouquets to the wealthy passengers. The first bellhop is sent with a bouquet to the Astors. The second bellhop is sent off with several gifts to Ben Guggenheim. In another scene, Guggenheim plays cards with several passengers.

Titanic *survivor Edith Rosenbaum (Russell) with actress Therase Thorne who played her in* A Night to Remember, *1958. Source: National Maritime Museum Archives*

The next *Titanic* film to be released was *A Night to Remember*, the most accurate and successful *Titanic* film ever made. There were historical mistakes regarding the sinking of the ship, but the film was made twenty years before the remains of the *Titanic* were found and based on the official inquiries. In all *Titanic* films before the 1980s, the ship sank in one piece, but only after the *Titanic* was found at the bottom of the Atlantic Ocean was it known that the ship had broken in two.

Several Jewish passengers are seen in *A Night to Remember*. Apart from reciting the *Shema* as the ship went down (as previously mentioned), there are other Jewish-related scenes and accounts.

Edith Rosenbaum appears several times in the film. In one scene, as the first-class passengers are taken to the lifeboats, Edith goes to her stateroom to fetch her lucky toy pig. A stewardess tells her to return to the Boat Deck. Edith is referred to as Miss Russell, her Americanized name. The stewardess says: "Miss Russell, I thought you had gone to the boats," to whom she replies: "My pig. I must have my lucky pig." She then unlocks her stateroom door, takes "Maxixe," her toy pig, and leaves. The drawers are left unlocked. In reality, she locked every trunk, drawer, and window and left with the toy pig and with nineteen keys.

Toward the end of the film, after the *Titanic* sinks, Edith is in a lifeboat holding the toy pig as it plays a tune. Doing so calms a frightened little girl. In reality Edith did calm several children with her toy pig.

After the ship sinks, there is a scene where a young woman cries: "My baby! My baby!" Of the 304 women survivors, only one lost her baby during the evacuation: Leah Aks, whose baby was torn away and thrown overboard. Not knowing that he landed safely in another lifeboat, Leah assumed that she has lost her baby forever. Many years later Walter Lord befriended Frank Aks. In his acknowledgments to his bestseller *The Night Lives On*, Lord mentions Frank and comments that "Frank Aks is as chipper as ever." Little baby Aks was fifty-seven at the time.

Walter Lord describes the famous Straus story in his book, and their story is depicted in the film. This time, several other passengers try to convince Ida to enter a lifeboat. In this scene, Ismay tried to urge people to get into the lifeboats.

Isidor faces Ida: "Please, Rachel, get in the boat."*

Isidor's friend Colonel Archibald Gracie adds: "Yes, Mrs. Straus, you must."

This is one of the most famous goofs in A Night to Remember. *Mrs. Straus's name is Ida, but in this particular scene she is accidently referred to as Rachel.*

Ida faces him and replies: "I've always stayed with my husband, Colonel, so why should I leave him now?"

Isidor: "Please be sensible."

Ida: "We have been living together for many years, Isidor. Where you go, I go."

Archibald Gracie: "I'm sure nobody would object to an old gentleman like Mr. Straus going in a boat. I'll ask the officer."

Isidor: "No! I will not go before the other men."

Ida: "We stay."

The couple is last seen holding on to a rail and to each other.

Jewish actress Helen Misener (1907–1960) portrayed Ida, and Jewish actor Meier Tzelinker (1894–1980) portrayed Isidor. Both actors portrayed Jewish characters in several films and Yiddish plays throughout their careers.

Isidor's heavy Jewish-German accent is noticeable in the film. Several Jewish film critics were offended by this, as were descendants of Ida and Isidor. Their claim was that the film described Isidor as an old-fashioned Jewish-German immigrant, yet he had been born in the United States and spoke English without an accent.

That was not the worst or most embarrassing portrayal of Isidor on screen. In 1957, in an episode of the American television series *Telephone Time*, the Straus's are depicted as an ultra-religious Jewish couple. In one scene, after Ida decides to stay with Isidor, the two are seen in their stateroom together. In this extremely inaccurate scene, Isidor is dressed as a rabbi, with a *talit* and a huge *kippah*, sitting at his desk, reading out of a Jewish book to Ida, who is sitting beside him. If the scene in *A Night to Remember* was inaccurate, insulting, and offensive, the scene in *Telephone Time* is even worse. It is distasteful and shows ignorance.

In *A Night to Remember*, Benjamin Guggenheim was played by Jewish actor Harold (Israel) Goldblatt (1899–1982), born in Manchester, England. He later moved to Belfast where he joined the Jewish congregation. In a scene in *A Night to Remember*, a steward assists Guggenheim with his life vest, yet Ben is uncomfortable and wants his valet. In a later scene, chief engineer Thomas Andrews sees Guggenheim in the first-class reception room and tries to convince him to wear a life vest. Guggenheim replies with his famous line: "It was uncomfortable. We have dressed now in our best and are prepared to go down like gentlemen."

Another Jewish passenger depicted in *A Night to Remember* is Charles

Stengel, seen in Lifeboat 1 along with Sir Cosmo Duff Gordon. In one scene, they ask the officer for permission to enter the lifeboat. In another scene they discuss returning to the sinking ship to pick up survivors but decide not to. There are several mistakes in the Lifeboat 1 scenes in *A Night to Remember*. For example, in the film, three men (not two) enter the lifeboat after Sir Cosmo Duff Gordon and his wife.

A Night to Remember became a great hit in England and United States and still continues to receive praise. The film has won several awards, including the Samuel Goldwyn International Award at the Golden Globe Awards ceremony in 1959. Until the ship was found in 1985, the film was considered one of the most accurate of all *Titanic* films.

The first *Titanic* film in color was the television film *S.O.S. Titanic,* shown in England and the United States in 1979. Jewish passengers portrayed in *S.O.S. Titanic* were Henry and René Harris, Ida and Isidor Straus, and Benjamin Guggenheim.

In 1992 Jewish actor Leonard Nimoy narrated a *Titanic* documentary about the wreckage; it included footage of the expedition that searched for the lost ship. Eva Hart, one of the few living survivors at the time, was interviewed for the documentary.

Dozens of *Titanic* films and documentaries have been produced yet the most famous and successful was the 1997 blockbuster *Titanic* directed by Canadian filmmaker James Cameron; it won eleven Academy Awards, including Best Picture and Best Director. Cameron hired a team of underwater researchers that used a Russian research vessel, the *Keldysh*, and the *Mir* submersibles to dive to the wreck, film it, and add the footage to the film.

In Cameron's *Titanic*, Guggenheim's last words are said, but this time with a little twist. After he is offered a life vest, he replies, "No, thank you. We are dressed in our best and are prepared to go down as gentlemen. But we would like a brandy." Then he is shown sitting in a chair at the Grand Entrance, watching in horror as the water draws near.

Again Ida and Isidor are shown together as the ship sinks. This time the two share their final moments embracing in bed as the room floods, with the hymn "Nearer My God to Thee" playing in the background. Cameron decided that it would be more dramatic this way.

In Cameron's *Titanic*, Ida Straus was played by Jewish-American actress Elsa Raven (Rabinowitz); Isidor was played by American actor Lew Palter.

The famous "where you go I go" scene is not in the 1997 *Titanic*, nor is the Straus couple seen on the Boat Deck during the night. Yet the famous scene with the two was added in the 2012 rerelease of the film. This version, known as *Titanic in 3D*, was part of the one hundred-year commemoration of the disaster.

Isidor: "Get into the boat."

Ida refuses: "No! We have been together for forty years, and where you go, I go."

Then Ida adds: "Do not argue with me, Isidor; you know it does no good."

Isidor nods his head in consent and the two embrace. End of scene.

As the women and children are loaded into lifeboats, there is a scene where a father tells his daughter: "Hold Mommy's hand and be a good little girl." This is a reference to the Hart family from second class. Those were almost the exact words that Benjamin spoke to Eva as she went into the lifeboat with her mother, Esther. An interview with Eva was included in a documentary about the film.

Besides film and documentaries, plays were also dedicated to the *Titanic* tragedy. In 2012 the Jewish-Canadian actor David Eisner portrayed Benjamin Guggenheim in a short television series named *Titanic* (a four-part television drama based on the passengers during the sinking). Eisner is the cofounder of the Harold Green Jewish Theatre in Toronto. In 1997 Jewish-American actress Alma Cuervo portrayed Ida Straus in *Titanic*, a Tony Award-winning musical.

Television shows also have paid tribute to the tragedy. In 1966 the first episode of *The Time Tunnel* was dedicated to the *Titanic*. Arriving on board the ship one day before the disaster, the two time travelers try in vain to warn the captain and crew. Other shows have paid homage to the *Titanic* story, including *Futurama* (1999), in which the largest spaceship ever built, called the *Titanic*, is torn in half by a black hole on its maiden voyage, and *Doctor Who* (2007), about a luxury space cruiser, *Titanic*, that crashes into a time machine.

The *Titanic* was no longer just a sunken ship or the story of an ocean liner colliding with an iceberg and sinking with 1,500 people on board. It became a myth.

16

THE *TITANIC* AS A METAPHOR

In 1998 the Jewish-American Hall of Fame created a special commemorative medal in honor of the *Titanic* Jews. Portraits of Ida and Isidor Straus appear on one side. On the other is radio operator David Sarnoff sitting in his radio station. In a catalog the medal is described this way:

> Following the *Titanic* disaster, young 21-year-old David Sarnoff remained glued to his wireless earphones in New York for 72 hours straight, and was one of the first to relay the names of the survivors from the *Carpathia's* telegraph operator to newsmen and frantic family members.[225]

Ida's famous quote "Where you go, I go" is inscribed on the medal, which was designed by Alex Shagin and Mel Wacks.

Over the years, the *Titanic* has become a metaphor, a symbol, an allegory. While being built, and as her maiden voyage drew near, she was described as a modern Tower of Babel. After the disaster the comparison deepened. Many people viewed the *Titanic* as a failure of humans against nature, a fight against God, an attempt to create a man-made machine that could not be handled. A century later the *Titanic* is viewed as an allegory for bad habits of those

Commemorative medal struck by Jewish American Hall of Fame. Dedicated to the victims of the Titanic *and to Jewish hero David Sarnoff. Photo credit: Eli Moskowitz*

who are blind to the warnings that surround them, blind to their friends who try to save them. It's an allegory for the habits of those who sail blindly and thus collide into their very own iceberg or those who sail to their unavoidable bitter end. Rabbis, philosophers, publicists, writers, and politicians used the *Titanic* as a proverb to warn their followers and return them to the right track.

Prior to the Israeli 2012 elections, the left-wing publicist Uri Avnery used the *Titanic* allegory to describe the political situation in Israel under the right-wing government. In an article named "Mutiny on the *Titanic*," published in *Haaretz*, he compared the situation in the state of Israel to the *Titanic's* collision with the iceberg:

> The State of Israel is similar to the *Titanic*. A luxurious ocean liner, whose owners proudly announced is unsinkable. The iceberg is already seen in the horizon, but on the ship's bridge they are arguing. About what? The crew wants to re-elect a new captain. The captain claims that only he can sail the ship to safety. What is his proof? He has never grounded his ship before.[226]

Avnery describes the situation in the ship (and uses the *Titanic* as a metaphor for the country). The crew demanded higher wages and better food. The passengers complained about the cramped conditions; they demanded social justice and an end to the discrimination between the classes. Avnery described the situation in Israel and suggested his solution for the political problem. He concluded, "If the ship does not change course, she will hit the iceberg. The inevitable end is known."[227]

Other Israelis used the *Titanic* for political reasons too. Former *Knesset* member Haim Ramon once compared the *Titanic* to the corrupt situation in the *Histadrut* (the Israeli organization of trade unions), which he directed at the time. In 2003 he said:

> The truth is that I inherited a large ocean liner with a long and magnificent history. But this *Titanic* was hollow and rickety. And she was on her way to the bottom of the sea. Her passengers were still partying and dancing on the decks . . . that was the true picture of the *Histadrut*.[228]

Nine years later, Ramon himself was compared to the *Titanic* in an article in *Makor Rishon*, as he was attempting to become a *Knesset* member again, this time with the *Kadima* party:

> Those who board the new ship that Haim Ramon is building need to take into account... this is not *Noah's Ark*. This ship is not a sanctuary during a great flood that will engulf the *Kadima* members. Whoever boards Ramon's ship will board the *Titanic*.[229]

Even the disappearance of *Kadima* from the Israeli political world was compared to the *Titanic*. A political blogger wrote in 2012 about the arrogance and lack of cooperation among the members of *Kadima*: "They flee *Kadima* like rats that flee a sinking ship. *Kadima* is the *Titanic* of Israeli politics."[230]

During the struggle against the Israeli Disengagement from Gaza in 2005, there were *Titanic* allegories. The right-wing parties and movements

"Sharon is sinking the country!" An inflatable "Titanic" used as a visual concept at a demonstration against the dismantling of Israeli settlements from the Gaza Strip. Photo credit: Avigdor Shatz

tried in vain to dissuade Prime Minister Ariel Sharon and his government from uprooting Israeli settlements in the Gaza Strip. In one of the major demonstrations held across the street from the *Knesset* building, a large inflatable *Titanic* was erected alongside a banner that read: "Sharon is sinking the country!" In the months before the Disengagement, many other comparisons were made, some less subtle, such as the use of the yellow Star of David and other Holocaust symbols. The Disengagement was also compared to the expulsion from Spain in 1492 and the destruction of the Second Temple in Jerusalem. Sharon was compared to Titus.

Hasidic movements also use the *Titanic* allegory, comparing today's world Jewry to a sinking ship. In the Chabad movement, *Eretz Yisrael* is the lifeboat where all the Jews will find refuge from anti-Semitism, religious persecution, assimilation, and loss of Jewish identity. When Rabbi Menachem Mendel Schneersohn (1902–1994), the seventh (and last) Lubavitcher Rebbe and one of the most influential Jewish leaders of the twentieth century, was asked why he did not make *Aliyah* (immigrate to Israel), he said that first the weak and faltering Jews should be taken to Israel, and only then could he and his devotees follow. The Lubavitcher Rebbe's repetitive theme is that the captain (the rabbi) will save his community, his followers, before he saves himself, similar to the *Titanic's* captain.

In a meeting with an Israeli Army official, the Lubavitcher Rebbe said that every army general should march at the front of his troops, but when a ship sinks, the captain cannot be in the front because he needs to stay back until his passengers are safe. The *Titanic* was a great example for the Lubavitcher Rebbe. The passengers were like the assimilating Jews, and the lifeboat is *Eretz Yisrael*. Although he himself did not make *Aliyah,* he encouraged Jews to come to Israel.

In their sermons, many rabbis talk about the dangers of assimilation in the Diaspora. The sinking ship represents assimilation and mixed marriages, while the lifeboats symbolizes Jewish education, maintaining a Jewish home, and keeping a strong bond to Israel and Jewish identity.

On May 21, 2012, a segment on *60 Minutes*, a television program broadcast by CBS, focused on Tel Aviv and compared the city to the *Titanic* before the disaster. The segment was not about assimilation or anti-Semitism. It was about the behavior of the citizens of Tel Aviv. After so many terrorist attacks on the city (the Iraqi scuds during the Gulf War, the Palestinian suicide bombers in the streets, the missile threat from Hezbollah in the north, and the missile threat from Hamas in the south), residents of Tel Aviv were apathetic, living as if there were no tomorrow. Bob Simon, the interviewer, asked: "Do you ever feel like you are dancing on the *Titanic*?" questioning why people in Tel Aviv were not worried. Simon also commented, "There are more bars than synagogues in this city."[231]

Viewing the *Titanic* as careless or immoral behavior is also found in Hasidic children's books. *The Amazing Journey to Noble Values* describes a fictional ship, the *Ga'avtanic,** which sails the seas of deeds. Passengers behave badly and selfishly, and only by being good can they save their ship. The drawings of ships in this children's book resemble the *Titanic*.[232]

Another example is a Hasidic two-part comic book series about a fictitious rich secular Jew named Moshe Gross who turns religious after surviving the *Titanic* disaster. Much of the plot takes place on board the ship, and many details of the disaster are inaccurate.[233]

The *Titanic* is frequently used metaphorically and compared to other maritime disasters. In January 2012, when the cruise ship *Costa Concordia* capsized and sank after hitting an underwater rock, the disaster was compared to the *Titanic*. The technological systems were much more sophisticated, and so were maritime safety regulations. The *Costa Concordia* had enough lifeboats for all passengers and crew. The ship carried over 4,200 passengers and crew at the time, and "only" thirty-two people who were trapped in the ship's hull died.[234]

Several Jews from the United States and England and seven Israelis were among the passengers of the *Costa Concordia*. Moshe Ashkenazi, one of the Israeli survivors, said: "The whole time the *Titanic* went through our minds. We hoped that this will not end in the same way." All Israelis were saved. Some American Jews went missing. Also it is said that an Italian survivor of the *Costa Concordia* was a granddaughter of a *Titanic* survivor.[235]

The disaster was extensively covered by international media. the *Costa Concordia* disaster happened only three months prior to the 100th year anniversary of the sinking of the *Titanic*. Several *Costa Concordia* survivors claimed that as the ship was sinking, the song "My Heart Will Go On" was

---

*The word Ga'avtanic is a compound word. Ga'ava is Hebrew for "pride," or "arrogance." The ending nic is a reference to the Titanic. The word Ga'avtanic is a Hebrew play on words.

playing on the ship's loudspeakers. (The song, sung by Celine Dion, was the main theme of Cameron's blockbuster in 1997.)

There are conspiracy theories surrounding the *Titanic's* sinking. One of the most famous of them is the one where the *Titanic* never sank at all. According to this particular theory, the White Star Line had to cover up the damage after the *Olympic* collided with the *Hawke*. The accident occurred several months before the *Titanic's* maiden voyage, so the company decided it would cost less to sink the *Olympic* deliberately and collect the insurance rather than to risk using a damaged ship.[236] To do so, they switched the two ships, which were identical, and intentionally sailed the *Titanic* into an iceberg-infested area. The switch was possible in the beginning of 1912 when both ships were docking side by side in Belfast. If this conspiracy theory was true, the ship that collided with an iceberg and sank on April 14 was actually the *Olympic*.[237]

Another theory, even more far-fetched, is one involving the Jesuits. According to this conspiracy theory, one goal of the Jesuits is to accumulate wealth. J. P. Morgan, one of the owners of the White Star Line, was a Jesuit. In 1910 he tried to convince some of the most influential men of his day to establish a powerful central bank. Benjamin Guggenheim, Isidor Straus, and John Jacob Astor opposed the idea, and the White Star Line decided to eliminate the three. They were persuaded to travel on the company's new and luxurious ocean liner. Captain Smith, who was also a Jesuit, was instructed to sail the ship into an iceberg and deliberately sink it, killing the three men. According to this conspiracy theory, the *Titanic* was built for this purpose.[238]

It is hard to understand how such a magnificent ship sank on her maiden voyage, and the disaster has fascinated many people. Conspiracy theories were developed to understand the disaster better by believing the collision was on purpose. As stated, though, if only the crew had binoculars or paid careful attention to the ice warnings, the ship would have arrived in New York. Since there were so many ways the disaster could have been averted, this is why the *Titanic* is so interesting.

17

LIFE AND DEATH OF THE *TITANIC* JEWS

Titanic passengers came from more than thirty countries. Most were British or American, but many were from Russia, Finland, Canada, and Sweden. Some were from Thailand, Peru, Mexico, Syria, India, and Portugal. Most Jewish passengers were British, American, or immigrants from Russia and Eastern Europe.

Benjamin Hart, Eva Hart's father, was born in 1869 in England to Solomon and Rhoda Hart, Jewish immigrants from Poland. Benjamin married Esther (Ada) Hart (nee Bloomfield), born in 1863. They lived in Ilford, England. Eva was born in 1905 and was their only daughter. In 1912 they decided to immigrate to Winnipeg, Canada. Esther did not want to leave, but Benjamin had trouble supporting the family. In Canada it was possible to improve their lives. Benjamin was a carpenter and planned to work in the construction business in Canada. Benjamin, Esther, and Eva boarded the *Titanic* in Southampton and traveled second class. Their ticket cost them 26£ 5s. After helping his wife and child into the lifeboat, Benjamin remained on deck, and his body was never found.[239]

Jewish diamond dealer Jacob Birnbaum was born in 1887 in Krakow, Poland, the second son of nine children of Joachim Yerucham (1856–1931) and Hannah Theophilia Birnbaum (1863–1931). Jacob was single and quite religious. The family immigrated to Antwerp, where Jacob worked in diamond trading. He became the family representative in San Francisco. In 1912 he visited his family on a business trip, and they insisted that he stay in Antwerp for Passover. He agreed to stay for *Seder* night and then postponed his trip a second time due to the coal strike. The first available ship was the *Titanic,* which he boarded at Cherbourg. He traveled first class and his ticket cost him 26£. His family asked him not to go on a ship's first voyage, but although Jacob reassured them that the ship was unsinkable, he died when the ship went down.[240]

Sinai (Sehua) Kantor, a furrier, was born in 1878 and his wife, Miriam Kantor (nee Sternin), was born in 1888. Both were Jewish and both were from Witebsk, Belarus. Sinai and Miriam decided to immigrate to the Bronx, New York. They took several crates with furs to sell in New York. With the money they planned to study dentistry. Both were university graduates. They boarded the *Titanic* at Southampton and traveled second class with a shared ticket that cost them 26£. Miriam survived, but Sinai drowned.[241]

Jewish businessman Emil (Franklin) Brandeis was born in Manitowoc, Wisconsin, in 1864. His parents, Jonas (1834–1903) and Francesca (1845–1905), immigrated to the United States from Bohemia in 1856. Jonas Brandeis sold dry goods in a store called J. L. Brandeis & Sons. After Jonas's death, Emil ran the store with his brothers, Arthur and Hugo. The family moved to Omaha, Nebraska. In January 1912 Emil, who was single, went to Europe and saw his niece Ruth (Arthur's daughter) in Italy. He also traveled to Switzerland, Spain, and the Middle East. He planned to return to the United States in May, but when he realized that he could sail on the *Titanic's* maiden voyage, he altered his plans. He boarded the *Titanic* at Cherbourg and traveled first class. He paid 50£ 9s for stateroom B10. While on board he met several good friends, including Henry and René Harris and John Bauman. In a letter he wrote before departure, he mentioned that he planned to meet Isidor Straus as well. That was his last letter, as Emil drowned.[242]

René Harris (nee Wallach) was born in 1876 in New York. She studied law, worked as a secretary in a law firm, and was an actress. In 1898 she married Henry (Birkhardt) Harris, born in 1866 in St. Louis, Missouri, who managed the Hudson Theater in New York. His parents Rachel (nee Freefield) and William Harris were also in the theater business. Henry and René did not have children. The theater was successful, and they opened theaters in Chicago and Philadelphia. Both René and Henry were Jewish. Henry had warm feelings toward his Jewish background and was a trustee of the Hebrew Infant Asylum in New York. In April 1912 Henry and René were returning to New York after a tour in Europe. They boarded at Southampton and traveled first class, with tickets which cost them 83£ 9s for stateroom C83. The Harrises were good friends with other Jewish passengers including

Emil Brandeis, John Bauman, and the Strauses. Similar to many couples, René survived the disaster, but Henry died.[243]

Edgar Josef Meyer was born in 1884 in San Francisco. His father Eugene, born in Germany, was a merchant and later a banker. Edgar's mother, Harriett Meyer (nee Newmark) was born in New York. Both Edger's parents were Jewish. Edger, the youngest of eight children, studied mechanical engineering and was vice president of a copper company in New York. Edgar married Leila (Leah) Saks, who was born in 1886 in Baltimore. Her parents were Andrew and Jennie Saks (nee Rohl), both Jewish. Andrew Saks founded a men's clothing and dry goods house by the name Saks & Co. Leah had two siblings. Edgar and Leah Meyer had a daughter, Jane, who was born in 1911. While Jane was home in New York, Edgar and Leah traveled to Europe and spent the winter there. Hearing that Leah's father, Andrew, had passed away in New York after a long illness, the two bought tickets to sail back home. The first available ship was the *Titanic,* and their ticket cost them 82£ 3s. They boarded at Cherbourg and traveled first class. During the disaster, Edgar convinced Leah to enter a lifeboat only after reminding her of their baby waiting for her at home. Edgar did not survive.[244]

Leopold Weisz was born in 1875 in Veszprém, Hungary, to Jewish parents. He immigrated to England and studied architecture. He married Mathilde, a Catholic woman from Belgium. Both sets of parents opposed the marriage. The two lived in England for a while, but Leopold sailed on board the *Lusitania* in 1911 to immigrate to Montreal, Canada, where he found work in architecture. Among the buildings he built were the Montreal Museum of Fine Arts and the Dominion Square Building, both of which are still standing today. He returned to England to bring his wife back with him to Canada. The two planned to sail the *Lusitania* but were transferred to the *Titanic* due to the coal strike. They boarded at Southampton

Birth certificate of second class passenger René Jacques Lévy. Born in Paris, 1875. Courtesy: Olivier Mendez

and traveled second class. Their ticket cost them 26£. Leopold died after helping his wife into a lifeboat.[245]

Jewish chemist Dr. René Jacques (Jacob) Lévy was born in 1875 in Nancy, France. His parents, Naphtali and Henrietta, originally came from Alsace, but after the region was annexed by the German Empire in 1870, the family was forced to move west.

René studied science in the Chemical Institute of Nancy. In 1897 he

moved to Manchester, England, where he practiced science for five years. He worked for a company that specialized in color-dying army uniforms. Eventually the company produced uniforms for British troops in World War I. Among the scientists René worked with was Dr. Haim Weizmann, who later became the first president of the State of Israel. René returned to France in 1903, married, and moved to Quebec, Canada. By 1910 he had three daughters: Simone, André, and Yvette. He returned to France in the winter of 1912 to attend a family funeral.

Second-class Jewish passenger, Dr. René Jacques (Jacob) Lévy.
Source: Royal Society of Chemistry

He planned to sail back to Canada on April 20, but after realizing he could return ten days earlier, he decided to travel on the *Titanic*. He purchased a second-class ticket for 12£ 17s and boarded at Cherbourg. He shared a room with two strangers. The three became friends and spent much of their time together during the voyage. After the collision, René managed to get into a lifeboat but climbed back out to make room for a woman. René died in the sinking.[246]

Morris Sirota was born in 1892 in Russia. When he was a little boy, his parents Solomon and Eva, both Jewish, immigrated to England where they had two more children, Rachel and Newman. The family lived in a Jewish neighborhood of Russian refugees in London. Solomon Sirota was a tailor. Morris became a tailor too and worked for his father. According to the census records, Morris spoke Hebrew, Yiddish, and English. At age twenty he decided to immigrate to New York. He boarded at Southampton as a third-class passenger. His ticket cost him 8£ 1s. He never made it to America.[247]

Harry Corn (Cornblatt) was born in 1882 in Warsaw and married Rebecca, also from Warsaw, in 1904. Rebecca's parents fled from Russia to New York because of the pogroms and anti-Semitism. Harry and Rebecca fled, too, and they lived in London where Harry worked as an upholsterer. They had three children, one son and two daughters: Morris, Fanny, and Yetta. Morris died as an infant. Harry and Rebecca decided to join Rebecca's parents in New York. In the winter of 1912, one of the two remaining children was ill, so they decided that Harry would travel alone and the family would go later. Harry boarded at Southampton with a third-class ticket that cost him 8£ 1s. His body was never found.

David Livshin was born in 1887 in Liepāja, Latvia (then part of the Russian Empire). His parents Moses (Moshe) and Zlata, were Orthodox Jews. David served in the Russian Army for a short while. He immigrated to Manchester in 1911 and married a young Jewish Lithuanian named Hannah (nee Hodes) in early 1912. David was a jeweler, and Hannah made and sold scarves and shawls for Jewish women. The young couple decided to immigrate to Montreal where two of David's sisters, Elka and Rosa, lived. David went first because Hannah was pregnant. David arranged passage on board the *Grampian* which was to set sail in March but had to postpone the trip due to the coal strike. David felt lucky as he preferred to stay home in England with his pregnant wife for Passover. He exchanged his ticket for the *Titanic* under the name Abraham Harmer, probably because he had purchased his ticket from a man with that name. As a third-class passenger, he made it to the Boat Deck after most of the lifeboats were gone. As the ship went down, he was able to hold on to Lifeboat B, yet he died during the night. His body was taken on board the *Carpathia,* and he was buried at sea.[248]

Emil Taussig was born in 1857 in Eisenbrod, Bohemia. His parents, Solomon and Rosie (nee Pick), were both Jewish. Solomon Taussig was a manufacturer of children's clothing. Emil had two siblings and six half-siblings from his father's second marriage, as Rosie died when Emil was very young. The family immigrated to America in 1866 and settled in Manhattan. Emil worked as a disinfectant manufacturer, and at age twenty-three, he married Tillie (nee Mandelbaum), born in 1872 in Manhattan. Her parents, Herman and Rosa, were Jewish immigrants from Germany. Emil and Tillie Taussig had one daughter, Ruth, who was born in 1893. In the winter of 1912, Emil, Tillie, and Ruth were in Vienna. They boarded the *Titanic* at Southampton as first-class passengers. Their ticket cost them 79£ 13s. Emil and Tillie were in stateroom E67, Ruth in E68. Tillie and Ruth survived, while Emil died.[249]

Jewish surgeon Dr. Henry Frauenthal was born in 1863 in Wilkes-Barre, Pennsylvania. His parents, Samuel and Henrietta (nee Lowenstein), immigrated to the United States from Germany. Henry had five siblings: Isaac, Herman, Isidor, Rose, and Carrie. Henry studied analytical chemistry and worked as a chemist in New York while studying medicine. He became a doctor in 1890 and worked as an orthopedic surgeon for eleven years, then entered private practice. He developed a new technique for treating chronic joint diseases. In March 1912 he married Clara (nee Heinshimer) in France. Clara was born in 1869 in Ohio, the daughter of David and Natalie, two Jewish German immigrants. Henry and Clara returned to America on board the *Titanic*. They boarded at Southampton, traveled first class, and their ticket cost them 133£ 13s. Henry's brother Gerald (Isaac) Frauenthal studied law and worked as a lawyer in New York. He joined his brother and new wife at Cherbourg. His ticket cost him 27£ 14s and he occupied stateroom D40. All three survived.

First-class Jewish passenger Gerald (Isaac) Frauenthal. Source: New York Herald, *April 17, 1912*

Woolf Spector (Spectorovski) was born in 1889 in Zambrów (a *shtetl* in Poland) to Jewish parents. He came to England, was single, and worked as a cabinetmaker. He lived with his sister Rachel Leah Ludiski, her husband Banda, and their three children. Woolf apparently changed his name from Spectorovski to Spector while living in England. Woolf boarded the *Titanic* at Southampton as a third-class passenger, and his ticket cost him 8£, 1s. He was traveling to New York to live with Frances Hersch Yellin, his aunt. Unfortunately he never made it.

Abraham Josef Hyman was born in 1878 in Russia to an Orthodox family. He fled with his family during the pogroms to Manchester, where he became part of the Jewish community. In 1902 he married Esther, a Jewish woman from Manchester. By 1911 they had five children: Julius, Ann, Lillian, Morris, and Ena. In 1912 at age thirty-four, the family decided to immigrate to America. As many other Jewish immigrants at the time, it was decided that Abraham would travel alone and send for his wife and children after he was settled. At the immigration office he registered as a frame maker. Although his brother Harry lived in New Jersey, Abraham's destination was Springfield, Massachusetts. Abraham believed that the streets in America were covered in gold and he would gain a large sum of money very quickly in order to bring his family to America. He boarded the *Titanic* at Southampton as a third-class passenger. His ticket cost him 7£ 17s. Abraham Hyman was one of the only Jewish third-class survivors.[250]

Jennie Dropkin was born in Mogilev Region (Belarus) in 1887 to a Jewish couple, Masha and Jacob Dropkin. She boarded the *Titanic* at Southampton as a third-class passenger, and her ticket cost her 8£ 1s.

Herbert Klein was born in 1878 in Bradford, England. His parents, Daniel, a tailor and Bertha (nee Rash), were both Jewish. In 1901 Herbert was working as a barber in Leeds. In 1902 he married a young Jewish Englishwoman named Leah Nora (nee Goldman). The wedding ceremony was held at the Great Orthodox Synagogue, also known as the Old Hebrew Congregation, in Leeds. In 1905 their first daughter, Bella, was born. The Kleins moved to Southampton in 1911, where Herbert worked as a barber on ships of the White Star Line. Their second daughter, Flora, was born toward the end of 1911. Before signing on to the *Titanic* on April 6, the last ship Herbert worked on was the *Teutonic*. On the *Titanic*, he worked as the second-class barber. He received only a shilling a week from the company and lived mostly on tips from the passengers. Not including Charles Kennell, Herbert Klein was the only known Jewish crew member. He died in the disaster.[251]

Not all of the Jews of the *Titanic* are known. Many of the *Titanic's* passengers, especially among the third class, died anonymously. Their memory sank with them.

After the disaster, many survivors tried to rehabilitate their lives in the United States. Others returned to England. The Red Cross, HIAS, and other organizations supported the survivors, funded their transport fares, and assisted them in getting to their destinations. Many survivors lost all their belongings in the disaster. Many lost loved ones and had to start a new life. Tilli Taussig, for example, lost her husband, Emil. In 1920 she remarried Morris Samuel, a Jewish clothing merchant from New York. Some survivors stayed anonymous, while others remained in the spotlight for many years after the *Titanic* sank.

After living for several weeks at the Hebrew shelter (HIAS) and testifying at the American Senate inquiry, Berk Trembisky (Picard) went to San Francisco

Tombstone of Titanic *survivor Hannah Abelson (Bolton), New Montefiore Jewish Cemetery, Long Island, New York.*
Photo credit: Helaine Larina

and lived there for the rest of his life. He remained single and died on May 25, 1940. The blanket he took with him from his cabin and wore on the night of the disaster was sold in 2012 at auction in London for 5,500£. The blanket was embroidered with the letters WSL (White Star Line).

After recuperation at the Hebrew shelter (HIAS), Hannah Abelson lived with her late husband Samuel's family in New York for a while. Later she remarried and became Mrs. Michael Bolton. The two had one daughter, Tessie. Hannah Bolton (late Abelson) died in Brooklyn, New York, on December 22, 1963, and is buried in Montefiore Jewish Cemetery, Long Island.

After the disaster Ruth Dodge lived in New York and died in 1950. Her death certificate has the name *Nathaniel* mistakenly written in the "name of father" box. Nathaniel Vidaver was her brother.

Sarah Roth married her fiancé one week after the disaster. They had one son, Albert. The family lived in Manhattan and moved to New Haven, Connecticut, in the late 1930s. Sarah died on July 4, 1947.

It was difficult for the widows of the victims. After the disaster Klein's widow, Leah, claimed 300£ compensation from the White Star Line. The company argued that Klein was not an employee. The case went to court, and Leah Klein won.

In September 1912, four months after the disaster, David Livshin's widow, Hannah, had a baby son. She named him David after his father. Hannah received a one-time grant from the Liverpool Relief Fund and transport money to return to her hometown in Russia. She decided not to immigrate to America but to settle in England. She planned to visit her family in Russia and return to England. Unfortunately, with the outbreak of World War I, her plans were ruined and she remained in Russia throughout the war. Afterwards Hannah returned to England. She made a living from making women's hats and shawls, as well as from grants and funds. Her son, David, grew up in the Orthodox community in Manchester and became president of his synagogue. He worked as a doctor, married a Jewish woman, the daughter of Russian immigrants, and the couple had three children: Michael, Naomi, and Deborah. David Livshin died in 1992 in Manchester. Several of his descendants made *Aliyah* and live in Israel today.[252]

Harry Corn's widow, Rebecca, never remarried. She remained in England for the rest of her life. She died in 1959 and was buried in East Ham Jewish Cemetery, Newham, London. Harry is commemorated on her tombstone:

In loving memory of
Rebecca Corn
Died 5th May 1959
Aged 74
Deeply mourned by her sorrowing
Daughters Fay and Stella
Son in law Alec, grandchildren,
Relatives and friends
Relict of Harris Corn
Lost at sea
In the "Titanic" disaster 1912
May her dear soul rest
In peace

Some of the survivors, especially the men, had to deal with feelings of guilt. In several cases, society looked upon them as selfish men who dared to save themselves while abandoning women and children. So was the case of Jewish passenger Adolphe Saalfeld.

Saalfeld was a businessman, a chemist, and a perfume maker. He was born in 1865 in Germany and immigrated with his family to England, where he married Gertrude. They had no children. Saalfeld was a member of the Reform congregation in Manchester. In April 1912 he was in Europe, and to return home he boarded the *Titanic* in Southampton. His ticket cost

Adolphe Saalfeld with his wife Gertrude, London. Courtesy: Astra Burka Collection

him 30£ 10s and he occupied stateroom C106. He was one of the wealthier Jewish passengers. Although he survived the disaster, his dream to open a pharmacy in America sank to the bottom of the Atlantic Ocean, along with his perfume samples. After the disaster, he returned to England. He tried to forget his past and the fact that he was a *Titanic* survivor, which haunted him. In a 2012 film made about his life, his niece said that he felt as though his life was worthless. He felt that society condemned him and held the fact that he survived the *Titanic* against him. He suffered from insomnia. Several years later he moved from Manchester to London, hoping for a fresh start. Although he felt rejected by society, he remained a member of the Reform

Tombstone of Titanic *survivor Adolphe Saalfeld, Golders Green Jewish Cemetery, London. Source: Encyclopedia Titanica*

community in London. He aged early, and in 1926 he died at the young age of sixty-one, only fourteen years after the disaster. He was buried in Hoop Lane Jewish Cemetery in Golders Green, London.[253]

After discovering the *Titanic* in 1985, Dr. Ballard tried to keep the exact location of the wreck a secret in order to prevent salvaging. He feared that private companies and investors would try to sell *Titanic* artifacts. Although he did what he could to prevent other expeditions from reaching the wreck, the location became known. With the development of technology, it became possible to reach the bottom of the ocean using submarines and to retrieve artifacts from the wreck. Some expeditions caused damage to the ship, while some scraped her hull. Others retrieved pieces of the ship, personal belongings, and other artifacts.[254] In a 2000 expedition, Saalfeld's perfume samples were found and recovered. The leather bag containing the glass bottles was in bad shape, but several of the bottles were surprisingly intact. Some even still contained the scent of the perfume. The leather bag and some of the perfume bottles were put on display in *Titanic* exhibitions around the world.[255]

Perfume bottle samples belonging to Adolphe Saalfeld, recovered from the Titanic *wreck. Source: unknown*

Some *Titanic* stories had an optimistic end,

even years after the disaster. René Lévy (Jewish chemist Dr. René Jacques Lévy) was in a lifeboat when he realized that women were still on board. He made room for a woman in the lifeboat and climbed back on the sinking ship. His death, although tragic, is not as well-known as Ida Straus'. But his valor, his kindness, and his research in chemistry eventually earned him a special posthumous award. In 2012 The Royal Society of Chemistry in England awarded him with the President's Award for his heroic act and his contributions to science. When describing what Dr. René Lévy did, the Royal Society of Chemistry wrote:

> Moments after he gave up his seat on one of the *Titanic's* lifeboats for a fellow female passenger, Lévy bid farewell, stayed on deck and was never seen again.[256]

The award, an engraved silver plate, was received by one of his relatives. The president of the Royal Society said it was rare to award someone posthumously, but in the case of Dr. Lévy, it was the right thing since his act was so outstanding and should be commemorated.

After recuperating from the disaster, Bella Moor left the Hebrew shelter (HIAS) along with her son, Meyer. They moved to Canada, then to Chicago, and finally Texas. Bella suffered from heart disease, died at age seventy-six in 1958, and was buried in B'nai Zion Jewish Cemetery, El Paso, Texas. Meyer, who was only seven when the *Titanic* sank, married Henrietta in 1937. For many years Meyer worked in wholesale. Although he enjoyed parties and a rich social life, he always refused to go on boat trips. He stated: "If you're born to be hanged, you'll never be drowned or shot." Meyer Moor died on *Titanic's* 63rd anniversary, April 15, 1975. He was buried alongside his mother in B'nai Zion Jewish Cemetery, El Paso.[257]

After he testified at the American inquiry, Charles Stengel's adventures were not over. Con man George Brayton tried to convince Stengel to bet on illegal horse racing. When they met in New York, Stengel realized that Brayton was trying to con him into illegal activity. Stengel refused, and the men got into a fight. Brayton escaped before the police arrived, and Stengel never saw him again. Stengel died in April 1914, only two years after the disaster, at age fifty-six. He was buried at Fairmount Cemetery, Newark, New Jersey.

Several years after the disaster, Annie Stengel described her injury incident in a letter she wrote:

One of them was a Hebrew doctor, another was his brother . . .
I was rendered unconscious and two of my ribs were very badly
dislocated.[258]

Annie Stengel was eighty-seven years old when she died in 1956 from
pneumonia. She was buried alongside her husband, Charles.

After the disaster, Abraham Salomon (rescued in Lifeboat 1) continued to
work in sales. Although he assimilated into American culture, he experienced
anti-Semitism. After the disaster, he seldom spoke of the *Titanic*. At family
gatherings he usually kept to himself. His wife, Hattie, died in 1943. Abraham's
daughter, Helen, cared for him until his death at age ninety in 1959.

Miriam Kantor stayed in New York for a while. Then she moved to Boston
where she stayed with relatives. She successfully finished medical school and
became a dentist. She never remarried. She died in 1939 and was buried in
Mount Zion Jewish Cemetery, Queens, New York, alongside her husband,
Sinai, who died in the disaster.

The trauma of the disaster accompanied many survivors for the rest of
their lives. Of 712 survivors, eight committed suicide. One of them was first-
class survivor, Jewish physician Dr. Henry Frauenthal.

Several days after the *Titanic* sank, Dr. Frauenthal gave an interview to the
Denver Post. He told his tale of his escape from the sinking ship. He said that
he was sleeping at the time of the collision. His brother, Isaac, woke him and
the two brothers went to the Boat Deck to investigate. They ran into Captain
Smith, who said the ship had hit an iceberg. After helping his wife, Clara,
into a lifeboat, she threatened to jump back onto the deck if he did not join
her. Thinking that all the other women were safe in lifeboats, he jumped (and
broke Annie Stengel's ribs). He added that:

> I would rather have stayed, too, than know that women went down
> with the *Titanic*, but I swear we thought every woman on the ship
> had been placed safely in the boats.

He also described that it was impossible not to hear the terrifying screams
of men in the water.[259]

After he, his wife, and his brother were saved, Dr. Frauenthal returned to
work in his hospital in New York. He developed mental health problems, and

in 1927 he jumped from the seventh floor of the hospital. Clara, too, suffered from mental illness and was admitted to an asylum, where she lived until her death in 1943. They had no children.[260]

After the *Titanic* disaster, Isaac Frauenthal was among the survivors who formed a committee to reward Captain Rostron of the *Carpathia* for his bravery. They gave him an inscribed silver cup. They also awarded the entire crew with medals. Isaac Frauenthal never married and died from heart failure at age sixty-four in 1932.

In an era when divorce was rare, it is not surprising that the divorce rate among the survivors was relatively high. In one case a *Titanic* survivor divorced her husband because she was ashamed to be married to a man who survived. Many male survivors suffered from social banishment. Men like Adolphe Saalfeld were rejected by society. Bruce Ismay, chairman of the White Star Line, had to resign and spent the rest of his life in solitude. Many survivors lost their jobs, their sanity, and their friends. Some suffered from hearing loss, nightmares, insomnia, sensitivity to cold, and other side effects.

First-class Jewish passenger William Greenfield.
Source: Encyclopedia Titanica, photo credit: Nell Greenfield

These post-traumatic effects also haunted Jewish survivors. Blanche Greenfield suffered from nightmares, haunted by the screams of people in the water. She also had hearing loss due to exposure to freezing water. She died in 1936 after a long illness and was buried in Salem Field Jewish Cemetery, Brooklyn, New York. Her son, William Greenfield, twenty-three at the time of the disaster, served in the United States Army during World War I. He married a Jewish woman, Flora (nee Stern), and they had two daughters. He lived in New York and died at age sixty-one in 1949. His grave lies next to his parents in Salem Field Jewish Cemetery.

Shortly after the disaster, Jewish passenger Samuel and his Christian wife, Nella Goldenberg, returned to Nice, France. They divorced, and Samuel remarried a woman named Edwige, who died in 1935. Samuel died in 1936 from heart failure and was buried alongside Edwige in Cimiez Cemetery, Nice, France. Unfortunately, Samuel's assimilation was so deep that his tombstone is not marked as a Jew but of a Christian, with a large engraved cross on the stone. Nonetheless, the mayor of Nice, being an anti-Semite, refused to attend a recent ceremony at the gravesite.[261]

A week after the disaster, René Harris, who was a good friend of Emil Brandeis, met with Emil's sister-in-law, Mrs. Arthur Brandeis, and explained how Emil died. She also told her that they ate together on the day of the sinking. Following the meeting, Mrs. Brandeis wrote:

> Emil and Mr. and Mrs. Harris enjoyed a hearty dinner together Sunday night… The men all stood together on deck as the women were lowered in lifeboats. When Mrs. Harris was ten minutes out at sea she saw the steamer sink with all those fine men aboard. They remained without fear.[262]

Several months after the disaster, René went to a doctor. Her arm was still in a sling, and she was still in pain from her unfortunate injury on the grand stairway. At the doctor's office, René cried for the first time since the disaster. Her husband, Henry, died in the sinking, and René believed that his body had been found. She believed that after he was found, his valuables were stolen, and he was tossed back into the sea. Her explanation was that he carried many valuables with him. She also explained that Emil Brandeis and Isidor Straus were with Henry in the final moments, and their bodies were found, so Henry's body must have been found too. Her claim has never been proven.[263]

René shared her *Titanic* experiences with Walter Lord. In a five-page letter, she described in detail the injury that happened several hours before the disaster. She told Lord that after she was treated, she returned to her stateroom. Half an hour later she and Henry went to dinner. On their way they met Captain Smith, who noticed that her arm was in a sling. The captain told René how brave she was. René also told Lord that Captain Smith told them about the temperature drop and his concern about icebergs. After dinner her pain grew, and she returned to her stateroom.

Like many other survivors who lost their loved ones or their belongings, René sued the White Star Line. Of all the claims, hers was the highest: a million dollars for Henry's death and all their belongings.

René continued her husband's theatrical business, managing the theater and producing plays. For a while she was successful. She remarried twice. In 1928 she traveled around the world, but when she realized that her business was failing, she returned home. The Great Depression destroyed her business. René was forced to sell many of her assets and the theatre closed. She died at the age of ninety-three in 1969.[264]

One prominent survivor was Edith Rosenbaum. During World War I, she was recruited by the American Red Cross as a journalist and was sent to Europe. For several months, she was with the troops in the European trenches, one of the first female journalists to do so. After the war she continued to work as a fashion journalist in New York and Paris. In honor of her acts in World War I, she received an award from the International Ladies' Garment Workers Union in 1925. She traveled to Europe often and lived well. Later in her life she became active in the *Titanic* story. She was interviewed numerous times and hosted many curious people who were interested in her story. In 1963 she was made an honorary member of the Titanic Historical Society and met other survivors such as Frank Aks. Edith showed Maxixe, the toy pig, to Frank. In one interview she said she was afraid to jump into the lifeboat because she was scarcely dressed.[265]

Titanic survivor Edith Rosenbaum (Russell) in 1911 and 1956. Courtesy: Randy Bryan Bigham

Edith spent her last years alone in a hotel room in London. She died at the age of ninety-five in 1975.[266]

After her death, Maxixe was given to *Titanic* researcher and author Walter Lord, who was a good friend of Edith's. After Lord's death in 2002, the toy pig was donated to the National Maritime Museum in Greenwich, London. Today, Maxixe is on display in the *Titanic* Remembrance Room with the slippers Edith wore on the night of the disaster.

Abraham Josef Hyman survived and arrived in New York, where he met his brother, Harry. In an interview in the *New York Times* he said:

> The forward deck was jammed with the people, all of them pushing and clawing and fighting, and so I walked forward and stepped over the end of the boat that was being got ready and sat down. Nobody disturbed me, and then a line of men gathered along the side and only opened when a woman or a child came forward. When a man tried to get through, he would be pushed back.[267]

After the disaster, his wife, Esther (nee Levi), who was still in England, refused to cross the Atlantic Ocean. While spending time in Jewish neighborhoods in New York, Hyman was inspired by the kosher restaurants and delis and

decided to open a kosher deli in England. He abandoned his dream to immigrate to America and returned home. A year later he opened a kosher deli and grocery store in Manchester with the compensation money he received from the Red Cross. His store was named J. A. Hyman Ltd, but locals referred to his store as Titanic's. Hyman himself was known as "the *Titanic* man."

The kosher deli, Manchester, England. Established and run by Titanic *survivor Abraham Hayman. Photo credit: Trevor Baxter*

Abraham Hyman seldom spoke about the disaster after returning to England. In addition to his five children from before the disaster, he had two more children afterwards (Jonas and Rachel). Esther died in 1927. Two years later Hyman married Esther (nee Rosengrass) in a ceremony at the New *Kahal Chassidim* Synagogue in Manchester. His second wife died in 1951. Abraham Hyman died in 1956 at the Victoria Memorial Jewish Hospital in Manchester.

The engraving on Hyman's tombstone is written in English and Hebrew. On the bottom of the tombstone are the letters M.H.D.S.R.I.P. (May His Dear Soul Rest In Peace). Beneath is a quote (in Hebrew) from the book of Zechariah referring to Hyman's survival from the *Titanic* disaster:

Is not this brand plucked out of the fire?

This biblical quote is often used by survivors of the Holocaust and other tragedies.

During the years when the deli was active, Jewish customers could be served kosher goods. The deli offered delivery throughout England and Scotland. Several outlets of the deli also opened. The deli and the restaurant were managed by the Hyman family under rabbinical supervision of the Manchester *Beth Din*.[268]

Tombstone of Titanic *survivor Abraham Joseph Hyman, Blackley Jewish Cemetery, Manchester, England. Courtesy: Trevor Baxter*

190

Hyman's Titanic's shop lost money due to harsh competition with major supermarkets in Manchester. By the end of 2016, the deli was forced to close, and thus ended an era.

After the disaster Jennie Dropkin lived in Brooklyn for a while. In March 1913 she married Russian-born Max Matlin, a Jewish tinsmith. They moved to Hartford, Connecticut, and had two sons. Jennie (Dropkin) Matlin died in 1951 at the age of sixty-four and was buried in Mount Hebron Jewish Cemetery, Queens, New York.

Shortly after arriving in New York, Gershon Cohen returned to England. He lived in Southend-On-Sea, Essex. In World War I, he served in the Royal Army and fought against the Germans. One night he was shot while standing at his post. Although the bullet hit his face and he lost an eye, he survived. Several years later he slipped and was badly hurt when leaving a train in London. He was exiting the train, took a bad step, and missed the platform. He also survived a major head

Tombstone of Titanic *survivor Jennie Dropkin (Matlin), Mount Hebron, Queens, New York. Courtesy: Helaine Larina*

injury. During World War II Gershon worked as a cloth buyer and owned a small shop. His shop was directly hit in the German *Blitz* over London. Luckily he was a few streets away, and he survived this too. Gershon's friends called him "the cat" since it was as though he had nine lives.[269] After surviving the *Titanic* disaster, a World War I injury, the London Blitz in World War II, an injury due to falling on the tracks at an underground station during a blackout, Cohen also survived a car accident on *Titanic's* fifty-year anniversary. That day he was on his way to a radio station for an interview. The taxi dropped him off, and as he was crossing the street, he was hit by a car driven by a drunk driver. Cohen survived that too. No wonder his nickname was "the cat"!

Gershon was interviewed numerous times and told his escape story over and over again. In one interview he expressed his feelings about the inconvenience of the discrimination between the classes. The third-class passengers felt they were not worth as much as other passengers. The quality of the food was not as good. The third-class passengers were restricted to "their" parts of the ship only. When asked about the small quantity of third-class survivors, Gershon nodded his head and said it was "because they were not allowed to go on to the first-class deck." In another interview he mentioned what he saw on his way to the lifeboats. As he made his way to the upper decks, he noticed a group of immigrants (he thought they were Italian). They were gathered in a corner of the third-class dining room. He never knew what happened to them. In another interview he talked about the band. He said that he noticed the band playing while he was on the Boat Deck, but he also noticed that the band was not playing when he was about to enter a lifeboat.[270]

Gershon saved the letters he wrote on the *Carpathia* and then donated them with other *Titanic* related items to various museums. He spent his last years in his apartment with the Thames visible from his bedroom window. Gershon Cohen was eighty-four when he died in his sleep in 1978.[271]

Another active *Titanic* survivor was Eva Hart, whose father, Benjamin, died. She and her mother, Esther, returned to Ilford, England, after a short stay in New York. Soon after arriving home, Esther was interviewed by the *Ilford Graphic*, a local newspaper. She described her ordeal in detail. She told of her concern before boarding the ship and of her insomnia during the voyage. She also said that she knew she would not feel safe until they landed in New York. Of her late husband, she said: "I knew that I had seen the last of my Ben, and that I had lost the best and truest friend." Esther described the events after the sinking:

And then a wonderful thing happened . . . the sea was as smooth as glass; it seemed as if the Almighty, in order that as many should be saved as possible had with a merciful hand, smoothed and calmed the waters... And the air was full of the awful and despairing cries of drowning men. And we were helpless to help, for we dared not go near them.

Describing her final moments with Benjamin, she added a very interesting remark: "He turned away for a few moments and said his Jewish prayers."

Then she described the long night on the cold Atlantic, the voyage to New York onboard the *Carpathia,* and the short stay in America before returning home with Eva. She concluded the interview with words about Eva's future. She would raise her all by herself. She said that "my lost Ben had such dreams of her future."[272]

Eva Hart was among the youngest survivors, but she remembered details of the disaster. Esther died in 1928 when Eva was twenty-three. After her mother's death, Eva began having nightmares. She decided to confront her nightmares by sailing the seas. She locked herself in her cabin for four days, and her nightmares disappeared. She sailed to Australia and lived there for a while. She lived most of her life in England.

Eva was interviewed numerous times. In one interview she said, "If a ship is torpedoed, that is war. If it strikes a rock in a storm, that is nature. But just to die because there weren't enough lifeboats, that is ridiculous." In an interview in 1979, she said, "I so clearly remember my mother saying to my father: 'Oh, this is the ship they say is unsinkable.' My father said, 'No, this is the ship that *is* unsinkable.'"[273]

Eva confirmed that the ship broke in two. When the ship was discovered in 1985, it turned out that Eva was right. In an interview in 1993, she said: "I never closed my eyes. I did not sleep at all. I saw it, I heard it, and nobody could possibly forget it. I can remember the colors, the sounds, everything. The worst thing I can remember are the screams." In regards to the *Californian*, she said that she saw the ship in the distance as the two ships were rather close. Eva believed that the crew of the *Californian* must have seen the distress signals and that if the *Titanic* shot rockets, the *Californian* should have seen them and taken action. In regards to the last song that the band played, she insisted that it was "Nearer My God to Thee."

After the exact location of the remains of the *Titanic* was known to the public, Eva was among the activists who called to stop the "grave robbery." She opposed attempts to retrieve anything from the site: "I hope severely that they will never attempt to raise part of it. I do hope they will remember this is a grave. A grave of 1,500 people who should never have died, and I do not think you should go down there and rob graves, and I'm very much opposed to it." She was an active survivor who promoted preserving the memory of the *Titanic* and the disaster. Eva belonged to various *Titanic* organizations and attended almost every meeting, conference, and convention.

She was in numerous television shows and documentaries about the *Titanic*. In 1982, she attended a convention held by the Titanic Historical Society to commemorate the seventieth anniversary, and in 1994 she published her autobiography. In 1995, when she was ninety, she dedicated a memorial garden plaque at the National Maritime Museum in Greenwich.

Eva Hart spent her last years in an old age home in Chadwell Heath, London. She died of cancer at age ninety-one in 1996, one of the last survivors with memories of the disaster.[274]

Leah Aks, whose son, Frank, was snatched from her on the night of the disaster and reunited with her on the *Carpathia*, spent a few days at the Jewish shelter (HIAS) to recuperate until her husband, Samuel, arrived. The Aks family left New York and moved to Norfolk, Virginia. A year later, Leah gave birth to a baby girl and decided to

Birth certificate of Sara Carpathia ("Titanic") Aks. In this document, her name is spelled "Sarah" incorrectly. Courtesy: Shelley Binder

name her Sara Carpathia in honor of the rescue ship. The nurses at the hospital

Samuel and Leah Aks 50 year wedding anniversary, Beth El synagogue, Norfolk Virginia, 1960. Courtesy: Shelley Binder

Tombstone of the Aks family, Forest Lawn Jewish Cemetery, Norfolk, Virginia. Courtesy: Shelley Binder

were so excited at the unique gesture that they accidently mixed up the name and registered the baby as "Sarah Titanic."[275] In 1915 the Akses had another son named Harry.

In a radio interview from the 1940s with *Ripley's Believe It or Not*, Leah Aks told her miraculous story. She described how she found her son in the arms of another woman on board the *Carpathia* four days after the disaster. Until that moment, she truly believed that her baby was dead. She described the man who snatched the baby and threw him overboard as a "maniac." In 1960 Leah and Samuel Aks celebrated their fiftieth wedding anniversary with their entire family and their local community in Beth El synagogue, Norfolk, Virginia.

Samuel and Leah Aks 50 year wedding anniversary (in center), Beth El synagogue, Norfolk Virginia, 1960. Courtesy: Shelley Binder

The cold from which Leah suffered during the fateful night caused permanent hearing loss. She died at age seventy-three in 1967 and was buried in Forest Lawn Jewish Cemetery, Norfolk, Virginia. The shawl Leah was wrapped with (given to her by Madeline Astor) was donated to the Mariner's Museum, Newport.

From the day little Frank Aks arrived in America with his mother, he led a religious life. As a young Jewish boy, he would walk with his father every Sabbath to *Bnai Israel*, the Orthodox synagogue on Cumberland Street in Norfolk. Frank married Marie (nee Miller). Both were active members in the Jewish community.[276] Frank was a member of Congregation *Beth El* and the Jewish community center. He was the

Frank Aks and wife Marie at a family celebration at Temple Beth El, Norfolk, Virginia. Courtesy: Shelley Binder

Tombstone of Leah Aks, Forest Lawn Jewish Cemetery, Norfolk, Virginia. Courtesy: Shelley Binder

president of Congregation *Brith Shalom,* and Marie was a member of Hadassah. Frank and Marie had two daughters, Judith and Barbara.

Although he was too young to remember the events of the disaster, Frank was very active with other survivors. He took part in many gatherings, conferences, and panels of various *Titanic* organizations. He helped Walter Lord with his research about the ship during the 1950s and 1960s and with Lord's *A Night to Remember* and with *The Night Lives On.*

Frank Aks was a *Titanic* memorabilia collector and owned one of the largest private collections of *Titanic* artifacts, souvenirs, and documents. He died at age eighty in 1991 and was buried alongside his parents in Forest Lawn Jewish Cemetery, Norfolk, Virginia.

His wife, Marie, continued his work and was involved with *Titanic* organizations in the United States until her death in 2003. Their children, grandchildren, and great-grandchildren continue the family legacy and cherish

Tombstone of Phillip Frank Aks, Forest Lawn Jewish Cemetery, Norfolk, Virginia. Courtesy: Shelley Binder

the memory of Frank Aks and the memory of the *Titanic.*

The sinking of the unsinkable *Titanic* and the deaths of 1,500 people were tragic. The death of dozens of Jews was a tragedy to the Jewish world but also is part of the global tragedy as well. The life and death of the *Titanic* Jews is only a part of the life and death of all the *Titanic* passengers and crew. The Jewish perspective is one part of the larger *Titanic* story which, unlike the ship is unsinkable, and will continue to fascinate the world for years.

EPILOGUE

Two major events happened in Israel during the summer of 2014. The first was the Protective Edge military operation, also known as the 2014 Israel Gaza conflict. During those intense few weeks, Hamas and other terrorist organizations shot hundreds of rockets and mortars from the Gaza Strip into Israel, causing much terror and the deaths of several Israeli civilians. Over seventy Israeli soldiers were killed. Many Israelis spent most of the summer in bomb shelters.

The second major event was the arrival of the *Titanic* exhibition in Tel Aviv. The RMS *Titanic* Inc. has the rights to retrieve *Titanic* artifacts from the bottom of the Atlantic. In recent years some artifacts have been displayed in major cities around the world. The first edition of my book was to be published in Israel in Hebrew at the time, and as a *Titanic* expert, I offered to share my knowledge for the benefit of the Israeli public during the exhibition.

Some artifacts on display belonged to Jewish passengers, including various documents belonging to George Rosenshine and the perfume samples of Adolphe Saalfeld. A plaque in English and in Hebrew was placed above the perfume samples, with the following words:

> Perfume bottles and labels from the original perfume case belonging to Adolphe Saalfeld. Despite more than nine decades on the ocean floor, these perfume bottles still emit the scent of the perfume samples they contained.

The *Titanic* exhibition was publicized in the Israeli media, but due to the war with Gaza, few people came to see it. Twice during the *Titanic* exhibition, I had to cut short a guided tour and lead the visitors to a bomb shelter because of missile attacks on Tel Aviv.

A few weeks later, the first edition of this book was published in Israel, and for the second time in weeks the *Titanic* story was in the Israeli spotlight for a short period of time.

Soon after my book was published, I received emails and phone calls from Israelis claiming that their grandparents or great-grandparents were on the *Titanic,* and they wanted me to identify them on the passenger list and add them to my book. Deep in my heart I hoped that some of them would actually be added to my list of confirmed Jewish names on the *Titanic*. I did all I could to confirm such claims, extensively researching the matter.

Sara Carpathia ("Titanic") Aks (left) during a visit to the old city, Jerusalem, 1967. Courtesy: Shelley Binder

I cross-checked people's names, names of towns, and years of birth, but unfortunately none of the names given to me matched. It is amazing how many people believe that they are descendants of *Titanic* passengers. One of the callers insisted over and over again that his grandmother was on the *Titanic,* and he told me that in his family her nickname was "the *Titanic* grandmother." The only case that I was able to confirm was the grandson of Jewish victim David Livshin. I already knew about him, so beyond knowing and meeting a Jewish descendant of the *Titanic*, it did not add to my research.

When I initiated my original research on the Jews of the *Titanic,* I had not considered the idea that there are Israelis who believe they are related to *Titanic* passengers, and this has led me to new Jewish *Titanic*-related questions. Questions such as: Did any of the survivors visit Israel? Are there any relatives of *Titanic* survivors (or of victims) living in Israel? Did any of them make *Aliyah*?

Several *Titanic* survivors visited Israel. After remarrying, Tilli Taussig toured Europe and the Middle East. Among the countries she visited was Israel

(Mandatory Palestine at the time). Relatives of the Straus family also visited Israel.

Another visitor to Israel was Sara Aks. In September 1967, several weeks after the Six Day War, she joined a group tour of the recently liberated old city of Jerusalem. As a member of Hadassah, and a devoted Zionist, it was a meaningful experience for her as she walked along the alleyways and ancient walls of the old city.

Sara Carpathia ("Titanic") Aks in her later years. Courtesy: Shelley Binder

One of the questions I tried to answer in my research was whether any of the Jewish survivors of the *Titanic* disaster had been killed in the Holocaust. I was fascinated by the idea that someone would have survived the *Titanic* disaster only to be killed by the Nazis. Other than the 1943 "Nazi Titanic" film, there are several connections between the *Titanic* and the Holocaust. Not surprisingly, several *Titanic* survivors were involved in or affected by World War II and the Holocaust.

One of them was Edmond Navratil (the older son of the man mistakenly buried in the Jewish cemetery in Halifax). In World War II, Edmond joined the French Army and became a member of the militia and collaborated with the Nazis. The group he belonged to was responsible of deporting and killing hundreds of people, including many Jews. He was arrested by the French and sent to prison. Over the next few years, his health deteriorated, and he died at the relatively young age of forty-three in 1953. His younger brother, Marcel, surpassed the age of ninety and died in 2001.

Another *Titanic* survivor associated with the Nazis was Dorothy Gibson (the actress), who was in France in the beginning of World War II. She publicly exposed her anti-Semitic beliefs and became a Nazi sympathizer and a supporter of the Italian Fascist Regime. None of that aided her in 1944 when she tried to flee to Switzerland and was arrested by the Germans. She was taken to a concentration camp. Eventually Gibson was taken to San

Vittore Prison. She described her experience in the camps as a "living death." She was smuggled out of prison and made it to Switzerland, where she was arrested as a Nazi sympathizer. After the war Gibson suffered from high blood pressure. She died in Paris in 1946 from a heart attack.[277]

When on April 16, 1945, Allied forces found looted treasures from the Rothschild Museum in a castle in Austria, The German guardian with the keys to the treasure was eighty-seven-year-old Alfred Teissinger, a *Titanic* survivor. He was a *Titanic* bedroom steward. On the night of the sinking, he assisted many passengers, including several Jewish passengers such as Guggenheim, Straus, and Taussig. He escaped in Lifeboat 11. After the disaster he returned to Germany.

One Jew who was on the *Titanic* died in the Holocaust. His name was Paul Danby, but he was neither a passenger nor a crew member. Danby toured the *Titanic* on the day she sailed but did not sail with the ship. He was a guest of his uncle, Adolphe Saalfeld, and the two of them had a great time together on deck before Danby went back to shore. While on board, Danby wrote a letter to his wife, Rose, who was in Manchester at the time. The letter was written in German on official White Star Line stationary paper. Amongst the things he wrote was:

> Uncle has a very large cabin nearly a living room with sofa and an electric ventilator. I will tell you all in detail later. I embrace you and kiss you dearly. Your very loving Paul. Love from Uncle.

Danby lived in England, but during World War I he was imprisoned because of his German background. After the war his family moved to the Netherlands. Thirty years after writing his letter on board the *Titanic,* the Nazis sent Danby and his family to Sobibór death camp, where he perished. His letter survived the Holocaust and was sold at auction in England in April 2016.[278]

None of the Jewish survivors of the *Titanic* were killed by the Nazis, but as mentioned, during the German blitz over London, Gershon Cohen's shop was hit by a German bomb. Luckily for Cohen, he was a few blocks away and was not injured.

Many Jews who fled the pogroms of Europe in the early twentieth century left their families behind. It would be no surprise if relatives of *Titanic* passengers would have stayed in Europe and been killed in the Holocaust.

In 2015 I learned of yet another Jewish story about the *Titanic*. I have seen and read this story in several places since then. Similar to the opening story of my book, this story also involves an Eastern European Jew and a rabbi. In this new story, the wise rabbi is Rabbi Israel Friedman (1854–1933), known as the Chortkover Rebbe. In contrast to the first story, this one is quite different. That is, the ending is different.

This new story is about a Jew who lived in Vienna and whose life was saved thanks to counsel he received from the Chortkover Rebbe.

This unknown man barely made a living and decided to immigrate to the United States. He purchased a ticket to sail to New York. Although not a Hasid, he decided to ask the Chortkover Rebbe for a blessing prior to his departure.

The Chortkover Rebbe blessed him but also gave him a unique message to carry with him to America. He told him to send his regards to "the God of America."

Amazed, the man asked, "Is not the God in America the same God here in Vienna?"

The rabbi answered: "Indeed. Why go to America? God can help you here . . ."

Although he already purchased the ticket, he got the hint and stayed in Vienna. The story ends with the ship's name: *Titanic*. The confidence the man had in the Chortkover Rebbe saved his life.[279]

And there we have it: A Jewish tale about the wisdom of a rabbi, about the most famous maritime disaster, and about saving the life of one Jew. And that is the story of the Jews of the *Titanic*.

NOTES

1. The Myth

[1] Bagad, Y. (1989) *Nahalei Ha'eshkolot* (in Hebrew) p. 17–22.

[2] Lord, W. (1987) *The Night Lives On*, p.11.

[3] Davenport-Hines, R. (2012). Titanic *Lives*, p. 169.

[4] Kushner, T. *Titanic's* Hidden Victims. *Jewish Chronicle*, 2012.

[5] Rigg B.M. (2002) *Hitler's Jewish Soldiers*.

2. Ship of Dreams

[6] Lynch, D. (1997) Titanic, *An Illustrated History*, p. 16–20.

[7] Lynch, D. (1997) Titanic, *An Illustrated History*, p. 16–20.

[8] Blake, J. (2011) Titanic: *A Passenger's Guide*, p. 5–6, 29–33.

[9] Lynch, D. (1997) Titanic, *An Illustrated History*, p. 35.

[10] Brewster, H. (1988) *882½ Amazing Answers to Your Questions about the Titanic*, p. 27.

[11] Matson, B. (2008) Titanic's *Last Secrets*, p. 128–130.

[12] Lord, W. (1987) *The Night Lives On*, p. 72–80.

[13] Davenport-Hines, R. (2012) Titanic *Lives*, p. 224–225.

[14] Lynch, D. (1997) Titanic, *An Illustrated History*, p. 34.

[15] Eaton, J. P. & Haas, C. A. (1994) Titanic: *Triumph and Tragedy*, p. 113–115.

[16] Brewster, H. (1988) *882½ Amazing Answers to Your Questions about the Titanic*, p. 42.

[17] Brewster, H. (1988) *882½ Amazing Answers to Your Questions about the Titanic*, p. 64.

[18] Ballard, R. D. (1987) *The Discovery of the* Titanic.

[19] Lynch, D. (1997) Titanic, *An Illustrated History*, p. 172.

[20] Eaton, J.P. & Haas, C.A. (1994) Titanic: *Triumph and Tragedy*, p. 178.

[21] Lynch, D. (1997) Titanic, *An Illustrated History*, p. 142–156.

[22] Eaton, J.P. & Haas, C.A. (1994) Titanic: *Triumph and Tragedy*, p. 228–235.

[23] Titanic Inquiry Project: www.titanicinquiry.org.

[24] Lord, W. (1987) *The Night Lives On*, p. 160–177.

[25] Lynch, D. (1997) Titanic, *An Illustrated History*, p. 193.

[26] Lynch, D. (1997) Titanic, *An Illustrated History*, p. 193.

[27] Brewster, H. (1988) *882½ Amazing Answers to Your Questions about the* Titanic, p. 78–79.

[28] Ballard, R. D. (1987) *The Discovery of the* Titanic, p. 45–51.

[29] *Titanic* Discoverer Launches Israel Sea-Floor Expedition, *Jewish Daily Forward*, 2010.

[30] Ballard, R. D. (1987) *The Discovery of the* Titanic, p. 53–57.

[31] Ballard, R. D. (1987) *The Discovery of the* Titanic, p. 80–85.

[32] Brewster, H. (1988) *882½ Amazing Answers to Your Questions about the* Titanic, p. 82–85.

[33] Brewster, H. (1988) *882½ Amazing Answers to Your Questions about the* Titanic, p. 83.

[34] *Titanic's* 83rd Anniversary Marked by Artifacts Exhibit Disaster, *Los Angeles Times*, April 16, 1995.

[35] Matson, B. (2008) Titanic's *Last Secrets*, p 58.

3. Immigration

[36] About Uncle Leyzer and That Iceberg, *Jewish Daily Forward*, April 17, 1998.

[37] (No author), *300 Years of Freedom* (in Hebrew), 1954.

[38] Sherman, Z. *United States Jewry*, (in Hebrew), 1956.

[39] Ziv, H. *B'nei Keshet: A Hundred Years of Struggle* (in Hebrew), 1998.

[40] Ziv, H. *B'nei Keshet: A Hundred Years of Struggle* (in Hebrew), 1998.

[41] Sherman, Z. *United States Jewry*, (in Hebrew), 1956.

[42] Davenport-Hines, R. (2012) Titanic *Lives*, p. 99–100.

[43] A Love Story Of Honor, *Dayton Jewish Observer*, March 20, 2012.

[44] A Love Story Of Honor, *Dayton Jewish Observer*, March 20, 2012.

[45] Jewish Heroes and Heroines in America, *Florida Atlantic University Libraries*, 1996.

[46] Many Waters Cannot Quench Love—Neither Can the Floods Drown It, Joan Adler, *Straus Historical Society Inc. Newsletter*, February 2012.

[47] A Philadelphia Jew on the Sunken *Titanic*, *Jewish Daily Forward*, April 10, 2012.

[48] Steerage Victim Lived Here, *Evening Bulletin*. April 23, 1912.

[49] A Philadelphia Jew on the Sunken *Titanic*, *Jewish Daily Forward*, April 10, 2012.

4. Sailing Day

[50] Davenport-Hines, R. (2012) Titanic *Lives*, p. 76–86.

[51] Sorrow in Jewish Home, *Leeds Mercury*, April 19, 1912.

[52] Brewster, H. (1988) *882½ Amazing Answers to Your Questions about the* Titanic, p 18–19.

[53] Davenport-Hines, R. (2012), *Titanic Lives*, p. 160.

[54] Lynch, D. (1997) Titanic, *An Illustrated History*, p. 64.

[55] Headstone Now Marks *Titanic* Victim's Grave, the *Canadian Jewish News*, April 2, 2012.

[56] Lord, W. (1987) *The Night Lives On*, p. 38.

[57] Lord, W. (1987) *The Night Lives On*, p. 38.

[58] Lynch, D. (1997) Titanic, *An Illustrated History*, p. 71–72.

[59] *Letter from* Titanic *Electrical Engineer William Kelly to His Mother.* Encyclopedia Titanica

[60] www.homersworld.blogspot.co.il/2012/04/ever-since-i-was-child-i-was-interested.html.

[61] Kushner, T. *Titanic's* Hidden Victims. *Jewish Chronicle,* 2012.

[62] *Titanic* Disaster in Yiddish and Hebrew Literature, (in Hebrew) *Herut*, June 22, 1962

[63] Kushner, T. Titanic's Hidden Victims. *Jewish Chronicle*, 2012.

[64] Two Families and One Lifeboat, *Jewish Daily Forward*, April 13, 2012.

[65] Eaton, J.P. & Haas, C.A. Titanic*: Triumph and Tragedy*, p. 92–93

[66] Davenport-Hines, R. (2012), Titanic *Lives*, p. 160, 168.

[67] My *Titanic* Uncle (2012) Astra Burka Design Production Company.

[68] Encyclopedia Titanica.

[69] My *Titanic* Uncle (2012) Astra Burka Design Production Company.

5. Eating Kosher on the Atlantic Route

[70] The Cat Recalls His Escape from the Sinking *Titanic, Mall Star*, April 12, 1972.

[71] Brewster, H. (1988) *882½ Amazing Answers to Your Questions about the* Titanic, p. 32–33.

[72] Kashrut Aboard the '*Titanic*' Sheds Light on Immigration, Marshall Weiss, *Dayton Jewish Observer*, April 12, 2012.

[73] Kashrut Aboard the '*Titanic*' Sheds Light on Immigration, Marshall Weiss, *Dayton Jewish Observer*, April 12, 2012.

[74] A Jewish Chapter in *Titanic* Saga, Marshall Weiss, *Dayton Jewish Observer*, April 6, 2012.

[75] A Jewish Chapter in *Titanic* Saga, Marshall Weiss, *Dayton Jewish Observer*, April 6, 2012.

[76] Blake, J. (2011*)* Titanic: *A Passenger's Guide*, p. 111.

[77] *Titanic's* Kosher Butcher Shop to Be Preserved, Kaplan, M, *Jewish Daily Forward*, January 1, 2014.

[78] A Jewish Chapter in *Titanic* Saga, Marshall Weiss, *Dayton Jewish Observer*, April 6, 2012.

[79] A Jewish Chapter in *Titanic* Saga, Marshall Weiss, *Dayton Jewish Observer*, April 6, 2012.

[80] A Jewish Chapter in *Titanic* Saga, Marshall Weiss, *Dayton Jewish Observer*, April 6, 2012.

[81] Eaton, J.P. & Haas, C.A. Titanic: *Triumph and Tragedy.*

6. Pleasure Cruise

[82] The Tale of the *Titanic* Told By a Rescued Ilford Lady, *Ilford Graphic*, May 10, 1912.

[83] Blake, J. (2011*)* Titanic: *A Passenger's Guide*, p. 51–53.

[84] Brewster, H. *882½ Amazing Answers to Your Questions about the* Titanic, p. 30–31.

[85] Davenport-Hines, R. (2012) Titanic *Lives*, p. 183.

[86] Brewster, H.(1988) *882½ Amazing Answers to Your Questions about the* Titanic, p. 38–39.

[87] Lord, W. (1987) *The Night Lives On*, p. 42.

[88] Davenport-Hines, R. (2012) Titanic *Lives*, p. 167–168.

[89] Other Midlanders aboard the *Titanic*, *Omaha World-Herald*, April 8, 2012.

[90] Davenport-Hines, R. (2012) Titanic *Lives*, p. 245.

[91] The Tale of the *Titanic* Told By a Rescued Ilford Lady, *Ilford Graphic*, May 10, 1912.

[92] The Cat Recalls His Escape from the Sinking *Titanic*, *Mall Star*, April 12, 1972.

[93] from an interview with Irene on April 23, 1932.

[94] Lynch, D. (1997) Titanic, *An Illustrated History*, p. 83–85.

[95] Blake, J. (2011) Titanic: *A Passenger's Guide*, p. 78.

7. Disaster

[96] Davenport-Hines, R. (2012) Titanic *Lives*, p. 275.

[97] Brewster, H. (1988), 882½ Amazing Answers to Your Questions about the *Titanic* , p. 42–47.

[98] Lynch, D. (1997) Titanic, *An Illustrated History*, p. 84.

[99] How Mrs. Meyer Escaped, *Le Journal*, April 20, 1912.

[100] My *Titanic* Uncle (2012) Astra Burka Design Production Company.

[101] Davenport-Hines, R. (2012) Titanic *Lives*, p. 169.

[102] Many Waters Cannot Quench Love—Neither Can the Floods Drown It, Joan Adler, *Straus Historical Society Inc. Newsletter*, February 2012.

[103] *Globe*, April 19, 1912

[104] Many Waters Cannot Quench Love—Neither Can the Floods Drown It, Joan Adler, *Straus Historical Society Inc. Newsletter*, February 2012.

[105] *Titanic* victims relative honors precious legacy, *New Jersey Jewish News*, August 27, 2012.

[106] Lord, W. (2012) *A Night to Remember*, p. 78.

[107] www.titanicgazette.blogspot.co.il/2008/02/edith-russell.html.

[108] www.charlespellegrino.com/passengers/mrs_harris.htm.

[109] How the Harrises Parted, *New York Times*, April 19, 1912.

[110] Other Midlanders aboard the Titanic, *Omaha World-Herald*, April 8, 2012.

[111] Proving Forman on *Titanic, New York Times*, May 15, 1912.

[112] The Tale of the *Titanic* Told by a Rescued Ilford Lady, *Ilford Graphic*, May 10, 1912.

[113] The Tale of the *Titanic* Told by a Rescued Ilford Lady, *Ilford Graphic*, May 10, 1912.

[114] Lynch, D. (1997) Titanic, *An Illustrated History*, p. 118–119.

[115] Lost & Found at Sea: The Story of Leah and Filly Aks, Marshall Weiss, *Dayton Jewish Observer*, March 20, 2012.

[116] Lost & Found at Sea: The Story of Leah and Filly Aks, Marshall Weiss, *Dayton Jewish Observer*, March 20, 2012.

[117] Lynch, D. (1997) Titanic, *An Illustrated History*, p. 118–120.

[118] What the Rescued Jewish Immigrants Have to Say, *Jewish Daily Forward*, April 1912.

[119] Hundreds Blown into Sea, *New York Herald*, April 19, 1912.

[120] Lord, W. (2012) *A Night to Remember*, London, p. 91–93.

[121] Lord, W. (2012) *A Night to Remember*, London, p. 94.

[122] About Uncle Leyzer and that Iceberg, Dovid Katz, *Jewish Daily Forward*, April 17, 1998.

[123] Sorrow in Jewish Home, *Leeds Mercury*, April 19, 1912.

[124] The *Titanic*: A Jewish Family's Story, Rachel Mines, *Outlook Magazine*, 2009.

[125] About Uncle Leyzer and that Iceberg, Dovid Katz, *Jewish Daily Forward*, April 17, 1998.

[126] Lord, W. (1987) *The Night Lives On*, p. 125–133.

8. On Board the *Carpathia*

[127] Eaton, J.P. & C.A. Haas (1994), Titanic: *Triumph and Tragedy*, p. 167–184.

[128] Lord, W. (1987) *The Night Lives On*, p 134–156.

[129] Lord, W. (2012) *A Night to Remember*, London, p.158.

[130] Eaton, J.P. & C.A. Haas (1994), Titanic: *Triumph and Tragedy*, p. 167–184.

[131] Lost & Found at Sea: The Story of Leah and Filly Aks, Marshall Weiss, *Dayton Jewish Observer*, March 20, 2012.

[132] A Story of a Pig and the *Titanic*, *Craig Daily Press*, October 24, 2007.

9. Reaction of the Jewish Press

[133] News of the *Titanic* Disaster, *Saturday Evening Post*, August 7, 1926.

[134] News of the *Titanic* Disaster, *Saturday Evening Post*, August 7, 1926.

[135] Brewster, H.(1988) *882½ Amazing Answers to Your Questions about the* Titanic, p. 66–67.

[136] Davenport-Hines, R. (2012) Titanic *Lives*, p. 325.

[137] www.billgladstone.ca/?p=2613.

[138] Disaster on the Sea (in Hebrew), *Hatzvi*, April 22, 1912.

[139] Nathan Straus in Jerusalem (in Hebrew), *Hamitzpe*, April 18, 1912.

[140] Telegrams (in Hebrew), *Hazman*, April 18, 1912.

[141] (in Hebrew), *Hazman*, May 20, 1912.

[142] To the Spirit of Time and Era (in Hebrew), *Machzike Hadas*, April 26, 1912.

[143] In Our World (in Hebrew), *Hazfira*, June 27, 1912.

[144] Letters from Overseas (in Hebrew), *Hazfira*, May 12, 1912.

[145] Agroy'se ship = Catastrophe (in Yiddish), *Der Mament*, April 17, 1912.

[146] The Wreck of the *Titanic*, *Jewish Chronicle*, April, 1912

[147] World Mourns *Titanic* Disaster, *Sentinel*, April 19, 1912.

[148] The *Titanic* Disaster, *Sentinel*, April 26, 1912.

[149] The Following Jews Were on Board the *Titanic*, *Bnai Brith Messenger*, April 26, 1912.

[150] The *Titanic* Disaster, *Sentinel*, April 26, 1912.

[151] *Washington Times*, April 20, 1912.

[152] Straus and Wife Drown Together as Vessel Sinks, *Humeston New Era*, April 24, 1912.

[153] About Uncle Leyzer and that Iceberg, Dovid Katz, *Jewish Daily Forward*, April 17, 1998.

[154] Davenport-Hines, R. (2012) Titanic *Lives*, p.167.

[155] Steerage Victim Lived Here, *Evening Bulletin*, April 23, 1912.

[156] Wants Information of Brandeis, *New York Times*, April 22, 1912.

[157] Senator Guggenheim Fearful that His Brother Is Dead, *Washington Times*, April 16, 1912.

[158] A Philadelphia Jew on the Sunken *Titanic*, *Jewish Daily Forward*, April 10, 2012.

10. Burial of the Victims

[159] Beth Israel Synagogue Cemetery, Years of Tradition: Beth Israel Synagogue in Halifax, Nova Scotia (official website): http://thebethisrael.com/index.htm.

[160] Eaton, J.P. & C.A. Haas. Titanic: *Triumph and Tragedy*, London, 1994.

[161] At Halifax's Jewish Cemetery: A *Titanic* Section, Marshall Weiss, *Dayton Jewish Observer*, March 18, 2012.

[162] Eaton, J.P. & C.A. Haas. Titanic: *Triumph and Tragedy*, 1994.

[163] Beed, B. Titanic *Victims in Halifax Graveyards*, 2001.

[164] Beth Israel Synagogue Cemetery, Years of Tradition: Beth Israel Synagogue in Halifax, Nova Scotia (official website): http://thebethisrael.com/index.htm.

[165] Lynch, D. (1997) Titanic, *An Illustrated History*, p. 170–171.

[166] Lynch, D. (1997) Titanic, *An Illustrated History*, p. 170–171.

[167] About Uncle Leyzer and that Iceberg, Dovid Katz, *Jewish Daily Forward*, April 17, 1998.

[168] Headstone Now Marks *Titanic* Victim's Grave, *Canadian Jewish News*, April 2, 2012.

[169] Queens Is Final Resting Place for Two *Titanic* Victims, *Western Queens Gazette*, Jason Antos, April 18, 2012.

[170] Queens Is Final Resting Place for Two *Titanic* Victims, *Western Queens Gazette*, Jason Antos, April 18, 2012.

[171] *New York Times*, May 11, 1913.

[172] *New York Times*, April 21, 1912.

[173] *Emergency and Relief Booklet,* American Red Cross, 1913.

[174] Other Midlanders aboard the *Titanic, Omaha World-Herald*, April 8, 2012.

[175] *Titanic* Victims Relative Honors Precious Legacy, *New Jersey Jewish News*, August 27, 2012.

[176] Masliansky, Z.H. (1926) *The Sermons of Rabbi Zevi Hirsh Masliansky.*

11. The *Agunot* Issue, a Rabbinical Dilemma

[177] Minzberg, Y. (1944) Agunah's *Pamphlet* (in Hebrew).

[178] Epshtein, A.L. (1936), *Question of the* Agunah (in Hebrew), p 3–7.

[179] Rat, A. (2013) *With Might and Strength* (in Hebrew), p 163–183.

[180] Water Without End, *Hazman*, May 21, 1912.

[181] Meskin, Y.(1940), *Beis Yaakov* (in Hebrew), p 128–138.

[182] *New York Herald*, April 19, 1912

12. Arrival of the Survivors in New York

[183] Ties Bind Jewish Charities to *Titanic*, N. Zeveloff, *Jewish Daily Forward*, April 13, 2012.

[184] List of Jews in Third Cabin of *Titanic* Reaches Chicago, *Chicago Jewish Tribune*, April 18, 1912.

[185] 11 Jewish Names among Rescued Steerage Passengers, *Jewish Daily Forward*, April 10, 2012.

[186] Ties Bind Jewish Charities to *Titanic*, N. Zeveloff, *Jewish Daily Forward*, April 13, 2012.

[187] Hadassah's 100th Anniversary and Its Link to the *Titanic* Recalled at Temple Emanu-El, *Jewish Daily Forward*.

[188] Hadassah's 100th Anniversary and Its Link to the Titanic Recalled at Temple Emanu-El, *Jewish Daily Forward*.

[189] Lynch, D. (1997) Titanic, *An Illustrated History*, p. 166–169.

[190] Encyclopedia Titanica.

[191] Cupid Wins Out, *Daily Banner*, April 23, 1912.

[192] Ties Bind Jewish Charities to Titanic, N. Zeveloff, *Jewish Daily Forward*, April 13, 2012.

[193] What the Rescued Jewish Immigrants Have to Say, *Jewish Daily Forward*, April 1912.

[194] What the Rescued Jewish Immigrants Have to Say, *Jewish Daily Forward*, April 1912.

[195] Gus Cohen, *Evening Echo*, August 7, 1978.

[196] Women Revealed as Heroines by Wreck, *New York Times*, April 20, 1912.

[197] Kosher Deli in England a *Titanic* Survivor's Legacy, Marshall Weiss, *The Dayton Jewish Observer*, March 21, 2021.

13. Inquiries

[198] Brewster, H. (1988) *882½ Amazing Answers to Your Questions about the Titanic*, p 72–73.

[199] Lord, W. (1987) *The Night Lives On*, p 164.

[200] Brewster, H. (1988) *882½ Amazing Answers to Your Questions about the Titanic*, p 72–73.

[201] *Titanic* Inquiry Project: www.titanicinquiry.org. Day 14, Testimony of Berk Pichard.

[202] *Titanic* Inquiry Project: www.titanicinquiry.org. Day 14, Testimony of Berk Pichard.

[203] *Titanic* Inquiry Project: www.titanicinquiry.org. Day 11, Testimony of Charles E. Stengel.

[204] *Titanic* Inquiry Project: www.titanicinquiry.org. Day 11, Testimony of Charles E. Stengel.

14. Eulogies, Memorials, and Lamentations

[205] The *Titanic* and Jews, David Geffen, *Jerusalem Post*, April 4, 2012.

[206] *New York Herald*, April 22, 1912

[207] Tribute to Straus Paid in Synagogues, *New York Times*, April 21, 1912.

[208] A Real *Titanic* Love Story, Philip Getz, *Jewish Ideas Daily*, April 18, 2012.

[209] Sorrow in Jewish Home, *Leeds Mercury*, April 19, 1912.

[210] The *Titanic* and Jews, David Geffen, *Jerusalem Post*, 2012.

[211] *Titanic* Disaster in Yiddish and Hebrew Literature, (in Hebrew) *Herut*, June 22, 1962.

[212] *Brooklyn Daily Eagle*, April 22, 1912.

[213] Levin, J. M. (1917), *To the House of David*, (in Hebrew), p. 89–94.

[214] Anzenberger, H., *Downfall of the* Titanic (in Hebrew), 1977.

[215] Signature of the *Titanic* in Prayer and Tehina (in Hebrew), Levin, Y. *Makor Rishon*, April 13, 2012.

[216] Biel, S. (1998). *The Disaster of the Century in Poetry, Song and Prose.*

[217] *Titanic* Disaster in Yiddish and Hebrew Literature, (in Hebrew) *Herut*, June 22, 1962

[218] *Titanic* Disaster in Yiddish and Hebrew Literature, (in Hebrew) *Herut*, June 22, 1962

[219] Lord, W. (1986) *The Night Lives On*, p. 106–118.

[220] www.youtube.com/watch?v=Mcy7NgoJP8Y.

[221] Lord, W. (1986) *The Night Lives On*, p. 106–118.

[222] www.poetrysoup.com.

15. Film Adaptations

[223] Lord, W. (2012) *A Night to Remember*, p. 179.

[224] *Palestine Post*, May 14, 1937.

16. The *Titanic* as a Metaphor

[225] Jewish American Hall of Fame: www.amuseum.org/jahf/virtour/page27.html#davidsarnoff.

[226] Mutiny on the *Titanic*, Avnery, A. *Haaretz*, October 1, 2011.

[227] Mutiny on the *Titanic*, Avnery, A. *Haaretz*, October 1, 2011.

[228] Ramon, H. (2003) *The Histadrut and the Health Insurance Law* (in Hebrew). p. 2–3.

[229] Crowded in the Middle (in Hebrew), Ron-Moria, S. *Makor Rishon*, July 4, 2012.

[230] www.po-liti.blogspot.co.il/2012/12/blog-post_5.html.

[231] Tel Aviv: *Titanic* or Pompeii or Sodom, Gal Bekerman, *Jewish Daily Forward*, May 21, 2012.

[232] Chait, B. (2001). *The Amazing Journey to Noble Values* (in Hebrew).

[233] Ohayon, A., (2015) Titanic *Comics*, (in Hebrew).

[234] Onboard the *Concordia*: A *Titanic* Survivor's Granddaughter, (in Hebrew) *Maariv*, January 18, 2012.

[235] Onboard the *Concordia*: A *Titanic* Survivor's Granddaughter, (in Hebrew) *Maariv*, January 18, 2012.

[236] Gardiner, R. Titanic: *The Ship That Never Sank?* 2009.

[237] Matson, B. (2008). Titanic's *Last Secrets*, p. 34.

[238] Matson, B. (2008). Titanic's *Last Secrets*, p. 34.

17. Life and Death of the *Titanic* Jews

[239] The Tale of the *Titanic* Told by a Rescued Ilford Lady, *Ilford Graphic*, May 10, 1912.

[240] Encyclopedia Titanica.

[241] Encyclopedia Titanica.

[242] Other Midlanders aboard the *Titanic*, *Omaha World-Herald*, April 8, 2012.

[243] www.charlespellegrino.com/passengers/mrs_harris.htm.

[244] Encyclopedia Titanica.

[245] Headstone Now Marks *Titanic* Victim's Grave, the *Canadian Jewish News*, April 2, 2012.

[246] www.rsc.org/AboutUs/News/PressReleases/2012/Rene-Levy-Titanic-chemist.as.

[247] Encyclopedia Titanica.

[248] The *Titanic*: A Jewish Family's Story, Rachel Mines, *Outlook Magazine*, 2009.

[249] Encyclopedia Titanica.

[250] Kosher Deli in England a *Titanic* Survivor's Legacy, Marshall Weiss, *Dayton Jewish Observer*, March 21, 2021.

[251] Sorrow in Jewish Home, *Leeds Mercury*, April 19, 1912.

[252] The *Titanic*: A Jewish Family's Story, Rachel Mines, *Outlook Magazine*, 2009.

[253] My *Titanic* Uncle (2012) Astra Burka Design Production Company.

[254] Hopper, T. Stealing the *Titanic*: Artifacts auction draws accusations of grave robbery. *National Post*, 2012.

[255] My *Titanic* Uncle (2012) Astra Burka Design Production Company.

[256] www.rsc.org/AboutUs/News/PressReleases/2012/Rene-Levy-Titanic-chemist.as.

[257] Two Families and One Lifeboat, *Jewish Daily Forward*, April 13, 2012.

[258] *The Story of the Titanic as Told by Its Survivors*, p. 232.

[259] Panic Terrible Just Before Vessel Sank, *Denver Post*, April 19, 1912.

[260] Encyclopedia Titanica.

[261] Gowan, Philip, "*The Goldenbergs*" (2013) www.wormstedt.com/Titanic/Goldenberg.html.

[262] Encyclopedia Titanica.

[263] https://www.charlespellegrino.com/passengers/mrs_harris.htm.

[264] Mrs. Henry B (Renee) Harris Dies, *Variety*, Robert Landry, September 10, 1969.

[265] www.youtube.com/watch?v=Mcy7NgoJP8Y.

[266] Edith Russell Obituary, *New York Times*, May 6, 1975.

[267] *New York Times,* April 19, 1912.

[268] A Jewish Chapter in *Titanic* Saga, *New Jersey Jewish Standard*, April 6, 2012. Also: Kosher Deli in England a *Titanic* Survivor's Legacy, Marshall Weiss, *Dayton Jewish Observer*, March 21, 2012.

[269] Gus Cohen, *Evening Echo*, August 7, 1978.

[270] www.youtube.com/watch?v=Mcy7NgoJP8Y.

[271] Gus Cohen, *Evening Echo*, August 7, 1978

[272] The Tale of the *Titanic* Told by a Rescued Ilford Lady, *Ilford Graphic*, May 10, 1912

[273] www.youtube.com/watch?v=NQbIrrxoEAg&spfreload=10.

[274] Eva Hart, 91, a Last Survivor With Memory of Titanic, Dies. *New York Times,* February, 17, 1996.

[275] Lost & Found at Sea, M. Weiss, *Dayton Jewish Observer*, March 20, 2012.

[276] Tropper Yoshef. *Jew on Board* (2013). www.closetotorah.com/tag/leah-aks/.

[277] Curse of the *Titanic*: What happened to those who survived? Andrew Wilson, *Independent*, 2011.

[278] *Times of Israel,* April 9, 2016.

[279] Ish Le-Re'ehu, Machon Ahavat Emet, June 2016.

Bibliography and Sources

Every effort has been made to locate and credit all copyright holders. In case of omission or mistake, please contact the author for correction in future editions.

Books:

Anzenberger, Hans Magnus. *Downfall of the* Titanic (in Hebrew). Tel Aviv: Po'alim Books, 1977.

Archbold, Rick, and Dana McCauley. *Last Dinner on the* Titanic. New York: Hyperion Books, 1997.

Avieli, Katzia. *Journey to the Past: A Modern World Is Born* (in Hebrew). MTH, Tel Aviv, 2003.

Ballard, Robert D. *The Discovery of the* Titanic. Toronto: Madison Press Books, 1987.

Blake, John. *The* Titanic *Pocketbook: A Passenger's Guide*. London: Conway, 2011.

Brewster, Hugh, and Laurie Coulter. *882½ Amazing Answers to Your Questions about the* Titanic. Toronto: Scholastic Canada, 1988.

Caren, Eric and Steve Goldman. *Extra* Titanic. Castle Books, 1998.

Davenport-Hines, Richard. Titanic *Lives: Migrants and Millionaires, Conmen and Crew.* London: Harper Collins Publishers, 2012.

Eaton, John P., and Charles A. Haas. Titanic: *Triumph and Tragedy*. London: Patrick Stephens, 1994.

Epshtein, Arieh Leib. *Question of the* Agunah (in Hebrew). New York: Rabbinical Assembly, 1936.

Gardiner, Robin, Titanic: *The Ship That Never Sank?* London: Ian Allan Publishing, 2009.

Gardiner, Robin, *The* Titanic *Conspiracy*. Secaucus, N.J.: Carol Publishing Corporation, 1995.

Halperin, Yisrael. *Jews and Judaism in Eastern Europe* (in Hebrew). Jerusalem: Magnes Pub., 1969.

Levin, Josef Meir. *To the House of David* (in Hebrew). Cincinnati: Rames Press, 1917.

Lord, Walter. *A Night to Remember: The Sinking of the* Titanic, Centenary Edition. London: Penguin Books, 2012.

Lord, Walter. *The Night Lives On: The Untold Stories and Secrets Behind the Sinking of the "Unsinkable Ship* – Titanic. New York: Harper Collins Publishers, 1987.

Lynch, Don, and Ken Marschall. Titanic: *An Illustrated History*. Toronto: Madison Press Books, 1997.

Marshal, Logan. *The Sinking of the* Titanic *and Great Sea Disasters*. Philadelphia: Universal Book & Bible House, 1912.

Masliansky, Zevi Hirsh, and Edward Herbert. *The Sermons of Rabbi Zevi Hirsh Masliansky*. New York: Hebrew Publishing Company, 1926.

Matson, Brad. Titanic's *Last Secrets: The Further Adventures of Shadow Divers John Chatterton and Richie Kohler*. New York: Hachette Book Group, 2008.

McCluskie, Tom. *The Wall Chart of the* Titanic. San Diego: Thunder Bay Press, 1998.

Meskin, Rabbi Yaakov. *Sefer Beis Yaakov* (in Hebrew). New York: REM Press, 1940.

Minzberg, Yisrael. Agunah's *Pamphlet* (in Hebrew). Jerusalem: EretzYisrael Print, 1944.

Sherman, Charles. *United States Jewry* (in Hebrew). Tel Aviv: Am Oved, 1956.

Winocour, Jack. *The Story of the* Titanic *as Told by Its Survivors*. New York: Dover Publications, 1960.

Ziv, Hani. *B'neiKeshet: A Hundred Years of Struggle* (in Hebrew). Tel Aviv: Ministry of Defense, 1998.

(No author). *300 Years of Freedom* (in Hebrew). Tel Aviv: American Information Office, Haaretz Press, 1954.

Articles:

Adler, J. "Many Waters Cannot Quench Love – Neither Can the Floods Drown It." *Straus Historical Society Inc. Newsletter*, 2012.

Antos, J. "Queens Is Final Resting Place for Two *Titanic* Victims." *Western Queens Gazette*, April 18, 2012.

Arnold, J. "Headstone Now Marks *Titanic* Victim's Grave." *Canadian Jewish News*, April 1, 2012.

Avnery U. "A Rebellion on the *Titanic.*" *Haaretz*, October 22, 2012.

Beckerman, G. "Tel Aviv = *Titanic* or Pompeii or Sodom?" *Jewish Daily Forward*, May 21, 2012.

Brody, S. "Jewish Heroes and Heroines in America." *Florida Atlantic University Libraries*, 1996.

Dalby, S. "Disaster Memories Pay Off at Auction." *Guardian*, May 6, 2000.

Fuerstenberg-Lidsky, G. "The Techinah and the *Titanic.*" *Canadian Jewish News*, February 7, 2012.

Gearan, A. "*Titanic*'s 83rd Anniversary Marked by Artifacts Exhibit Disaster." *Los Angeles Times*, April 16, 1995.

Geffen, D. "The *Titanic* and Jews." *Jerusalem Post*, April 15, 2012.

Getz, P. "A Real *Titanic* Love Story." *Jewish Ideas Daily, April 18, 2012.*

Gottesman, I. "The *Titanic* in Yiddish Folklore." *Jewish Daily Forward*, April 20, 2012.

Green, D. "An Esteemed Jewish Couple Goes Down With the *Titanic.*" *Haaretz*, April 15, 2013.

Hazard, S. "*Titanic* Victims Relative Honors Precious Legacy." *New Jersey Jewish News*, August 27, 2012.

Hirsch, M. "Titan of the Sea Meets Its Match." *Jewish Daily Forward*, April 9, 2012.

Hirsch, M. "Two Families and One Lifeboat." *Jewish Daily Forward*, April 11, 2012.

Hopper, T. "Stealing the *Titanic*: Artifacts Auction Draws Accusations of Grave Robbery." *National Post*, January 28, 2012.

Jeffay, N. "*Titanic* Discoverer Launches Israel Sea-Floor Expedition." *Jewish Daily Forward*, September 7, 2010.

Katz, D. "About Uncle Leyzer and That Iceberg." *Jewish Daily Forward*, April 7, 1998.

Kalmus, J. "He Survived the Titanic Shipwreck and Became a Manchester Legend." *Jewish Chronicle*, March 29, 2012.

Kaplan, M. "Titanic's Kosher Butcher Shop to Be Preserved." *Jewish Daily Forward*, January 1, 2014.

Kennedy, C. "The Cat Recalls His Escape from the Sinking *Titanic*." *Mall Star*, April 12, 1972.

Kennedy, M. "*Titanic* Artifacts Go on Display for First Time." *Guardian*, July 13, 2011.

Kushner, T. "*Titanic*'s Hidden Victims." *Jewish Chronicle*, April 11, 2012.

Landry, J.R. "Mrs. Henry B (Renee) Harris Dies." *Variety*, September 10, 1969.

Levin, Y. "Signature of the *Titanic* in Prayer and Tehina" (in Hebrew). *Makor Rishon*, April 13, 2012.

Leon, M. "Hadassah's 100th Anniversary and Its Link to the *Titanic* Recalled at Temple Emanuel." *Jewish Daily Forward*, March 1, 2012.

Mines, R. "The *Titanic*: A Jewish Family's Story." *Outlook Magazine*, July 1, 2009.

Prather, D. "A Story of a Pig and the *Titanic*." *Craig Daily Press*, October 24, 2007.

Robert, T. "Eva Hart, 91, a Last Survivor with Memory of *Titanic*, Dies." *New York Times*, February 16, 1996.

Ron-Moria, S. "Crowded in the Middle" (in Hebrew). *MakorRishon*, July 4, 2012.

Siegel, M. "A Love Story of Honor." *Dayton Jewish Observer*, March 20, 2012.

Weiss, M. "A Jewish Chapter in *Titanic* Saga." *Dayton Jewish Observer*, April 6, 2012.

Weiss, M. "At Halifax's Jewish Cemetery: a *Titanic* Section." *Dayton Jewish Observer*, March 18, 2012.

Weiss, M. "Kashrut Aboard the '*Titanic*' Sheds Light on Immigration." *Dayton Jewish Observer*, April 11, 2012.

Weiss, M. "Kosher Deli in England a *Titanic* Survivor's Legacy." NewYork: *Dayton Jewish Observer*, March 21, 2012.

Weiss, M. "Lost & Found at Sea: The Story of Leah and 'Filly' Aks." *Dayton Jewish Observer*, March 20, 2012.

Wilson, A. "Curse of the Titanic: What Happened to Those Who Survived?" *Independent*, 2011.

Zeveloff, N. "Ties Bind Jewish Charities to *Titanic*." *Jewish Daily Forward*, April 12, 2012.

(No author). "Gus Cohen." *Evening Echo*, August 7, 1978.

(No author). "Montreal Cemetery a Testament to the Past." *Jewish Tribune*, July 22, 2009.

(No author). "Other Midlanders aboard the *Titanic.*" *Omaha World-Herald*, April 8, 2012.

(No author). "What the Rescued Jewish Immigrants Have to Say." *Jewish Daily Forward*, April 10, 2012.

(No author). "What Those Rescued from the *Titanic* Experienced." *Jewish Daily Forward*, April 12, 2012.

(No author). "Edith Russell Obituary." *New York Times*, May 6, 1975.

(No author). "The British Courtesy Killed *Titanic*'s Passengers" (in Hebrew). *Walla News*, January 23, 2009.

Newspaper reports of the disaster:
"Agroy'se ship = Catastrophe" (in Yiddish). *Der Mament*, April 17, 1912.

"Disaster on the Sea" (in Hebrew). *Hatzvi*, April 22, 1912.

"How Mrs. Meyer Escaped." *Le Journal*, April 20, 1912.

"How the Harrises Parted." *New York Times*, April 19, 1912.

"Hundreds Blown into Sea." *New York Herald*, April 19, 1912.

"In Our World" (in Hebrew). *Hazfira*, June 27, 1912.

"Isidor Straus Buried in Beth El Cemetery." *World (Evening Edition)*, May 8, 1912.

"Last Will and Testament Lost on *Titanic.*" *Daily Chronicle*, April 1912.

"Letters from Overseas" (in Hebrew). *Hazfira*, May 12, 1912.

"List of Jews in Third Cabin of *Titanic* Reaches Chicago." *Chicago Jewish Tribune*, April 18, 1912.

"Mrs. Henry B. Harris Saved from Wreck." *Washington Times*, April 18, 1912.

"Mrs. Straus Would Not Leave Her Husband." *Exelsior*, April 20, 1912.

"Nathan Strauss in Jerusalem" (in Hebrew). *Hamitzpe*, April 18, 1912.

"News of the *Titanic* Disaster." *Saturday Evening Post*, April 7, 1926.

"Overseas" (in Hebrew). *Hazfira*, August 4, 1912.

"Panic Terrible Just Before Vessel Sank." *Denver Post*, April 19, 1912.

"Proving Forman on *Titanic*." *New York Times*, May 15, 1912.

"Resonance of the *Titanic* Disaster" (in Hebrew). *Hazman*, April 28, 1912.

"Senator Guggenheim Fearful That His Brother Is Dead." *Washington Times*, April 16, 1912.

"Sinking of the *Titanic* and Her Loses" (in Hebrew). *Hamitzpe*, April 22, 1912.

"Solomon Sadowitz Is Anxious about His Son." *Evening News*, April 16, 1912.

"Sorrow in Jewish Home." *Leeds Mercury*, April 19, 1912.

"Steerage Victim Lived Here." *Evening Bulletin*, April 23, 1912.

"Straus and Wife Drown Together as Vessel Sinks." *Humeston New Era*, April 24, 1912.

"Telegrams" (in Hebrew). *Hazman*, April 18, 1912.

"Tell Them No Woman Died Because I Was a Coward." *Washington Times*, April 20, 1912.

"The Catastrophe Details of the *Titanic*" (in Hebrew). *Hazfira*, April 21, 1912.

"The Following Jews Were on Board the *Titanic*." *Bnai Brith Messenger*, April 26, 1912

"The *Titanic* Disaster." *Sentinel*, April 26, 1912.

"The *Titanic* Disaster." *Aberdale Leader*, May 4, 1912.

"The *Titanic*'s Barber: Important Question in Compensation Law." *Hampshire Independent*, August 17, 1912.

"The *Titanic*'s Great Tragedy" (in Yiddish). *Jewish Daily Forward*, April 16, 1912.

"The Tale of the *Titanic* Told by a Rescued Ilford Lady." *Ilford Graphic*, May 10, 1912.

"The Wreck of the *Titanic*." *Jewish Chronicle*, April 19, 1912.

"*Titanic*" (in Hebrew). *Hazman*, May 20, 1912.

"To the Spirit of Time and Era" (in Hebrew). *Machzike Hadas*, April 26, 1912.

"Tribute to Straus Paid in Synagogues," *New York Times*, April 21, 1912.

"Wants Information of Brandeis," *New York Times*, April 22, 1912.

"Who Is Guilty for the *Titanic* Disaster?" (in Hebrew), *Hazman*, April 23, 1912.

"Women Revealed as Heroines by Wreck." *New York Times*, April 20, 1912.

"World Mourns *Titanic* Disaster." *Sentinel*, April 19, 1912.

Online articles:

www.shturem.net/index.php?section=special&id=29&oldlang=english.

www.bh.org.il/jewish-community-antwerp-belgium.

www.wormstedt.com/Titanic/Goldenberg.html.

www.billgladstone.ca/?p=2613 (2013).

www.rsc.org/AboutUs/News/PressReleases/2012/Rene-Levy-Titanic-chemist.asp.

www.closetotorah.com/tag/leah-aks/.

www.enchantedTitanic.com/children-of-the-Titanic/Titanic-passenger-typkia-friedberg/.

www.charlespellegrino.com/passengers/mrs_harris.htm.

Online archives:

American Jewish Historical Society: www.ajhs.org.

Encyclopedia Titanica: www.encyclopedia-Titanica.org.

Family Tree & Family History: www.geni.com.

Find A Grave—Millions of Cemetery Records: www.findagrave.com.

Genealogy, Family Trees & Family History Records: www.ancestry.com.

Hebrew Immigrant Aid Society: www.hias.org.

Historical Jewish Press: www.web.nli.org.il.

International Titanic Society: www.Titanicinternationalsociety.org.

Jewish American Hall of Fame: www.amuseum.org/jahf.

Jewish Virtual Library: www.jewishvirtuallibrary.org.

Library of Congress: www.loc.gov.

Straus Historical Society: www.straushistoricalsociety.org.

Titanic Historical Society: www.titanic1.org.

Titanic Inquiry Project: www.titanicinquiry.org.

Archives, museums, libraries:

Maritime Museum of the Atlantic, Halifax, Nova Scotia.

Merseyside Maritime Museum, Liverpool Waterfront, Liverpool.

National Library, Givat Ram, Jerusalem, Israel.

National Maritime Museum, Park Row, Greenwich, London.

Titanic Museum, Queens Island, Belfast, Northern Ireland.

The *Titanic* Museum, Main Street, Indian Orchard, Massachusetts.

Yad Va-Shem Holocaust Museum and Library, Jerusalem, Israel.

Films:

Mime Misu, *In Night and Ice*. Continental Kunstfilm, 1912.

Ewald André Dupont, *Atlantic*. British International Pictures, 1929.

Werner Klingler, *Titanic*. Universum Film AG, 1943.

Jean Negulesco, *Titanic*. Twentieth Century Fox, 1953.

Roy Ward Baker, *A Night to Remember*. Rank Organization, 1958.

William Hale, *S.O.S. Titanic*. EMI films, 1979.

Stephen Low, *Titanica*. IMAX, 1995.

James Cameron, *Titanic*. A James Cameron Film, Twentieth Century Fox, 1997.

Other:

Burka, A, (writer/director), *My Titanic Uncle,* Astra Burka Design Production Company, 2012.

www.youtube.com/watch?v=Mcy7NgoJP8Y www.youtube.com/watch?v=MD5J43Z9AWI.

Acknowledgments

Before I thank all who helped me throughout my research and writing, I wish to thank a special woman; without her none of this would have been possible. Thanks from all my heart to my dear wife, Tirza, mother of my five children, who guided me and escorted me throughout the entire process. She was there for me from research through writing and publishing. She gave me the mental relaxation I needed so much during these past years. Anything I required she granted, including my absence from home and hours on end with the books, the old newspapers, and the computer. She listened to my stories, my indecisions, and my frustrations and helped me pass these intensive years in the best and most comforting and enjoyable way possible.

The whole process of my research, from rough draft to publication, became possible with the assistance, support, and encouragement of many individuals and organizations. To them, I owe my gratitude. I wish to thank the following for permission to use their material: Charlie Haas from the *Titanic* International Society, Valery Bazarov from the Hebrew Immigrant Aid Society, and Joan Adler from the Straus Historical Society Inc. I also thank Naomi Zeveloff from the *Forward*, and Jason Antos from the *Western Queens Gazette*.

Thanks to the staff of the following institutes for their aid and guidance: National Maritime Museum in Greenwich, Merseyside Maritime Museum in Liverpool, and the National Library in Jerusalem.

Thanks to *Titanic* researchers and historians for assisting me, each one in a special way: David Gardner, Bill Wormstedt, Phil Gowan, and George Behe. Thanks to all the individuals who shared photos, documents, and knowledge with me: Trevor Baxtor, Peter Engberg, Evgueni Mlodik, Olivier Mendez, Helaine Larina, and Marta Dawes.

Special thanks to three individuals who not only gave me permission to use their material about the *Titanic*, but also agreed to read my manuscript and share their opinions with me. The three are: Marshall Weiss from the

Dayton Jewish Observer, historian Randy Bryan Bigham, and *Titanic* expert Don Lynch.

I wish to thank the relatives and descendants of *Titanic* victims and survivors for the information they shared with me about their loved ones and for permission to use their work, information, documents, and photos: Stanley Gilinsky, relative of *Titanic* victim Eliezer Gilinski; Astra Burka, great-grandniece of *Titanic* survivor Adolphe Saalfeld; Rachel Mines, grandniece of *Titanic* victim David Livshin; and Richard Hyman, great-grandson of *Titanic* survivor Abraham Hyman.

Special thanks to Shelley Binder, great-granddaughter of *Titanic* survivor Leah Aks and great-niece of *Titanic* survivor Philip Aks.

On the technical side, I wish to thank several people. Thanks to Noa Netanel, my copyright consultant who took care of all my copyright matters, for her professional help in all the references and copyright issues and for her general remarks. Thanks to Michal Schwartz, my editor of the Hebrew edition, who escorted me though the entire process of the research and initial writing.

Turning my book from Hebrew to English was a challenging mission as well. I wish to thank Yael Kollet and Henrietta Mann from Halifax, Canada, who gave me the inspiration and pushed me into translating the book, and for their support along the way. Literally, without their support, this book wouldn't have been possible. Also I thank Deanna Ryan-Meister from *Titanic* Society of Atlantic Canada.

Finally I wish to thank the entire staff of Hybrid Global Publishing for the smooth transition from manuscript to printed book. Special thanks to Joe Potter for the cover design, Claudia Volkman for the editing and typesetting, and Karen Strauss for everything else.

All Jewish passengers and crew on board the Titanic[1]

Name	Born	Class	Gender	Lifeboat
Abelson, Hannah (Henya)	1884	2	F	10
Abelson, Samuel	1882	2	M	—
Aks, Frank Philip	1911	3	M	11
Aks, Leah	1894	3	F	13
Banewer, Solomon	1870	2	M	—
Baumen, John	1852	1	M	—
Birnbaum, Jacob	1887	1	M	—
Brandeis, Emil	1864	1	M	—
Cohen Christi, Alice	1867	2	F	12
Cohen Christi, Julia	1887	2	F	12
Cohen, Gershon (Gus)	1893	3	M	12
Cook, Jacob	1871	3	M	—
Corn (Cornblatt), Harry	1882	3	M	—
Dodge, Ruth	1878	1	F	5
Dodge, Washington Jr.	1907	1	M	5
Dropkin, Jennie	1887	3	F	13
Emanuel, Ethel Virginia	1907	3	F	13
Forman, Benjamin	1881	1	M	—
Frauenthal, Clara	1869	1	F	5
Frauenthal, Henry	1862	1	M	5
Frauenthal, Gerald (Isaac)	1868	1	M	5
Friedberg, (Hershel?)[2]	?	3	M	—
Friedberg, Typkia (Tikvah?)	?	3	F	—
Gilinski, Eliezer (Leslie)	1890	3	M	—
Goldenberg, Samuel	1864	1	M	5
Goldsmith, Nathan	1875	3	M	—
Greenberg, Samuel	1860	2	M	—
Greenfield, Blanche	1867	1	F	7
Greenfield, William	1888	1	M	7

[1] Names marked in bold are survivors of the disaster.
[2] The Friedberg's names were not on the passenger list. They both sailed under unknown alias names. The husband's true name remains unknown. It is possible that the couple never actually sailed the *Titanic*.

Name	Born	Class	Gender	Lifeboat
Guggenheim, Benjamin	1866	1	M	—
Harris, Henry Birkhardt	1876	1	M	—
Harris, René	1876	1	F	D
Hart, Benjamin	1869	2	M	—
Hyman, Abraham Josef	1878	3	M	C
Jacobsohn, Amy	1888	2	F	12
Jacobsohn, Sidney (Samuel)	1870	2	M	—
Kantor, Miriam	1888	2	F	12
Kantor, Sinai (Sehua)	1878	2	M	—
Kennell, Charles	1882	crew	M	—
Klaber, Herman	1867	1	M	—
Klein, Herbert	1879	crew	M	—
Kutsher, (Lithman) Simon	1886	3	M	—
Lewy, Ervin	1881	1	M	—
Lévy, René Jacques (Jacob)	1875	2	M	—
Livshin, David	1887	3	M	B[3]
Maisner, Shimon	1878	3	M	—
Mayer, Edger Joseph	1884	1	M	—
Mayer, Leah (Leila)	1886	1	F	6
Moor, Bella (Beila)	1882	3	F	14
Moor, Meyer (Meier)	1904	3	M	14
Nesson, Israel	1886	2	M	—
Pinski, Rosa	1880	2	F	9
Pulner, Uscher (Asher)	1894	3	F	—
Rosenbaum, Edith	1879	1	F	11
Rosenshine, George	1866	1	M	—
Roth, Sarah	1885	3	F	C
Rothschild, Martin	1865	1	M	—
Saalfeld, Adolphe	1865	1	M	3
Sadowitz, Harry	1894	3	M	—
Sirota, Maurice (Moshe)	1892	3	M	—
Slocovski, Zalman	1892	3	M	—

[3]He died during the night and was buried at sea the next day.

Name	Born	Class	Gender	Lifeboat
Salomon, Abraham	1868	1	M	1
Spector (Spectorovski), Woolf	1889	3	M	—
Stengel, Annie May	1867	1	F	5
Stengel, Charles	1857	1	M	1
Straus, Ida Rosalie	1849	1	F	—
Straus, Isidor	1845	1	M	—
Taussig, Emil	1860	1	M	—
Taussig, Ruth	1893	1	F	8
Taussig, Tilli	1872	1	F	8
Trembisky, Berk[4]	1880	3	M	9
Troupiansky, Moshe Aaron	1888	2	M	—
Weisz, Leopold (Aryeh)	1880	2	M	—
Weller, (Veller) Aaron	1875	3	M	—
Zimerman, Leo	1883	3	M	—

[4]Berk Trembisky changed his name to Benoît Picard.

Notable *Titanic* passengers and crew who might have been Jewish[5]

Name	Born	Gender	Class	Lifeboat
Cavendish, Julia	1886	F	1	6
Flegenheimer, Antoinette	1863	F	1	7
Murdlin, Josef	1890	M	3	—
Pennal, Thomas Frederick	1879	M	crew	—
Rheims, George A	1879	M	1	A

[5]Unfortunately, by the time my book was ready for publication, I was not able to determine if these passengers where Jewish or not. Some researchers claim that they are; others claim that they are not.

Possible names of Jewish passengers
(None appear on White Star Line or official *Titanic* list)[6]

Name	Gender	Survived?
Badman, Herman	M	?
Barawitch, George	M	Y
Barawitch, Harren	M	Y
Barawitch, Marian	F	Y
Holman, Sucha	M	?
Trantinsky, Bercka	F	Y

[6]Although these names do not appear in the passengers list, they are all mentioned in Jewish newspapers shortly after the disaster as Jewish passengers of the Titanic. It is possible that these Jews sailed with assumed names. It is also possible that they were not onboard the Titanic and their names were mistakenly added to the lists.

Jewish *Titanic* victims whose bodies were found and buried

Name	Body #	Cemetery
Birnbaum, Jacob	148	*Machzikey Hadat* Jewish Cemetery, Putte, the Netherlands
Brandeis, Emil	208	Pleasant Hill Jewish Cemetery, Omaha, Nebraska
Gilinski, Eliezer	47	Buried at sea[7]
Greenberg, Samuel	19	Jewish Cemetery, Bronx, New York
Kantor, Sinai	283	Mount Zion Jewish Cemetery, Queens, New York
Livshin, David	—	Buried at sea[8]
Rosenshine, George	16	Bayside Cemetery, Queens, New York
Straus, Isidor	96	Woodlawn Cemetery, Bronx, New York
Weisz, Leopold	293	Baron de Hirsch Jewish Cemetery, Montreal, Canada

[7]Although his body was found by the Mackay-Bennett, he was buried at sea after identification.
[8]He died during the night in Collapsible Lifeboat B. His body was transferred to Lifeboat 12, then transferred to the Carpathia and was buried at sea the next day.

Titanic victims buried in Baron de Hirsch Jewish Cemetery, Halifax

Name	Body#	Class	Jewish?
Navratil, Michel[9]	15	2	No
Wormald, Frederick William[10]	144	crew	No
Unknown male	78	crew	Probably not
Unknown male	248	crew	Probably not
Unknown male	136	crew	Probably not
Unknown male	291	crew	Probably not
Unknown male	289	crew	Probably not
Unknown male	264	crew	Probably not
Unknown male	214	crew	Probably not
Unknown male	278	crew	Probably not

[9]Navratil sailed under the alias name Louis Hoffman, a Jewish-sounding name. That is why he was accidently identified as a Jewish victim and buried in the Jewish cemetery. His family decided

[10]Wormald was identified many years after burial. He was a member of the crew. He was not Jewish. His family decided that his body should remain as it is.

INDEX

CPSIA information can be obtained
at www.ICGtesting.com
Printed in the USA
LVHW020312250721
693448LV00004B/5